Mahir A. Aziz was educated at the University of Salahaddin, the University of Baghdad and Birkbeck College, London, and holds a PhD in Kurdish Studies from the University of Exeter. He previously taught at the University of Salahaddin, Erbil and the Kurdistan University, Hawler, and is currently the Deputy Director General of Scholarships and Cultural Relations at the Ministry of Higher Education and Scientific Research for the Kurdistan Regional Government.

THE KURDS OF IRAQ

Nationalism and Identity in Iraqi Kurdistan

Mahir A. Aziz

I.B. TAURIS
LONDON · NEW YORK

Revised paperback edition published in 2015
6 Salem Road, London W2 4BU
175 Fifth Avenue, New York NY 10010

www.ibtauris.com

Distributed in the United States and Canada
Exclusively by Palgrave Macmillan
175 Fifth Avenue, New York NY 10010

First published in hardback in 2011 by I.B.Tauris & Co Ltd

ISBN 978 1 78453 273 4

A full CIP record for this book is available from the British Library
A full CIP record for this book is available from the Library of Congress

Library of Congress catalog card: available

Printed and bound by CPI Group (UK) Ltd, Croydon, CR0 4YY
Camera-ready copy edited and supplied by the author

For Alan, Rawaz, Sara and Zoe

CONTENTS

TABLES

FIGURES

Maps

APPENDICES

A NOTE ON THE
TRANSLITERATION AND
TRANSLATION SYSTEM USED

Except for some Arabic, Kurdish, Persian or Ottoman words, terms and names, which have been standardized in English (such as *Sunna*, *Shi'a*, *Jihad*, Hussein, Salahaddin, *Qur'an*, *Pasha*, *Agha*, *Hiwa*), the non-English words or names used have been transliterated according to the system used by the *International Journal of Middle Eastern Studies*, which is a modified version of the *Encyclopaedia of Islam* where *Qaf* = Q, not K.

The spellings reflect neither pronunciations, which vary from Arabic to Kurdish, Persian, or Turkish, nor accepted English spellings, which often reflect the way a word sounds in English rather than how it is spelled in Arabic or other languages. It might be useful to note that Kurdish, Persian and Turkish make use of all of the five English vowels (*a, e, i, o* and *u*), whereas Arabic uses only three vowels (*a, i* and *u*).

All non-English words, except the well-known terms or names such as Islam, Ali, Mohammad or Hussein, are italicized. Words and geographical names familiar to English readers are given in the English version and not in transliteration. Regarding the pronunciation of Arabic words, the Arabic linguistic system of *al-Hruf al-Qamariaya* and *al-Huruf a Shamsiya* was not followed. So a word like *al-Siyasiya* should be pronounced as *As-Siyasa*, or *As Suleimaniya* as a name of Suleimaniya city.

The article (*al*) was put in front of the noun to make it easier for the reader, unless it was different in the original text. This transliteration system has not been applied to the maps as the spellings on the maps sometimes differ from those in the text. For instance, on some maps, one might see the name 'Irbil' instead of 'Erbil' or 'Arbil.' Or one might see 'Hawler' rather than 'Erbil', 'Irbil', or 'Arbil'. For the Kurdish terms and names, the Sorani written style was adopted, as it is the style used in Iraqi Kurdistan, e.g., the name *Hiwa* is distinguished from *Hevi* or *Hiva*. Translations from Kurdish and Arabic language sources are my own unless otherwise specified.

ABBREVIATIONS AND GLOSSARY

ABSP   Arab *Ba'th* Socialist Party founded in 1947 as a secular Arab nationalist Party. The official name of the *Ba'th* party.

ADM   Assyrian Democratic Movement. A political party representing the Chaldo-Assyrian (Christian) community headed by Yondam Youssef Kanna.

Algiers Accord An agreement reached in 1975 between the Shah of Iran and Iraqi President Saddam Hussein (Vice President at the time), whereby the Shah agreed to cut off support for Iraqi Kurdish rebels in exchange for an Iraqi territorial concession.

CARDI   Committee against Repression and for Democratic Rights in Iraq.

CPA   Coalition Provision Authority, headed by Ambassador L. Paul Bremer.

CSO   Civil Society Organization.

CW   Chemical weapons.

FCO   Foreign and Commonwealth Office.

FO   Foreign Office.

ICP   Iraqi Communist Party, founded in 1934.

IGC   Iraqi Governing Council, appointed by the CPA to provide guidance and advice on governing Iraq during the period 13 July 2004–1 June 2005.

IIG   Interim Iraqi Government, formed after the elections of 30 January 2005. Replaced on 3 May 2005 by the Iraqi Transitional Government. Iyad Allawi served as prime minster with Gazi al Yawer appointed president.

IKF   Iraqi Kurdistan Front. Political front formed in 1987 of leading parties based in Kurdistan.

ILK	Islamic League of Kurdistan.
IMIK	Islamic Movement of Iraqi Kurdistan.
IMK	Islamic Movement in Kurdistan.
INF	International Islamic Front.
IO	India Office.
IRGC	Iranian Revolutionary Guard Coup.
KAR	Kurdistan Autonomous Region.
KCP	Kurdistan Communist Party.
KDP	Kurdistan Democratic Party. One of the two main parties founded in 1946 and headed by Mas'ud Barzani.
KDP (PC)	Kurdistan Democratic Party Provisional Committee.
KDP (PL)	Kurdistan Democratic Party, Provisional Leadership.
KF	Kurdistan Front.
KIL	Kurdish Islamic League.
KIU	Kurdistan Islamic Union. A moderate Islamic party founded in 1994 under leadership of Salahaddin Baha'adin.
KNA	Kurdistan National Assembly. The 105-seat legislature of the Kurdistan Region of Iraq was first assembled in 1992.
KNF	Kurdistan National Front.
KRG	Kurdish Regional Government. The unified government established in Kurdistan by the Kurdish Front after the 1992 elections. It was divided in 1993 and reunified in 2006.
KSP	Kurdistan Socialist Party. One of several small Kurdish parties in northern Iraq.
KTP	Kurdish Toilers' Party.
KUP	Kurdistan Unity Party.
Lausanne Treaty of 1923	Superseded the 1920 Treaty of Sèvres, giving most of Kurdistan to Turkey.
No Fly Zone	Area established under UN auspices in which Iraq was not allowed to fly non-commercial fixed-wing aircraft. There were two such zones in Iraq, one above the thirty-sixth parallel in the north and one below the thirty-third parallel in the south.
NGO	Non-governmental organization.
OFFP	The United Nations Oil for Food Programme.
OPC	Operation Provide Comfort. The name given by the US military to the operation that returned Iraqi Kurdish refugees to their homes in the wake of the 1991 rebellion.

OPEC	Organization of Petroleum Exporting Countries. Formed in 1960 by Middle East oil-exporting countries and a few others, such as Venezuela, Indonesia and Nigeria. OPEC is dedicated to protecting the oil-price structure in the interests of exporters.
PUK	Patriotic Union of Kurdistan. One of the two main Kurdish parties in Kurdistan. Founded in 1975 it has since been led by Jalal al-Talabani.
RCC	Revolutionary Command Council. The highest legislative and executive authority in Iraq from 1968–2003.
Resolution 687	The UN cease-fire resolution that concluded the Gulf War and stipulated the requirements that Iraq had to fulfil before troops were withdrawn. Chief among these was the destruction of Iraq's weapons of mass destruction (WMD). Sanctions would be maintained until this was satisfactorily accomplished.
Resolution 688	The UN resolution that instructed Iraq to cease repression of its population and to allow the international community to assist Kurdish refugees in returning to Iraq.
Resolution 986	The UN resolution, known as 'Oil for Food,' that allowed Iraq to export a certain amount of oil in order to purchase food, medicine and other essentials for its population, despite sanctions.
TAL	Transitional Administrative Law. An interim constitution signed on 8 March 2004 by IGC.
UAE	United Arab Emirates.
UAR	United Arab Republic. A political union formed by Egypt, Syria and Yemen in 1958. The UAR lasted until 1961.
UK	United Kingdom.
UKDP	United Kurdistan Democratic Party.
UKH	University of Kurdistan in Hawler (Erbil).
UN	United Nations.
UNSCOM	United Nations Special Commission. A body created in 1991 to conduct inspections in Iraq for biological weapons and long-range missiles.
USA	United States.
WMD	Weapons of mass destruction, whether chemical, biological or nuclear.

GLOSSARY OF KURDISH AND ARABIC TERMS

Agha	A chieftain or a tribal leader or landowner among the Kurds.
Anfal	'Spoils.' The term is taken from the eighteenth *Sura* of *Qur'an*, where it refers to the spoils of battle. In Iraq it is the code name for a campaign by the central government against Kurds in 1978–9 in the aftermath of the Iran–Iraq war, in which chemical weapons were used.
Arbil, Erbil, Irbil, (or Hawler in Kurdish)	The current capital of the Kurdish autonomous region.
Ashertalaf Immigrants	The Arab Iraqis who received 10,000 dinars from Saddam in 1980 to immigrate to Kirkuk.
Assyrians	A Christian minority in northern Iraq, sometimes referred to as Nestorians.
Ba'th	'Renaissance, rebirth.' Refers to the *Ba'th* Party, a pan-Arab party founded in Syria in 1946 that took root in Iraq in the 1950s and was in power 1968–2003.
Bayan Athar	March proclamation.
Emir or Amir or Mir	A leader of an emirate or principality.
Emirate or Mirnishin	A semi-independent principality.
Gurani	A group of Kurdish dialects, including Hawrami, spoken around the Hawraman area of southern Kurdistan.
Hiwa, Hiva, Hevi	Hope, a Kurdish political party founded by the leftists in early 1940s in Iraqi Kurdistan.
Hukmdar	Governor.

Ittifaq	Agreement.
Ittihad Ikhtiyari	Voluntary union.
Jash	'Little donkeys,' Kurdish militia who serve the state government.
Kirmanj	Northern Kurd, speaker of Kirmanji, peasant.
Kirmanji	Dialect of Kurdish, spoken north of the Greater Zab River.
Madrasa	School that teaches religious science and Islamic jurisprudence.
Millet	A religious minority or ethnic group based on the Ottoman system of administration.
Mulla or Mala	Clerical office in *Sunni* Islam.
Naqshbandiya	A Sufi brotherhood order, widespread in Kurdistan.
Pasha	A Kurdish and Turkish feudal title.
Peshmargas	'Those who face death.' Militias attached to Kurdish political parties, especially the KDP and the PUK.
Qaderiya	A Sufi brotherhood order, widespread in Kurdistan.
Qadi or Qzi	Muslim judge.
Qanun al-Hukm al-Thati	Autonomy law agreement of 11 March 1970 – offered by the *Ba'th* government and accepted by Mustafa Barzani.
Rapareen	Uprising.
Sanjaq or Sinjaq	Administrative territorial unit in the Ottoman Empire.
Sheikh	Head of a tribe of Arabs. In Kurdistan this is a leader of the *Sufi* order.
Shi'a	Muslims who follow the 'party' of Ali, that is, who believe that Ali, the Prophet Muhammad's cousin and son-in-law should have succeeded the Prophet as the leader of the Muslims.
Sorani	A dialect of Kurdish spoken south of the Greater Zab River. It is the dialect of Erbil, Suleimaniya and Kirkuk.
Sufi	Mystical order in *Sunni* religious doctrine.
Sunna	Traditions of Prophet Muhammad including his sayings (Hadith).
Sunni	The word comes from *Sunna*, which means words and actions.

Tariqa	In the *Sufi* brotherhood this is one of the most persistent forms of religious adherence.
Thalug	Deepwater channel in the centre of a river; used in a specific sense to denote the (disputed) boundary between Iraq and Iran in the Shat al-Arab.
Ulama	Clergies or Islamic scholars knowledgeable in Islamic law and theology.
Uruba	'Arabness'.
Wilaya, Vilayat or Wilayat	State or province; a unit of government under the Ottoman Empire.

PREFACE

A decade ago while studying for the Master of Science degree in politics and sociology at Birkbeck College, University of London, I came across David McDowall's book, *A Modern History of the Kurds*. While not the first I had read on the subject of the Kurds and Kurdish history in English, this was the book that aroused my interest and curiosity in Kurdish nationalism and national identity. It led me to further study in the wider context of Kurdish nationalism.

In my later studies I discovered that while Kurdish nationalism had been studied from various angles and disciplinary perspectives, there was no study in Kurdish, Arabic, or English, that concentrated on the history and culture of the Iraqi part of Kurdistan. This is a serious deficiency in the literature. As a social scientist and native researcher who has first-hand knowledge of the Kurdish and Arabic languages, I thought that this study would fill a void in the literature while adding an insider's view to the study of nationalism and national identity in the Kurdistan region of Iraq.

FOREWORD

The situation in the Kurdistan Region of Iraq, also referred to as Iraqi Kurdistan or, by those unwilling to recognize the constitutional reality of the Kurdistan Region, 'Northern Iraq', is a subject that swiftly arouses commentary and speculation grounded at best in dated analyses of Iraqi and Kurdish political life or, in the worse cases, highly loaded and at times dangerously inaccurate views and misconceptions. These views and misconceptions are legion. Whether focusing on the supposed aspiration to secede from Iraq and establish an independent state in the heart of the Middle East, or viewing the Kurdish leadership being in some form of alliance with the US and her allies to ensure that the wider Middle East region remains in a fragmented condition, easy to influence, control, and coerce. Opinion about the internal dynamics of the Kurdistan Region's politics and society are similarly varied, with the Kurdish leadership seemingly being either a mirror-image of the deposed Ba'th regime of Saddam Hussein, or the only true Western-style democrats between Europe and Australia.

Whatever the relative truth or fiction of these views may be, one theme underpins all of them, and that is the sense that the Kurds in Iraq now exist as a discrete unit, with the capability to engage in partnership with neighbours inside and outside Iraq, and with the ability to self-determine, to a degree not previously seen, their own future. This existence is commonly viewed in a classic statist manner – or *de facto* statist manner, more accurately – in so far as 'the Kurds' are often considered *en masse*, with little consideration given to the domestic political and social realities that serve to build the edifice of the Kurdish geopolitical reality in the international setting. This lacuna constitutes a particular problem, as it is filled by many assumptions. How the political parties operate; how processes of democratization are or are not being implemented; how do young Kurds view their situation and their future; how do people in the Kurdistan Region envisage their own identities and, more importantly, how do they view the identities of those around them, are just a few of the issues that are formatively important not only to the Kurdistan Region itself, but the wider geopolitical theatre of the Iraqi, Turkish, Syrian, and Iranian borderlands.

It is on the question of national identity that Mahir Aziz focuses upon. Accepting that identities are mobile and changeable, needing to be remembered and constantly revisioned and reconstructed, Mahir's research focuses not upon those most commonly studied in terms of Kurdish politics – the political elites – but upon those who will arguably be the dynamos of change and development in the future – University students. His choice of sample is important – young people, born in the autonomous Kurdistan Region established in 1991, and exposed largely to a distinctly 'Kurdish' narrative of culture, social processes, and historical and political development. How this cohort of society views themselves, those around them, and their future allows those interested in Iraq and the Kurdish place within (or outside) it to understand, empirically rather than merely anecdotally, the current situation and the demands and aspirations of a critical grouping (students) within a vital region (Kurdistan) of a state (Iraq) of immense geopolitical significance in the region and internationally. Aziz's contribution is therefore not only to the literature on nationalism, identity, and the Kurdistan Region of Iraq – clear though this is. It is also a contribution to the wider field of Middle East Politics, and wider strategic and geopolitical concerns.

Gareth Stansfield
Professor of Middle East Politics
Director of the Institute of Arab and Islamic Studies
Co-Director of the Centre for Kurdish Studies
University of Exeter

INTRODUCTION

This book is concerned with the development of Kurdish ethnonationalism and Kurdish citizens' perceptions of national identity in the Kurdistan region of Iraq. After introducing the major theoretical approaches on nationalism and national identity, the discussion concentrates on the development of Kurdish nationalism and contemporary Kurdish national identity beginning with the 1990s. After the establishment of the Kurdistan Regional Government (KRG) in 1992, the two major political parties, namely the Kurdistan Democratic Party (KDP) and the Patriotic Union of Kurdistan (PUK), achieved a *de facto* state. The new generation of Kurds in Iraq has grown up since the 1991 Kurdish uprising, which is an absolutely different political climate than that which their parents experienced. The parents' generation was dominated by the *Ba'th* party, which along with the Iraqi state was the hegemonic power. The youthful Kurdish generation does not remember this and as a result has little interest in Iraqi politics or Arabic culture.

The historical development of Kurdish national identity is contextualized within an understanding of Kurdish nationalism that spans the twelfth century to the present time. This research supports Anthony Smith's theory of historical ethno-symbolism, which explains the origins and development of nations as a long-term process subject to a great variety of influences. Political, economic, social and emotional elements converge as conditions in the respective communities evolve, requiring the ruling elites to continually adjust their means and goals, not only to remain in power, but to consolidate and reinforce the sense of nationalism and national identity among the people.

This investigation explores attitudes towards national identity using a sample of university students from the three largest universities in Iraqi Kurdistan. It is not suggested that nations and national identity are naturally occurring phenomena; they are not. My concern is to explore how notions of 'nation' and 'national identity' are used by students to position themselves in relation to others and how such actions are partly responsible for the ongoing perpetuation of the cultural outlook within the nation. The research explores answers to the following questions: (1) Do the Kurds, specifically the young Kurds, have more than one identity simultaneously? (2) Is 'identity' a confusing term for them? (3) How do the young Kurds identify themselves? (4) What does it mean to be *Kurdistani* or Iraqi? (5) To what extent is Kurdish identity linked with Kurdistan and *Kurdistanism*? (6) Which identity is more predominant in Kurdistan: national, tribal, Islamic or local?

With regard to the pre-1990s era when there was much confusion over long-term prospects, an examination was made as to whether the Kurds in the stateless nation of Iraqi Kurdistan have managed to retain a sense of distinct culture and national consciousness, despite subjection to forceful and unforgiving assimilating forces.

From the basic elements that make up the Kurdish sense of 'nationhood', it is my contention that a unified nationalist political movement has sprung up over the years, especially since 1960, which seeks power, ranging from limited control over certain aspects of the nation's affairs, to the dream of complete independence. This unified nationalist movement fragmented between 1975 and 1988 and resurged after 1998.

Data from the experiences of 450 graduate students from three major universities in the region were used from which to draw inferences. The data was collected through quantitative and qualitative research instruments based on questionnaires and interviews which were then analysed from a nationalistic framework. The participants generously interpreted various aspects of their responses as well as their recollection of the acquisition of such during the years of their upbringing. The findings demonstrate that several factors have played a role in consolidating a sense of Kurdish national identity. These include the national, territorial, political and linguistic factors.

This book has been divided into two parts. Part One deals with the theoretical approaches to nationalism and national identity and chronologically contextualizes the development of Kurdish nationalism in Iraq.

Chapter 1 provides background information to the study and to Kurdistan in general, the questions of concern and a review of the current literature. This chapter also deals with the construction of Kurdish national identity in Iraqi Kurdistan. It assesses the national identity of young urban kurds, whilst the remainder of the chapter is devoted to a description of Iraqi Kurdistan's population, religion, the economy in the post-1990s era and the development of higher education.

Chapter 2 conceptualizes and explores the most important terms and concepts used in the study, such as nationalism, national identity, nation state, stateless nation and political culture.

Chapter 3 addresses the modern theoretical debates and approaches to nationalism and national identity. The dichotomy of civic versus ethnic conceptions of national identity and nationalism is considered. Anthony Smith's ethno-symbolism and his six dimensions of ethnic community are analysed and applied to Kurdistan as an appropriate model by which to understand Kurdistan's case. A critical reading of other scholars' responses to Smith's approach is debated as well. The remainder of the chapter outlines some of the most important contributions to the debate on nationalism and national identity as represented in the works of Benedict Anderson by assessing Anderson's views on language, imagination and imagined communities.

Chapter 4 contextualizes Kurdistan's history from the pre-modern to the twentieth century by use of territorial and linguistic approaches. The early phase of Kurdish nationalism is detailed, which covers the period from the twelfth to the end of the nineteenth centuries. This chapter also assesses Kurdish proto-national identity and the rise of the 'imagined community'.

Chapter 5 outlines the historical and socio-political conditions for the development of Kurdish nationalism from 1921–91. Ten sections cover the following topics: (1) losing the game of state formation; (2) rebellion in Kurdistan; (3) the meeting of tribalism and nationalism from 1930s–58; (4) Political Developments in Iraq and Kurdistan; (5) the Kurdish nationalist movement in the republican era: 1958–68; (6) Kurdish nationalist mobilization in the *Ba'th* era: 1968–90; (7) the Agreement of 11 March 1970; (8) the Algiers Agreement of 1974–5 and the Kurdish Revolution; (9) the Internal Displacement; and (10) militant Kurdish nationalism: 1976–90.

Chapter 6 explores the reconstruction and consolidation of Kurdish national identity. Section one assesses the uprising (*Rapareen*) of March 1991 in Kurdistan and its causes and consequences. The second section presents a socio-political reading of the 19 May 1992 elections and discusses the power-sharing system which was in place from 1992–8. The third section assesses the political power structures, power-sharing system and Kurdish national identity from 1998–2008. The fourth section illuminates the notion of *Kurdistanism* (*Kurdistaniyeti* in Kurdish) as a new form of asserting modern national identity from 1998–2008. It also assesses Kurdish nationalism after 1998 until the present time.

Part Two consists of three chapters which present the conclusions and findings of the present study. Chapter 7 describes the method of the study and the design of the questionnaire which was administered in March–June

2007 at the universities of Salahaddin, Suleimani and Dohuk. The demographic variables of the students are discussed along with those of their families, including place of family residence, place of birth, age and gender of respondents, marital status, parents' occupation, education, income and social status, family size and other characteristics.

Chapter 8 is devoted to students' attitudes towards identity in a variety of dimensions: tribal, local, territorial, religious and national. Here the issue of *Kurdistanism* (*Kurdistaniyeti*) is investigated while exploring students' attitudes towards Iraqi Kurdistan, the *Kurdistani* flag versus the Iraqi flag, politics and political parties in Kurdistan. Chapter 9 discusses the study's findings and outlines recommendations for further study.

This book could not have been written without the effort and encouragement of many people. I would particularly like to thank my mentor and friend, Professor Gareth Stansfield. Without his help, commitment to the project and keen insights, this work would have been vastly more difficult to complete. I have a special appreciation for Professor Tim Niblock for his assistance, encouragement, ideas and advice and criticism and suggestions. I would like to express my deep gratitude to my friend Farouk Muhammad Amin in the Netherlands for his advice and for refreshing my knowledge of statistics.

In the Kurdistan region many people have helped and supported me, especially in the survey process. I would like to thank my students at the universities of Salahaddin, Suleimani and Dohuk who were forthright, honest and patient in answering the many questions. I thank Prof Nadje AL-Ali of SOAS, London University for reviewing the questionnaire and I'm grateful for Mr. Falah Mustafa Bakir the Director of Foreign Affairs in Kurdistan Region in Hawler for the support he offered during the last five years. I would particularly like to thank Dr. Fuad Mawlood Shareef for providing me with the books I needed from the Library of Queen Mary College at the University of London and Dr. Sharon Linzey for her assistance during the revision and final editing process. I would like to thank my mother, brothers and near relatives who have encouraged me along the way. The devotion and enduring encouragement, patience and unwavering support of my family, especially my wife and my son Alan, enabled me to cope during tense moments and the long commitment of working on the PhD. To them I am utterly grateful. I would be remiss if I did not mention the long hours of editing that Mrs. Valerie Dal Pozzo spent on my behalf. And to the editors at I.B.Tauris, Joanna Godfrey and Maria Marsh, I express my sincere gratitude for their help and patience. There are others that I am sure I have forgotten to mention and I apologize in advance for this oversight. Any errors of fact or interpretation are, of course, my sole responsibility.

PART ONE

1

THE CONSTRUCTION OF KURDISH NATIONAL IDENTITY IN IRAQI KURDISTAN

Much contemporary work on the politics of identity has concentrated on either (1) the study of ethnicity and ethnic community, or (2) the analysis of national identity and nationalism. Over time these two fields have converged, a process which has led scholars to study the phenomena of ethnicity and nationalism as intimately related. Nowhere is this truer than in cases of ethnonationalism.[1]

The term 'ethnonationalism' was coined by Walker Connor who defines a nation as a self-conscious ethnic group.[2] One may ask how the term 'ethnonationalism' is distinguished from 'nationalism'. For Connor the term 'nationalism' refers to loyalty to the ethnic group, but it is usually mistaken to refer to loyalty to the state. The term 'ethnonationalism' must be distinguished from 'patriotism'. The latter is often synonymous with the nationalist projects of post-colonial states.[3] The study of the ethnonational must thus 'focus on the groups' own cultural boundaries and the ways in which they use their cultural resources to affirm their distinctiveness and promote their interests.[4]

My concern here is whether the theoretical approaches to nationalism provide an adequate framework within which to understand the Kurdish ethnonationalist movement and its current *de facto* state in Iraqi Kurdistan.

Mainstream scholarship generally takes the view that nationalism is a modern phenomenon in both the West and the Middle East. Accordingly, it was thought to have developed first in Europe 200–300 years ago and then spread to the Middle East. Rogers Brubaker dates the birth of 'nationhood' to 1792 and considers it to have died in 1992.[5]

Walker Connor states: 'Europe's presently recognised nations emerged only very recently, in many cases centuries later than the dates customarily assigned for their emergence.'[6] There is no consensus on the origins or timing of nationalist ideologies. Hans Kohn refers to 1642, whereas Acton points to 1772 and the period of the partition of Poland as the date for the birth of this phenomenon. Kedourie offers the year of 1806 when Fichte published his call to the German nation. For most, the late eighteenth century and the period of the French and American revolutions mark the birth of nationalism.[7]

Toward the end of the twentieth century questions of national identity became highly relevant in both Eastern Europe and the Middle East.[8] Modern societies tend toward a form of identity that finds expression in the *nation* concept. As a result, understanding how national identity is constructed is an enormously important task on the road to understanding a people's social and political culture. And nationalist movements are vital for understanding how national identities are constructed.

The good news is that the tools used to understand the construction of national identities are available within the community. Sometimes they are invented. Concepts such as common culture, shared history, common myth, traditions, national essence, the flag, the national anthem, language, spirit of the people and folklore, are all imaginary creations that provide a group with a sense of 'togetherness.' It is this sense of 'togetherness' and the belief that the people of a given locale share a lot in common that serve to unify the group.

For at least half a century, nationalism has given the Kurdish people the most effective answer to questions of identity and connectedness in an amorphous and fluid world. In recent decades political developments in Kurdistan have been dominated by 'nationalistic' oriented, or 'nationalistic' types of questions.

Nation versus National Identity

The Kurds appear to be the largest ethnic group in the world without a state of their own.[9] Therefore, as the largest stateless nation in the Middle East, they are a growing regional and international problem—as well as an embarrassment. They have suffered discrimination, marginalization and assimilation in each of the states in which they reside: Turkey, Iran, Iraq and Syria. In each of these countries, the nationalism of the sovereign dominant ethnic group has fed the official ideology and each national ideology has endeavoured to establish a homogeneous nation state. In every case the Kurds have been excluded, sidelined, or outright had their existence denied.[10]

Iraqi Kurdistan has existed since 1991 when a new political era brought about a strengthening of the Kurds' sense of national identity. Gareth

Stansfield asserts that this period may be a decade of development 'in which the political system was finding a measure of equilibrium in the milieu of the geopolitical forces affecting it.'[11]

National Identity of Young Urban Kurds

The 1990s introduced a significant change in Kurdish thinking about themselves. The term 'Kurd' had previously referred to ethnicity. But after the 1990s the young educated Kurds began to understand their Kurdish-ness in a new way, as *Kurdistani*.[12]

The political events of the 1920s, 40s, 60s, 70s and 90s consolidated Kurdish national identity and strengthened Kurdish pride in Kurdistan. The 1990s was a period of growing *Kurdistani* identity. Thus, the central argument for this work may be stated as follows:

The political changes that took place in Iraqi Kurdistan after 1991, the 19 May 1992 election and the existence of the *de facto* Kurdish state since 1992 coalesced to cause a sense of political and national cohesiveness among urban and literate Kurds in which a widely accepted identity as '*Kurdistanis*' displaced the former self-designation of 'Iraqi Kurds' or 'Iraqis'.

Historical memory, language and territory as characteristic features of Kurdish national identity play an important role in stimulating national historical consciousness and ethnic solidarity. Kurdish national identity is not treated as an idea or discourse, but rather as empirically observable political and social units.

Tribal affiliations and religious loyalties no longer exercise a major influence in post-1990s Iraqi Kurdistan, especially among the younger educated generation. Today, professional, civic and ethnic allegiances proliferate and they involve ever larger cross-sections of the populace in Kurdistan, especially educated youth.

The provinces of Erbil, Suleimaniya and Dohuk constitute the three governates or provinces of Iraqi Kurdistan.[13] The majority of the Iraqi Kurds live in the Kurdish cities of Erbil, Suleimaniya, Dohuk and Kirkuk, while a significant number live in other Iraqi cities such as Mosul, Baghdad and Diyala. Of course, there are a significant number in exile.

Kurdish nationalism before the 1990s in Iraq was primarily a reaction to policies denying them Kurdish national identity and to the systematic processes and policies promoting 'de-Kurdification', assimilation, 'Arabization', discrimination, terror and ethnic cleansing of the Kurds and their interests.

As a consequence of the second Gulf war in 1991, the Kurdish *Rapareen* and the *Shi'i intifada* in the south rebelled against Iraq. Later the USA established a 'safe haven' for the Kurds to keep Saddam's troops from carrying out further operations as part of his nefarious *Anfal* campaign which destroyed thousands of Kurdish villages and cost multiple thousands of Kurdish lives.[14]

The Gulf war of 1991 marked for Iraqi Kurds the turning point in their understanding of contemporary politics and history. The *de facto* Kurdish state was the result of the political vacuum left when Saddam withdrew from Kurdistan. The US established a 'no fly zone' which protected the region from future Iraqi army attacks. At the same time Kurdistan was politically dominated and economically controlled by the two major Kurdish political parties: the Kurdistan Democratic Party (KDP), led by Mas'ud Barzani and the Patriotic Union of Kurdistan (PUK), led by Jalal Talabani.

Since the creation of Iraq by the British in 1921 and throughout most of modern and contemporary Kurdish history, it was 'the patchy and ambivalent recognition of Kurdish identity' by various Iraqi political systems, together with 'territorial institutionalization of the Kurdish resistance, that made Iraqi Kurdistan an important centre for the development of modern Kurdish politics and culture for the whole region'.[15] The Kurdish political elites sought affiliation with regional or external powers, rather than relying on indigenous power bases, primarily because they had no better alternatives. Even those dramatic events that brought the establishment of the Mahabad Republic in Iranian Kurdistan in 1947, or the collapse of the Kurdish nationalist movement of 1974 in Iraqi Kurdistan, might be interpreted this way.

After the establishment of the Kurdistan Regional Government (KRG) in 1992 and the declaration of the Transitional Administrative Law (TAL) on 8 March 2004, Kurdish nationalism became more consolidated than ever. A new generation of Kurds grew up and and was educated with little or no knowledge of Arabic culture and language. This is relevant to explain why they also seem to have little knowledge, understanding, or interest in the construction of Iraqi society and politics.

Why Study Kurdish National Identity in Iraqi Kurdistan?

There are at least two compelling reasons why Kurdish national identity in Iraqi Kurdistan should be closely examined: (1) to better understand key components of the political culture in the Kurdistan region through the younger generation's perception of national identity and (2) to better inform debates about the prospects for consolidation of this national identity.

The modes of collective behaviour and national identity evident in Kurdistan differ from those noted in Iraq or elsewhere in the Middle East. This reflects the differences in cultures in terms of political development.

On the one hand, the study of Kurdish national identity presents an important research task in its own right. Identity politics takes the form of nationalism, which represents an attempt at task-specific utilization of cultural resources of a certain large group of people defined as a nation. On the other hand, the character of nationalism exhibited in post-1990s Kurdistan is an offshoot of a political culture that had little place for pluralistic values heretofore and is not ready to cope with their immediate introduction or insistence now. Kurdish nationalism, therefore, must be looked upon as a political/cultural phenomenon in its own right.

Oftentimes newly liberalized or democratized nations compensate for state incapacity and the underdevelopment of civil society by constructing a political orientation and ideology to serve as the basis of its state nationalism. One might ask the fundamental question: Does Kurdistan possess a political tradition of its own? The answer is, yes, it does, although Kurdistan has never been 'independent' in the full sense of the word.

In recent years there have been a plethora of scholarly books and articles regarding the Kurds. The arguments made on behalf of Kurdish nationalism and national identity have been largely theoretical and most studies have dealt with the Kurdish cases in Turkey, Iran or Syria separately, or in Kurdistan generally, which includes Turkey, Iran, Iraq and Syria. Discussions of nationalism within Kurdistan have been largely undertaken within an area studies framework and they have not been integrated into the theoretical literature on nation-building, identity and nationalism. My approach differs in that I offer a general picture of Iraqi Kurdistan's population, religion, the economy after the 1990s and the development of higher education.

The Background of the Iraqi Kurds

The Kurds in Iraq speak Kurdish. The Kurdish language is an Indo-European language that has Sorani and Bahdinani (Kirmanji) dialects. The Kurds are ethnically Aryan and claim descent from the Medes. The majority of Kurds are predominantly *Sunni Shaf'ites* who converted to Islam in the sixteenth century.[16] Thus, Kurdish society cannot be seen as a homogeneous one since there are other small minorities who also live in the region e.g., Assyrians, Chaldeans, Turkmen and Armenians. Demographically the region has a young growing population with 36 per cent aged 0–14 years and only four per cent aged over 63. The median age in Kurdistan is just over 20. More than 50 per cent are less than 20 years of age, so it is a relatively young population.[17] There are no exact figures for the number of Kurds living in Iraq due to the fact that previous Iraqi political systems downplayed their numbers, especially since the 1940s.

According to the UN estimate, there are 3,757,058 Kurds in Iraq. The population in each of the region's three provinces is estimated to be: Erbil: 1,033,176; Suleimaniya: 1,605,506; and Dohuk: 817,376.[18] (Table 1.1 illustrates a sampling of figures used.)

The Kurds claimed that their population in 1990 was 27.4 million in all parts of Greater Kurdistan. Most of the Kurds are in Turkey where their numbers run between 15 and 20 million, or about 23 per cent of the population. There are at least 4 million Kurds in Iraq (15 per cent of the population); it is believed that there are 7 million Kurds in Iran, or 15 per cent of the population; and over 1 million in Syria, or nine per cent of the population. In addition there are 75,000 Kurds in Armenia (1.8 per cent of the population), 200,000 in Azerbaijan (2.8 per cent of the population) and 300,000 in the Russian Federation.[19] The Kurds easily comprise the fourth-largest ethnic group in the Middle East.[20] The Kurds believe that they have the right to be considered a nation because they have all the attributes of nationhood: i.e., territory, language, culture, history, common myth, economic resources and population.

Demographically the region has witnessed significant changes in the last few decades. Previous Iraqi governments imposed migration policies which resulted in a forced urbanization process. At least 600,000 people in Iraq were internally displaced from 1970 to 2001. This included more than 100,000 people who were forcibly removed from Kirkuk in November 1991 and replaced by Arabs under the 'Arabization' policy of Saddam Hussein's Ba'th Party. In 1975 alone 279,000 Arabs were forcibly relocated to Kirkuk.[21] According to a UNDP survey 66 per cent of those living in Dohuk province were forced to change their residence at some point in their lives due to war. The figures in Suleimaniya and Erbil are 31 per cent and seven per cent, respectively.[22]

In the 1980s Saddam Hussein's regime destroyed over 5,000 Kurdish and Christian villages in clear violation of the International Covenant on Civil and Political Rights, which is now considered to be customary international law to be respected by all nations.[23] These thousands of displaced Kurds were forcibly relocated to collective towns. At least 2,620 of these villages were rebuilt after 1991 by the Kurdistan Regional Government (KRG), with the support of UN agencies and nongovernmental organizations.[24]

Kurdish population figures are at least as old as the nation states among which Kurdistan is divided (see Table 1.1). All of the numbers given, both from Kurdish and/or non-Kurdish sources, are rough estimates. In a few instances, they are based on early census data obtained under political and economic circumstances hardly conducive to accurate reporting.

Table 1.1 Estimates of Iraqi Kurdistan's Population

Author's Estimate	Population for Year Cited
League of Nations (1925)	500,000
M. Amin Zaki (1945)	600,000
W. Jwaideh (1953)	1,200,000
B. Nikitine (1956)	749,000
C.J. Edmond (1957)	900,000
A. Ghassemlou (1965)	3,300,000
Short and McDermott (1977)	3,400,000
M. Bruinessen (1978)	2,500,000
More (1984)	3,000,000
D. McDowall (1992)	4,100,000
K. Nezan (1996)	5,200,000
M. O'Shea (1996) (2004)	4,400,000
G. Stansfield (2003)	3,315,204
Muller and Linzey (2007)	4,000,000

Sources:
1 Most population statistics pertaining to the Kurds cannot be trusted because all the states in which the Kurds reside downplay their numbers for political reasons. The first four figures are quoted in Shakir Khasbak, *al Kurd wal-Mas'ala al- Kurdiyai fil Iraq*, (Kurds and the Kurdish Question in Iraq), (*Al Mu'asasa al Arabia le al-Dirasat wal- Nashr*).
2 Figures 2 and 4 are quoted in Wadie Jwaideh, *The Kurdish Nationalist Movement: Its Origins and Development*.
3 Figures 5–10 are quoted in Stansfield, *Iraqi Kurdistan*.
4 Figure 11 is quoted in Kendal, 'The Kurds'.
5 For Figure 12 see O'Shea, *Trapped Between* and McDowall, *A Modern History of the Kurds*.
6 Figure 13 is from Stansfield, *Iraqi Kurdistan*. This figure represents only the population inhabiting the Kurdistan region, whereas the other figures presented may include Kurds who live outside the region.
7 Figure 13 is taken from Muller and Linzey, *The Internally Displaced Kurds of Turkey*.

On the basis of this generalized data, some have conjectured or estimated the numbers of Kurds in the four states of habitation and these figures have then been used selectively by subsequent writers or politicians to diminish or enhance the numbers of the Kurds depending on their motives. Over time certain numbers (15, 20–25 million) became more or less accepted as 'official', but this was more due to repetition than based on sound research, accurate data or solid methodological accounting procedures.

Yet, the sizeable numbers of Kurds in the four states have always been a crucial component of the Kurds' argument for the right to self-determination and nationhood. The Kurds claim to be the largest nation without a state. Most observers agree that they constitute the fourth-largest ethnic group in the Middle East after the Arabs, Persians and Turks, who each lay claim to one or more countries. The unreliability of the data is commonly acknowledged as is the tendency of governments to minimize Kurdish population figures and of Kurdish nationalists' tendency to exaggerate them.

Religion in Kurdistan

In ancient times before the advent of Judaism and Christianity, many Kurds were followers of Zoroastrianism, Mithraism, or they were pagans who participated in tree and solar cults. The Kurds had absorbed some of these mystical aspsects into their cultural worldview by approximately 800 BC.[25] At the time the Arab conquests began in the seventh century AD, the Kurds fought against the forced practice of Islam. Eventually the Kurds submitted to the Arab armies and Islam became the dominant religion.

Since Islam's arrival in the seventh century, religious belief and practice haven't meshed with politics. Religion helped to provide spiritual cohesion in a disaggregated world, but it never provided the ideological foundation for an emerging nationalist identity. Modern *Kurdistani* political culture is deeply rooted in national rather than religious identity. Inasmuch as *Qur'anic* Islam fuses the sacred with the secular, the development of *Kurdistani* political identity that has simultaneous nationalist, modern and secular components is a contradiction in terms of both belief and practice. Having had its own indigenous belief systems, Islam was a foreign religion that was interjected into Kurdistan by conquest, rather than by trade, with the sword, rather than by choice, beginning in the seventh century AD when many Kurds had long before converted to Christianity or Judaism.[26]

Today Islam pervades virtually all aspects of life in Iraqi Kurdistan. The Kurds are not particularly religious people in the sense of abiding by dogma. For example, few Kurds, whether in the countryside or in the cities, say their prayers five times a day as Muslim religious teachings instruct, yet they may scrupulously observe prescriptions that are secondary from the point of view of religious doctrine, such as taboos concerning food and alcohol and practices such as circumcision and wearing the veil. These taboos, however, are not prevalent in today's urban life in the major cities of Kurdistan. Rites associated with pagan beliefs, sacred stones and other forms of divine intervention that may be practised in the most rural areas provide a sense of proximity to God for their practitioners. Such practices are far removed from the orthodox strictures of the *Qur'an* that remain remote, inaccessible and impenetrable for most country folk.[27]

For much of their pre-modern history, the most salient non-local identity for many Kurds was that of membership in the community of Islam. The Islamic *Umma* links its members by means of a common faith, ritual practice and sacred language. Islam introduced literacy into Kurdish, Arab, Persian and Turkish cultures. The successful spread of Islam was based not only on military power, but on the training of *Mulla* (*Mala* in Kurdish), from the newly absorbed linguistic communities in the law and the language of the *Qur'an*. These new local elites were often instrumental in facilitating not only the spread of the Islamic faith but the Arabization of convert cultures as well. The Kurds were able to resist assimilation by such a dominant cultural force due to the isolation and autonomy that the mountainous environment of Kurdistan afforded them. The development of its indigenous forms of religious observance facilitated this resistance as well.[28]

After the Kurds' aristocratic leaders were removed in the nineteenth century, popular Sheikhs became the most powerful leaders of Kurdish rebellions against the Ottoman state and are generally credited with encouraging the rise of popular Kurdish nationalism. In later years they posed such a threat to the Kemalist forces in Turkey that Kemal Ataturk banned the *madrasa* and *tariqa* in order to eliminate their power base. A smaller number of Kurds belong to the *Shi'a* sect. Religious minorities in the region include Christians, Jews and Yezidi *Ahli haq* and *Ali Allahi*. There is little religious dissension in Kurdistan in Iraq unless one converts from Islam.[29] Since 2003 the UN High Commissioner for Refugees reported that 1.5 million refugees have fled Iraq on account of religious persecution. Although Christians in Iraq make up approximately three per cent of the total population, they currently account for 40 per cent of the refugees living in nearby countries and another 2 million are internally displaced in northern Iraq.[30]

Currently it is estimated that 80 per cent of contemporary Kurds are *Sunni* Muslims belonging to the *Shafi'i* school of religious doctrine (*madhab* or *mazhab* in Kurdish).[31] One of the most persistent forms of religious adherence among Muslim Kurds has been the *Sufi* brotherhoods (*tariqa*), particularly the *Naqeshbandiya* and *Qadriaya* orders. Popular veneration of the *Sufi* Sheikhs has been intense and even fanatical during certain periods of Kurdish history, particularly among the peasant and urban lower classes.[32]

The Economy of Post-1991 Kurdistan

Before the 1990s the Iraqi government's policies towards Kurdistan were to marginalize the economy and deliberately neglect its infrastructure. The economy in the Kurdistan region was dominated by the oil sector, agriculture and tourism. Since the establishment of the Kingdom of Iraq in 1921 up to the 90s, the Kurds never controlled their economy, as it was always under the central government's hegemony. In the 1990s the Kurdistan Regional Government (KRG) received 13 per cent of the oil revenues garnered from the Oil-for-Food Programme under UN Security Council Resolution 986.[33]

Because of the numerous adversities and obstructions caused by the *Ba'th* regime, the Oil-for-Food Programme was installed later than designed. The intention was to provide some sort of humanitarian relief (i.e., medical and food support) for civilians when sanctions on Iraq were first imposed. This was also expressed in Resolution 661 that implemented the sanctions in 1990. However, it was not until March 1997 that the first shipments of food arrived in Iraq and reached the needy. The first oil that was exported after the oil trade blockade was put in place took place in December 1996. It is notable that the delivery of food supplies took quite some time to reach the needy even after the oil had been delivered.[34] The reason why it took so long remains a mystery. In the initial stages of the programme, Iraq was permitted to sell $2 billion worth of oil every six months, with two-thirds of that amount to be used to meet Iraq's humanitarian crises. In 1998 the limit on the level of Iraqi oil exports under the programme was raised to $5.26 billion every six months, again with two-thirds of the oil proceeds earmarked to meet the humanitarian needs of the Iraqi people.

In December 1999 the ceiling on Iraqi oil exports under the programme was removed by the Security Council. When the UN implemented the programme on behalf of the government of Iraq, 72 per cent of the Iraqi oil export proceeds funded the humanitarian programme. Of that, 59 per cent was earmarked for contracts for supplies and equipment for the 15 central and southern governorates. The government of Iraq was to use 13 per cent for contracts on behalf of the three northern governorates. The balance included 25 per cent for a Compensation Fund for war reparation payments; 2.2 per cent for UN administrative and operational costs; and 0.8 per cent for the weapons inspection programme.[35] The Kurds overwhelmingly supported the Oil-for-Food Programme as Kurdish society benefited enormously from it.

Following the removal of Saddam Hussein's regime and the subsequent violence, the three provinces under the Kurdistan Regional Government's control were the only three in Iraq ranked 'secure' by the US military. The relative security and stability of the region allowed the KRG to sign a number of investment contracts with foreign companies. By 2003 the programme had disbursed $8.35 billion to the Kurdistan Regional Government. Iraqi Kurdistan's food security allowed for substantially more of the funds to be spent on development projects than in the rest of Iraq. By the programme's end in 2003, $4 billion of the KRG's Oil-for-Food funds were unspent and the KRG claims funds are owed them which were withheld by the Iraqi government.[36]

The stability of the Kurdistan region has allowed it to achieve a higher level of development than other regions in Iraq. In 2004 the per capita income was 25 per cent higher than in the rest of Iraq. The two chief cities of the region, Erbil and Suleimaniya, both have international airports serving destinations throughout the Middle East and parts of Europe. The Kurdish Regional Government continues to receive 17 per cent of the revenue from Iraq's oil exports and it will soon implement a unified foreign investment law. The KRG also has plans to build a media city in Erbil and free trade zones near the borders of Turkey and Iran.

In 2006 the first new oil well since the invasion of Iraq was drilled in the Kurdistan region by the Norwegian energy company DNO. Initial indications are that the oil field contains at least 100 million barrels of oil and can be expected to regularly pump 5,000 barrels per day. The KRG has signed exploration agreements with two other oil companies: Canada's Western Oil Sands and the UK's Sterling Energy.[37]

No detailed or reliable economic statistics are available for the Kurdistan region specifically, but the overall picture appears as follows. The per capita income in the Kurdistan Regional Government is estimated to be the equivalent of $3,500 per year, still barely middling by regional standards but modestly higher than in the rest of Iraq and growing lately at a healthy seven per cent annual rate.[38] This is due to rising oil revenues received from the central government. Beyond any of these figures is the simple reality that daily economic life for the people of the KRG is not hostage to constant severe security disruptions, as has been the case everywhere else in Iraq since 2003. As a result, the prospects for economic development in the region are reasonably good, though complicated by legal hassles, lack of transparency and logistical bottlenecks with other parts of Iraq. Though still a developing economy, if the KRG can find the right political paths to open up its very substantial oil and gas reserves, ideally in cooperation with Baghdad, Ankara and international energy firms, then its overall economic prospects could fairly rapidly become highly attractive.[39] At present the KRG relies almost entirely on oil revenues distributed by Baghdad to cover its expenses. The KRG depends on a month-to-month cash flow, with no margin of error. Until the cash arrives literally in hand, people do not get paid.[40]

Higher Education in the Kurdistan Region of Iraq

Universities tend to play a central role in political and cultural movements for self-governance. Education systems in general play important roles as they work to impose a specific cultural understanding based on a common language. The education system played a key role in the creation of a shared national identity in Kurdistan. Prior to the 1990s the previous Iraqi regime paid scant attention to Salahaddin University. Table 1.2 shows the slow growth of the number of students in attendance at Salahaddin University prior to 1990. It is important to note that nearly half of these numbers included Arab students who came from areas outside of Kurdistan, from Mosul to Basra. The total number of students at the University of Salahaddin for the 1990/1 academic year was 7,027.

After the 1990s higher education in Kurdistan underwent an enormous expansion. The numbers of students increased and the proportion of students aged 18–25 grew even faster (see Tables 1.2 and 1.3). Arab students from other parts of Iraq stopped attending Salahaddin University since the central government ceased recognizing it after 1992. The total number of students in 2005 was 9,005. They were all Kurdish students.

Until 1992 Salahaddin University was the only university in Kurdistan. It initially consisted of seven colleges: Medicine, Engineering, Science, Administration and Economics, Education, Arts and Law and Political Science. Table 1.3 shows the increase in universities and the numbers of students in Kurdistan for the last 15 years. Salahaddin University is considered the oldest and largest institution of higher education in the Kurdistan region. It was established in Suleimaniya in 1968 as the University of Suleimani. The central government transferred the university to Erbil in 1981 and changed its name to Salahaddin University. The College of Law and Politics was added in 1985 and the College of Dentistry in 1995. The number of colleges reached 22 in 2004 and decreased to 18 the following year when the Colleges of Medicine, Dentistry, Nursing and Pharmacy separated and formed Hawler Medical University. Today there are 21 colleges, 17 for the morning classes and four for the evening. University employees number about 2,483 and faculty members total about 1,063.[41]

Table 1.2 Students attending Salahaddin University by College, 1968–90

	University of Salahaddin Colleges							
Year	*Science*	*Agriculture*	*Engineering*	*Arts*	*Administration & Economics*	*Education*	*Medicine*	*Law*
1968–9	243	116	–	–	–	–	–	–
1969–70	513	200	–	–	–	–	–	–
1970–1	596	301	–	–	–	–	–	–
1971–2	698	388	41	41	–	–	–	–
1972–3	715	401	40	160	–	–	–	–
1973–4	692	542	45	139	–	–	–	–
1974–5	646	620	11	252	–	–	–	–
1975–6	654	729	127	566	158	–	–	–
1976–7	814	864	169	377	185	180	–	–
1977–8	917	862	184	3521	201	193	90	–
1978–9	997	875	142	377	182	352	210	–
1979–80	1135	1003	187	464	185	323	145	–
1980–1	1188	997	155	545	194	259	458	–
1981–2	1160	990	446	562	169	246	486	–
1982–3	1105	918	728	642	258	184	528	–
1983–4	1116	–	923	753	902	197	579	–
1984–5	972	–	832	927	992	266	587	
1985–6	1305	–	997	1260	1385	289	782	88
1986–7	1279	–	862	1392	1310	322	771	101
1987–8	1236	–	871	1603	1463	356	780	145
1988–9	1244	–	973	1778	1260	372	746	174
1989–90	1272	–	992	1884	1307	421	767	189
1990–1	1254	–	986	1991	1373	437	785	201

Source: 2006 Field Survey, Department of Planning, Salahaddin University.

Table 1.3 Students attending Salahaddin University by College, 1991–2005

Year	*University of Salahaddin Colleges*							
	Science	Engineering	Arts	Administration &Economics	Education	Law	Law(evening)	Medicine
1991–2	1225	1345	1881	1269	569	530	194	741
1992–3	1278	1378	1894	1288	594	584	388	722
1993–4	1244	1409	2013	1308	522	572	599	778
1994–5	1269	1569	2341	1340	612	561	772	763
1995–6	1288	1523	2401	1386	914	529	785	744
1996–7	1298	1668	2565	1441	992	582	762	798
1997–8	1279	1701	2599	1482	1024	533	779	773
1998–9	1278	1663	2614	1599	1248	238	761	771
1999–0	1301	1672	2669	1704	1383	566	769	732
2000–1	1281	1649	2641	1788	1685	572	778	739
2001–2	1272	1678	2634	1881	1901	599	722	748
2002–3	1269	1645	2654	1922	1941	601	741	753
2003–4	1235	1628	2601	1999	1917	561	793	766
2004–5	1241	1602	2643	2024	–	571	764	721
2005–6	1272	1674	2665	2087	–	530	777	–

Source: 2007 Field Survey, Department of Planning, Salahaddin University.

In the Kurdistan region there are seventeen public and private universities. The three largest are Salahaddin University in Erbil, the University of Suleimani and the University of Dohuk. They offer studies in various subjects leading to specialized diplomas, Bachelor's, Master's and PhDs. The two more recently established institutions are the University of Koya and Hawler Medical University. Kurdistan also has two universities that teach exclusively in English: University of Kurdistan-Hawler, which was established with the support of the KDP, and the American University in Iraq-Suleimaniya, established in 2007 by the KRG with the support of the PUK, working in conjunction with American academicians.

The second-largest university established in Kurdistan was Suleimani University, which includes 15 colleges in different campuses in Suleimaniya city, Bakrajo Chamchamal and Kalar. The total number of students at Suleimani University was 15,329 in 2007 (see Table 1.4).

Table 1.4 Students attending Suleimani University by College, 2007

Name of College	Number of Students
Medicine	785
Dentistry	257
Veterinary	217
Nursing	105
Pharmacy	122
Engineering	1,032
Sciences	1,560
Agriculture	953
Humanities Education	1,402
Administration and Economics	925
Languages	1,184
Physical Education	521
Education / Kalar	1,227
Arts	123
Basic Education	865
Arts / Khanaqin	679
Education / Chamchamal	110
Law	448
Law / Evening	707
Political Sciences / Evening	360
Languages / Evening	419
Commercial / Evening	1,328
Scientific Education	N/A

Source: 2007 Field Survey, Department of Planning, Suleimani University.

The third university in the region is Dohuk University, which was founded in October 1992 by mandate of the KRG Parliament due to the fact that Salahaddin University in Erbil could not meet the demand for all who needed higher education (see Table 1.5). At first it consisted of two colleges: the College of Medicine, which had 48 students and the College of Agriculture, which had 146 students. The total number of students in 2007 was 7,235. Koya University was established in 2003 in the city of Koysinjak. Koya is geographically situated at the centre of Iraqi Kurdistan, almost equidistant from Erbil and Suleimaniya. Currently, Koya University consists of 10 colleges with 29 departments. There are approximately 4,000 undergraduate and postgraduate students (60 per cent male and 40 per cent female), taught by enthusiastic, dedicated and research-oriented academicians.

Table 1.5 Colleges and Departments at Dohuk University, 2007

Colleges	Departments	
	Morning Study (50)	*Evening Study (8)*
College of Medicine	General	
College of Agriculture	Agriculture, Animal Production, Forestry, Soil and Water	
College of Engineering	Civil Engineering, Water Source Engineering, Architecture Engineering, Electricity and Computer Sciences	
College of Arts	Kurdish Language, History, English Language, Geography	Kurdish, History, English Language
College of Administration and Economics	Economics, Administration, Financial and Bank Sciences, Accounting	General Administration, Administration, Accounting, Computer Sciences
College of Sciences	Computer Sciences, Mathematics, Physics, Chemistry, Biology	

Colleges	Departments	
	Morning Study (50)	Evening Study (8)
College of Education	Computer Sciences, Mathematics, Physics, Chemistry, Biology, History, Kurdish Language, English Language, Arabic Language, Education and Psychology	
Veterinary College	General	Politics
College of Law & Politics	Politics	
College of Basic Education	Kurdish Language, English Language, Sociology, Mathematics	
College of Physical Educ.	Physical Education	
College of Education – Zakho	Computer Sciences, Mathematics, Physics, Chemistry, Biology, History, Kurdish Language, English Language, Arabic Language, Education and Psychology	
College of Commerce – Zakho	Commerce	

Source: 2007 Field Survey, Department of Planning, Dohuk University.

Table 1.6 Students attending Universities in Iraqi Kurdistan, 2007

University	Year Established	Location	Number of Students in 2007
Salahaddin University	1968–81	Erbil	19,609
Suleimani University	1992	Suleimaniya	15,329
Dohuk University	1992	Dohuk	7,435
Hawler Medical University	2005	Erbil	2,105
Koya University	2003	Koysinjak	4,000
Kurdistan University-Hawler	2006	Erbil	234

Source: 2007 Field Surveys from the Planning and Registrar Offices of each University.

2

NATIONALISM, NATION, STATE, NATION STATE AND STATELESS NATION

There are as many different forms of nationalism as there are definitions of what constitutes a nation. Terms such as 'territory', 'language', 'culture', 'religion' and 'history' are all possible but not necessary elements that factor into the creation of a people's sense of national identity.[1]

The study of nationalism has produced a plethora of related terminology: 'nation', 'nation state', 'nation-building', 'nationhood', 'national identity', 'ethnicity' and more.[2] There is surprisingly little agreement on the nature of, expected stages of, or typology of nationalism. This diversity of understandings is inevitable given the fact that the birth of each nation takes place at different times and in differing geopolitical contexts. The literature emphasizes that the abstract concept of 'nationalism' is separate from its multifarious, particular, contextually determined origins, routes and implementations.[3] Anthony Smith's definition of nationalism is particularly pertinent to this study because it fully explicates the socio-political understanding of Kurdish national identity:

> Nationalism is a cultural doctrine and ideological movement for attaining and maintaining the *autonomy, unity and identity* of a nation.[4]

One of the major characteristics of nationalism has been its ability to stamp an identity on to each person. The success of the notion and process of nationalism is demonstrated by the fact that most people regard the person without a nationality as somehow defective.[5] The individual without a nationality, or a national personality, is a lost soul, or even a non-person, if such a thing is possible. At least the individual without a national identity is ill-defined and incomplete.[6]

The concepts of 'nation' and 'nationalism' cannot be clarified without focusing on the process of identification. Katherine Verdery points out that the future of the study of nations and nationalism lies in the consideration of national identities. She argues that the investigations of national identity must take into account that 'national identity exists at two levels: the individual's sense of self as national and the identity of the collective whole in relation to others of like kind.'[7] In other words, national identity may mean either the identity of individuals who claim to belong to a nation, or the collective identity of the nation which distinguishes it from other nations.

The term 'nationalism' is generally used to describe two types of phenomena: the first consists of the attitudes that the members of a nation have when they care about their national identity. This in itself raises questions about the concept of nation (or national identity), which is often defined in terms of common origin, ethnicity or cultural ties. The second type consists of the actions that the members of a nation take when seeking to achieve or sustain self-determination. These actions raise questions about whether self-determination should be understood as involving full statehood with complete authority over domestic and international affairs, or whether something less is adequate.

Nation, State, Nation State and Stateless Nation

The terminology surrounding the issues of nations, nationalism and states is both confused and confusing. Writers in international politics and in the popular media often use the terms 'nation' and 'state' interchangeably, as if they are synonyms.[8] The word 'nation' is used to describe a human community that has acquired national identity. Most definitions of nation have three main common elements: spatial, social and political.[9] The spatial element is the territory: nations are usually linked to a homeland. The social element pertains to common understandings, aspirations, myths, historical memories, symbols and traditions. The political element is akin to 'state' or 'government.'

The modern understanding of 'nation' may not be older than the 'eighteenth century, give or take the odd predecessor.'[10] It is commonly understood that every nation must have its own state. But is this always the case? Are there not many stateless nations, or nations without a state in today's world? Traditionally, 'nations' are distinguished from 'states'. A nation often consists of an ethnic or cultural community, whereas a state is a political entity with a varying degree of sovereignty. While many states are nations in some sense, there are other nations which are not fully sovereign states. In other words, there exist communities that consider themselves nations, but which are not recognized as such by other states or they are not granted the legitimacy, privileges, or acknowledgement of fully fledged states. These are 'nations in waiting', 'proto-nations', 'nations without states', or 'non-state nations'. Examples of these include the Kurds, Basques, Armenians, Palestinians, Québécois, Cree Indians, Scots, Welsh, Cornish ... and other people groups. What binds them together is that each somehow demonstrates a 'national conscience'.[11]

What, then, is national consciousness? National consciousness is the sense of belonging to a political and social community, which constitutes or wishes to constitute a nation organized as a state. It is the fundamental basis of the cultural or political nation. In principle, national consciousness is independent of the existence of a national state. Without national consciousness, however, a national movement would be doomed to failure.[12]

What, then, is the state? The concept of the state, like that of nation and nationalism, is problematic. In many cases the concept of state may be likened to vastly different concepts of the nation, such as the United Nations or the League of Nations.[13] Philip Abrams states clearly:

> We have come to take the state for granted as an object of political practice and for political analysis, while remaining quite spectacularly unclear as to what [it] is.[14]

David Held holds that the state is an 'apparatus of government'.[15] Referring to Weber Held notes that 'the very nature of the state crystallizes at the intersection of international and national conditions and pressures'.[16] The state may thus be defined as 'the institution, or grouping which possesses the monopoly of legitimate or physical violence over a territory'.[17]

Gareth Stansfield studied the political development of Iraqi Kurdistan in the late 1990s and found that it is not impossible to consider the Kurdish entity as state or stately 'entity' because it possesses the attributes of: population, territory, governmental and administrative institutions and significant informal and formal international relations. Yet, Kurdistan does not have a formal standing army; it is not recognized by the UN and it doesn't collect taxes from its citizens.[18] The 'stately attributes' that Kurdistan does possess, however, serve to consolidate the sense of belonging to one nation state among the younger generation in Kurdistan, as shall be seen.

What is National Identity? Meanings and Character

National identity is a particular form of collective identity in which, despite their routine lack of physical contact, people consider themselves to be bound together. They may feel bound together because they speak the same language or a dialect of a common language. Or they inhabit or are closely familiar with a defined territory and experience its economic system with the same understanding. Or they share a variety of customs, of collective history, which is experienced in the present with pride in the nation's achievements and, where necessary, a sense of shame at the nation's failings.[19]

Social psychologist Michael Billig explains national identity as a social concept which is derived through the habits, beliefs and behaviours of social life and it has a strong emotional component. In all of these descriptions identity is not conceived of as a 'thing', but is rather an understanding that allows people to speak about self and the community. Identity does not develop in a social void but in relation with other forms of existence. 'Identity is a form of life.'[20]

Anthony Smith points out that national identity's popularity is relatively recent. It has replaced earlier terms such as 'national character' and the later 'national consciousness' which were widely used in eighteenth, nineteenth and early twentieth centuries.[21] National identity is not regarded as something that 'is', but something that is constructed. National identity in this sense is in continual flux. No national identity is immutable, just as no culture can remain untouched by history. Identity is perceived as 'the action unit of culture'.[22]

Although national identity generally refers to an identity that is constructed and formed within the boundaries of a nation state, one cannot limit it solely to such an activity. For Parekh national identity is, first of all, identification with 'a particular community based on a shared loyalty.'[23] Nations without states or stateless nations also share common characteristics which differentiate them from other nations. An important aspect of both individual and collective identities is their dependence on 'the other.' There is no independent identity without taking into account its difference from the identity of others. The creation of 'the other' is as necessary as constructing one's own identity. Actually, 'identities are constructed through, not outside, difference'.[24]

The most important function of national identity is that it provides people with the knowledge of who they and others are and where they are from. Even though no definition may appear completely satisfactory, given the complexity and multi-dimensionality of national identity, a working definition is necessary for constructing a theoretical framework. For the purposes of this study, national identity is defined as a sense of national character or a set of national characteristics that are presented as distinctive or defining. Thus national identity is defined as the individual's national feeling, loyalty and connection to a national group.

I argue that national identity is imagined; it is a story people tell themselves, grounded in experience, structured by the social and economic context in which people are set. It is assigned and learned as well as invented.

Political Culture

Political culture embraces the dominant patterns of beliefs and values, which are acquired, but modify and change as a result of a complex process of socialization and feedback from the political system. So for our purposes political culture may be defined as the politically relevant values and attitudes of the members a society.[25]

The political culture may change rapidly through specific events.[26] Even so, the building blocks of political culture are the knowledge, beliefs, opinions and emotions of individual citizens toward their form of government.[27] If nationalism is about identity and national identity is based on emotional bonds, then national identity and political culture in Kurdistan are most likely complementary aspects of the same phenomena. Since nationality is politically shaped and reflects the national traditions of governance, political culture must be seen as an important aspect of national identity.

In the older Anglo-American literature the dominant concept of 'nation' simply related to the civic, state-oriented concept: all citizens of a state formed a nation. It was often contrasted with the Central European, ethnically oriented one for which a special term, 'ethno-nation', was coined. A group forms an ethno-nation if its members share, or believe that they share, origin, language and culture. Many combinations of underlying traits (common history, language, customs, values, common political understandings and geographical proximity) must be true for each separate group that claims to form a nation. For instance, the Kurds distinguish themselves from Arabs or Turkmens in the sense that they belong to another nation, mainly the Kurdish. They don't speak the same language as Arabs or Turkmen; they don't live in similar conditions; and they have no shared political history with their Arab neighbours, especially since the 1990s.

It is proposed that the term 'nation' denotes any group united through a common belief in the possession of common features like language, roughly common origins and history, ethnic ties and territory. Nationalism for the Kurds can be regarded as a state-seeking and nation-building movement, especially in the post-1990s era.

3

APPROACHES TO THE STUDY OF NATIONALISM AND NATIONAL IDENTITY

Anthony Smith's understanding of ethnicity, nation, nationalism, national identity and political culture are the focus of this chapter. Smith has popularized his six dimensions of ethnic community and I apply them to Kurdistan because they are particularly pertinent and fitting to the development of Kurdish understandings of nationalism.

The Civic–Ethnic Dichotomy

There are two ways to become a member of a nation. These two ways represent two separate and distinct kinds of nationalism: 'ethnic-genealogical' and 'civic-territorial.'[1] Scholars of nationalism point out that any nation has many elements that correspond to their particular notion of 'nation'. Sometimes civic elements dominate ethnic ones; other times the opposite occurs. Smith notes that there is a 'profound dualism at the heart of every nationalism and every nationalism contains civic and ethnic elements in varying degrees and different forms.'[2]

The bases of the civic model are the sense of territory and the sense of a legal-political community that is subject to common laws and institutions. These common laws and institutions are vital to the definition of the community of citizens who are legally and politically equal and who identify with the common culture.[3] Critical elements that make up the ethnic concept of nation are common descent and kinship ties. Ethnic demography is the route toward nationhood in this latter concept. This concept of the nation also emphasizes elements such as customs, traditions and dialects.[4] Ethnic nations appeal to existing customary and linguistic ties which they set out to standardize and elaborate, thereby developing rules and laws from customs and transforming dialects into languages.[5]

The focal point of the civic-territorial nation is the political community. Membership is based on juridical definitions of citizenship irrespective of ethnic ancestry. The common culture is based not on genealogical commonality but on shared components of the political culture, such as the rights and obligations of citizenship. The focal point of the ethnic-genealogical nation is genealogy *per se*; the route to membership is through descent or ancestry; and the common culture lies in shared components of native traditions and symbols.[6]

Belief in a unitary ethnic nation among the Kurds has produced an intensely felt collective sense of 'oneness' and has served a variety of functions in modern Iraqi Kurdistan. The distinction between cultural or ethnic and civic nationalism is difficult to ascertain in the Kurdish case because the boundary dividing them is unclear. Both types of nationalism look forward and backwards to seek to build a common destiny and obtain historical legitimacy.

Political or civic nationalism is explicitly concerned with the individual rights of each citizen, all of whom are equal, and it is based on cosmopolitan and rationalist conceptions of the nation in which educated individuals are united by common laws and mores. This nationalism anticipates a common humanity, which transcends cultural differences, but accepts the division of the world into different political communities. Its objective is the construction of a representative state for the community in order to participate as an equal nation in a developing cosmopolitan civilization based on reason. The vital elements in civic nationalism are the extension of legal rights and duties to all sectors of society. Therefore, citizenship is the most important factor in the civic conception of the nation.[7]

Cultural or ethnic nationalism imagines the nation to have a distinctive civilization based on a unique history, culture and territory. Nations are not merely rational political units, but organic beings that have been endowed with unique individuality, which should be treasured by all members. Nature and history, rather than mere consent or law, are the passions that bind individuals to the nation. Cultural nationalism rejects the ideal of universal citizenship rights and insists that presumed natural divisions between and within nations be respected. As such, cultural nationalists view the nation as an organic entity only in a metaphoric sense.[8]

Clearly, ethnic nationalism is a typology of nationalism that defines its nation's members based on consanguinity. Ethnic nationalists seek to establish the ethnic nation as the 'sole criterion of statehood'.[9] Therefore participation in the membership of ethnic nations is not based on free will but on the fixed inheritance of bloodlines. Historical memories and myths of descent are particularly important. As Smith points out, it is the particular mix of civic and ethnic elements that brings out the unique distinctiveness of each culture.

A unique sense of Kurdish national identity emerged when Kurdish society began to modernize. People came to define themselves in terms of ethnicity based on the myth of common ancestry. This meshed with civic identity and its acquisition of political rights. One can assume that ideas of civic nationalism spread along with the political transformation of the post-1990s. Ideas of human rights, democracy, the free market and individualism were spreading around the world during this time and they became the dominant mode of thinking for the Kurds after the 1990s.

Ethno-Symbolism and the Dimensions of Ethnic Community

Both critics and supporters of Smith's framework have focused on the specific, mostly historical, issues that his theory addresses: the origins of nations and nationalism, the importance of collective mythologies, the questions of ethnic election or ethnic survival and national identity. The nation as a homogeneous entity with shared characteristics is defined here in terms of its dialectic and discursive nature. Smith's definition of nation is:

> a named human community occupying a homeland, and having common myths and a shared history, territory, a common public culture, a single economy and common rights and duties for all members.[10]

Smith speaks explicitly in favour of an 'ethnicist' or 'culturalist' definition of nation and describes nations as 'cultural units'. Oftentimes mistakenly referred to as 'primordialistic',[11] Smith's view is that most nations are to a certain extent 'the heritage of older collective groups'. The French term *ethnie* as a unit of analysis is used as a synonym for 'ethnic community'. Smith feels it best captures the range of meanings embodied in the original Greek term *ethnos* which stresses the similarity of cultural attributes in a community rather than in biological or kinship-based factors. *Ethnie* serves to unite cultural uniqueness with historical continuity.[12]

> Though most latter-day nations are, in fact, polyethnic, or rather most nation-states are polyethnic, many have been formed in the first place around a dominant *ethnie*.[13]

Nations always require ethnic 'elements', These may, of course, be reworked and they often are. But nations are inconceivable without common myths and memories of a territorial home.[14]

'Any useful definition of the nation must do justice to both ethnic and territorial conceptions'.[15] The *ethnie* is defined by a set of features or dimensions that by now should be familiar:

> a named human community connected to a homeland, possessing common myths of ancestry, shared memories, one or more elements of shared culture and a measure of solidarity, at least among the elites.[16]

These six dimensions may be considered in relation to the Kurds generally and modern Iraqi Kurdistan specifically.[17]

Smith's Conception of Ethnicity, Nation, Nationalism, National Identity and Political Culture

Ethnicity is the basis of national identity for Smith. Hence, people who share some of these characteristics are entitled to form some sort of national identity. The movement that facilitates and brings nations into being is nationalism. Nationalism is defined as

> an ideological movement for attaining and maintaining autonomy, unity and identity on behalf of a population deemed by some of its members to constitute an actual or potential 'nation.'[18]

Smith's conception of nationalism as an ideology or core doctrine applies to the nation, not the state. He suggests that four vital propositions should be considered in defining the 'ideology of nationalism' or the 'core doctrine' of nationalism:[19] (1) the world has been divided into nations and each nation has its own history, destiny and individuality that make it unique; (2) all the social and political power belongs to the nation and allegiance to the state overrides all other loyalties; (3) if individuals want to be free and realize themselves, their identification must be with a nation; and (4) nations must be autonomous, united and free to attain their goals of security and peace.

Smith argues that although nations and nationalism are profoundly modern phenomena, they have deep roots in earlier ethnic communities and *ethnies*.[20] He considers the specificity of the *ethnie* to be embedded in its 'myth-symbol complex' which is very durable over time. This durability does not imply that myths and symbols have static meanings, but rather that they create a myth of 'common origins'.[21]

Ethnicity in itself may well be an imagined association, but for Smith, nations are more than artificial modern constructs. To see them as such is to deny prior social formations the fluidity of the present. Nations develop out of local traditions, institutions, economic and social structures and dialects as much they are created by an elite who 'hoodwink' the populace into accepting an ideology that is used as a tool for the maintenance of hegemony. The masses not only experience national consciousness, but they also participate in its formation.[22]

Smith argues that nationalisms and national identities develop within, and are shaped by, specific historical, cultural and territorial contexts. Nationalism 'depends for its power not just on the general idea of the nation, but on the presence and character of this or that specific nation' from which it is derived.[23] Nationalisms and national identities are thus embedded in 'pre-existing and highly particularized cultural heritages and ethnic formations'.[24] The political cultural patterns of pre-existing cultures necessarily inform national development. For example, cultural definitions of legitimate authority and community, and the individual's relationship to both, strongly shape national identity.

The 'myth of the modern nation' fails to grasp the continuing relevance and power of the role that pre-modern ethnic ties and sentiments play in providing a firm base for the nation-to-be.[25] The argument that nationalism is an exclusively political phenomenon inasmuch as its meaning cannot be found outside of the political realm is seriously mistaken. Nationalism cannot be reduced to the uniform principle that the cultural unit must be made congruent with the political unit. Not only does this omit a number of other vital nationalist tenets, but it fails to grasp the fact that the development of any nationalism depends on bringing the cultural and moral regeneration of the community into a close relationship, if not harmony, with the political mobilization and self-determination of its members.[26]

To neglect the vital link between culture and politics in nationalism is, therefore, 'to remove the mainspring of nationalism, the ideal of communal regeneration in any and every sphere of human life and substitute the "pure form" of the territorial nation for its emotional content, on the lines of that other hollow strategy, "national in form, socialist in content."'[27]

Smith's approach is grounded in a very different understanding of the roots of nations and nationalism. Nationalism derives its force from its historical embeddedness. As an ideology, nationalism can take root only if it strikes a popular chord and is taken up by and inspires particular groups and social strata. But nationalism is much more than an ideology. Unlike other modern belief-systems, it depends for its power not just on the general idea of the nation, but on the presence and character of this or that specific nation which it objectivizes. Its success, therefore, depends on specific cultural and historical contexts and this means that the nations it helps to create are derived from pre-existing and highly particularized cultural heritages and ethnic formations.[28] A nation is not merely a cultural 'artefact' or an invention by those with a nationalist agenda; nor are nations strategic reactions to modernization and late capitalism. To understand them, '[w]e must trace them back to their underlying ethnic and territorial contexts; we must set them in the wider historical intersection between cultural ties and political communities as these were influenced by and influence the processes of modernization'.[29]

Underlying the development and appeal of the national idea is a strong cultural legacy that incorporates patterns of authority, symbols, values, political and social traditions, myths and memories, all of which undergo reinterpretations throughout the generations and through political mobilization and actions. Smith calls the rediscovery of the ethnic past, and especially of a 'golden age' that can act as an inspiration for contemporary problems and needs, a 'cultural purification'. These 'pasts' become standards against which to measure the alleged failings of the present generation and the contemporary community.

Smith's analysis of the 'modern ethnic revival' revolves around the cultural history of groups. He argues that ethnonationalism grows out of ethnic consciousness, which is itself the product of a sense of common origin and destiny and of cultural markers.[30] The transformation of cultural markers into identities expressing political claims is a natural and necessary phenomenon. Consequently, he is sceptical of theories that view nations and nationalism as purely modernly constructed phenomena.

Along with ethno-history, vernacular symbolic codes and indigenous artifacts and achievements are rediscovered. Historians, archaeologists, philologists and others scour the documentary and material records of the community to reconstruct a picture of collective native life in earlier times from which the current community can derive a sense of connection, continuity and dignity. In so doing they draw the boundaries of the community on the basis of shared codes—often a vernacular language—which produces a strong sense of cultural community and sense of distinguishment of the group from others.[31]

'Authentication' involves 'sifting or determining what is and what is not distinctive, what is and what is not indigenous and what therefore can be deemed to be 'truly ours'. What is authenticated must then be 'reappropriated'. People must be encouraged to take possession of their authentic vernacular heritage and their genuine ethno-history. The history of several East European nationalisms reveals the ways in which intellectuals defined the cultural profile of their peoples through the reappropriation of an authenticated vernacular language and culture, even where elements of that linguistic culture long pre-existed the activities of the appropriating nationalist intellectuals.[32]

Thus there is a crucial 'relationship between culture and politics in nationalism', as nationalism's goals are far more complex than a basic desire to make the cultural and political unit 'congruent'.[33] To disregard its emotional and spiritual aspects is to seriously misunderstand nationalism's nature and appeal. One should not assume that the nationalist project, including the 'regeneration' of the community, leads Smith to assume the purity of nationalist intentions. Leaders may be unscrupulous. However, '[t]he ethnic past sets limits to the manipulations of the elites and provides the ideals for the restored nation and its destiny. In this way the nation remains embedded in a past that shapes its future as much as any present global trends'.[34]

The focus of analysis for nationalism 'can be neither the aims nor activities of the intellectuals, professionals and other elites, nor the mass sentiments and memories of the common people, but the often complex relationships between the two'.[35] By sustaining a sense of shared memory, a nation's cultural framework remains a vital force in both shaping nationalism's substance and providing its continuing appeal. The modernist-instrumentalist approach weds nationalism's essence and political appeal to the desire for an increasingly obsolescent nation state and it discounts the nationalist vision of culturally and historically anchored national identity as essentially imagined. It provides little significant theoretical insight into continuities in national perspectives over time or the continuing relevance of national identity and nationalist programmes for rational citizens of modern states.

Smith's approach provides a framework that incorporates elements of both the primordialist and instrumentalist approaches which are useful for exploring the character of Kurdish nationalism. The Kurds are an *ethnie* that aspires to become a full nation, with or without a separate state of their own. Even if it falls short of independent statehood, the Kurds of Iraq aim to form a single nation out of their *ethnie*.[36]

Applying Smith's Dimensions of Ethnic Community to Kurdistan

The first dimension, the necessity of having a collective name, fits Kurdistan very well. If one inspects Kurdish historical records, there is plenty of documentation that the Kurds and Kurdistan, as name and territory, can be traced back well over two thousand years.[37] A collective proper name is the hallmark of the ethnic community in the historical record. The historical record is more replete with collective names than descriptions of social and cultural structures of a given nation.[38] Kurdistan had a collective name for its ethnic community by which it distinguished itself and continues to distinguish itself from others. At the same time that name summarizes Kurdistan's essence to itself. It is as if within the name, 'Kurdistan', lay the magic of the ethnic community's existence and guarantee of its survival.[39]

The second dimension is the myth of common ancestry, which undergirds the sense of ethnic ties and sentiment for the members. Myths of origin and descent provide not only the means to collectively locate the nation in the world, but they provide the charter for the community's self-understanding which explains its origins, growth and destiny.[40] The myth provides an overall framework of meaning for the ethnic community, a *mythomoteur* which makes sense of the community's experiences and self-defines its 'essence'. 'Without a *mythomoteur* an ethnic group cannot define itself to itself or to others and the group cannot inspire or guide collective action'.[41]

> The study of ethnicity through ethnic myths, symbols, memories and values allows us to grasp the dynamic and expressive character of ethnic identity, and its long term influence on human affairs, while allowing for its changing content and meaning.[42]

The common myth of descent for the ancient Kurds can be traced to the memory of Kurdish common history, its golden age, heroes, myths and symbols. In light of the importance of these myths, memories and symbols, which are closely associated with Kurdish ethnic awareness of the nineteenth and twentieth centuries, light can be shed on a Kurdish 'golden age,' along with its myths and memories. These distinguish the Kurds from their neighbours. An example of the golden age is the citation of the Kurds to the dynasties and families who ruled various places in Kurdistan in premodern history, such as the *Shaddadis* who ruled 951–1174 in Transcaucasia, 1088 north of Kurdistan, the Caucasus and Armenia, and the *Hasanwayhids* who ruled 959–1095 in Dinawar. Likewise 990–1096 the *Marwandis* ruled Diyarbakir, Jazera and several towns in Armenia. A century later, between 1169 and 1250, the *Ayyubi* dynasty came to power.[43] Its founder was Salahaddin Ayyubi, a Kurd who formed an Islamic empire in both Egypt and Syria.[44] The Kurds also refer to the *Zand* dynasty who ruled Iran 1752–95. The founder of this dynasty was Karim Khan-e-Zand who became Shah of Persia.[45] The Seljuk Turks invaded these dynasties between the eleventh and twelfth centuries, the

Mongols invaded in the thirteenth century and their successors invaded until the fifteenth century.[46]

An example of remembering heroes as mythical symbols is the Kurds' popular memories of *Kaway Asinger*, *Mami Alan* and the ceremonies and celebrations of *Nawroz* on 21 March (New Year's Day).[47] The Kurds mark *Nawroz* on the first day of spring each year and celebrate it by going on picnics and setting large fires on the peaks of mountains. Until recently all the states in which the Kurds live, with the exception of Iran, prohibited the Kurds from celebrating this day. The Persians allowed the celebration because they also consider their new year to be on the first day of spring and they also celebrate *Nawroz*.

The celebration of *Nawroz* is historically related to the legend of *Zuhak* and of *Kaway Asinger*. The legend of *Zuhak* contains one of several folk myths pertaining to the origins of the Kurds. According to written Kurdish folklore, *Zuhak* was a tyrant who had snakes growing on his shoulders. Physicians were not able to cure this deformity. Satan appeared to the tyrant and told him that he would be cured if he would feed the snakes each day with the brains of two youngsters. The executioner appointed to the task of providing the brains took pity on his victims and each day spared one of them and substituted the brains of a sheep. The survivors fled to the safety of the mountains, where they became the founders of a new people, the forefathers of the Kurds.[48]

Zuhak himself was overthrown when one of the tyrant's intended victims rebelled against his fate and killed *Zuhak* instead. That person was *Kaway Asinger*. The day that tyrant *Zuhak* was killed is called *Nawroz*. Historically, the Kurdish calendar dates from the defeat of the Assyrian Empire at Nineveh, north of Mosul, by the forces of the Medes.[49] The myth of *Zuhak*, according to the Kurdish perspective, represents their existence as one of the ancient peoples of the region. The end of *Zuhak*'s tyranny represents a great deal of relief in the Kurds' collective memory.[50]

The myth of *Nawroz* was used by Kurdish nationalists to rally and galvanize Kurdish support against the newly created national states which were developing around them and encompassing the lands in which they were living. Many Kurds applied *Nawroz* and the myth of *Zuhak* as a symbol of freedom and victory of the people over the tyranny of *Zuhak*. This relates to Smith's third dimension of ethnic community in that there is a shared historical memory that everyone in the 'nation' knows about and feels emotionally toward. Smith points out that 'history must tell a story; it must please and satisfy as narrative; it must all be part of a piece ... and it must also educate.'[51]

For the Kurds the symbol of *Nawroz*, an essentially Kurdish practice, is requisite to their sense of ethnic identity. Thus, by engaging in these annual celebratory rituals, the Kurds differentiate themselves from their neighbours, the majority of whom do not celebrate *Nawroz*. The *Nawroz* festival as a shared historical memory can also be seen as an opportunity to practise Kurdish culture. *Nawroz* is a very important celebration for the Kurds because it is an opportunity for them to gather together as Kurds, whether in Kurdistan or in diaspora and to continue the celebration of their collective unique identity.

The fourth dimension refers to the elements of a shared culture. A distinctive shared culture serves to bind the members of an ethnic community and to distinguish them from outsiders. Language and religion have been the most commonly shared distinctive traits for an ethnic community.[52] Other than that, laws, dress, music, food and folklore all are providers of common cultural bonds. The Kurdish language for the Kurds is the main, but not the sole, differentiating mark of ethnicity. Though only Kurds practise the Yezidi religion,[53] since many Kurds belong to other religions, such as Islam, Christianity and even Judaism, religion for the Kurds would not qualify as the most distinguishing mark of ethnicity.[54] Hensler and Muller point out that given the wide diversity of religious practice in Kurdistan, 'religious belief doesn't play a major role in defining Kurdish distinctiveness'.[55] Language, however, allows for a clear differentiation between Kurds and the non-Kurds, such as Arabs or Turkmen.

Smith's fifth dimension of ethnic community is having an association with a specific homeland or territory. 'Territory is relevant to ethnicity because of an alleged and felt symbiosis between a certain piece of earth and "its" community'. This can be clarified through three aspects of ethnic homelands: sacred centres, commemorative association and external recognition.[56] Smith refers to Musasir as the sacred city of ancient Urartu in what is now northern Kurdistan.[57]

In the sixteenth century when Kurdistan as a homeland was divided by the external powers of the Ottomans and the Qajars, the link between the Kurds and their territory remained. This association itself became an essential part of the collective memory and identity of the Kurds. Greater Kurdistan as a land became part of the Kurdish lore and a focus of the Kurdish collective dream. When outsiders identify members of the community, they often do so with reference to their territorial 'origins'. So the term 'ethnic' acquires additional connotations of 'being from the same original home land'.[58]

The final dimension that pertains to ethnic community is perhaps the strongest in terms of evoking identity and national feeling. It is the sense of solidarity. In my view the feeling among the Kurds of belonging to Kurdistan is vital to demonstrate their national identity and political solidarity. The feeling of belonging, of being part of a group that shares the same characteristics and which also separates them from others allows individuals to acquire an identity outside of themselves and beyond their immediate environment. In times of stress and danger this strong sense of belonging can override class, factional or regional divisions within the community. This sense of solidarity must animate at least the educated upper strata to be effective as a solidarity-inducing factor.[59]

Identity then is conceptualized as 'sameness'.[60] The nation as a form of community implies both similarity among its members and difference from outsiders.[61] Political scientists in Kurdistan observe that national symbols as markers of national solidarity have played a vital role in consolidating national identity since the 1990s. National symbols, such as flags and national anthems, play crucial roles in nation-building and maintenance. National symbols are interactive aids through which people can and do participate and celebrate the nation and their linkages to it. People who are learning to identity as Kurds are invited not only to watch the Kurdish flag from afar, but to carry it in their hands or to wear flag pins and participate in flag parades and flag hoisting ceremonies.[62]

There is wide recognition that symbols are a potent source with which to aid political power and influence. They are capable of rallying support for state interests by evoking emotional sentiments relating to national identification, allegiance and self-sacrifice. For large and arguably 'imagined' communities,[63] like a nation where group members cannot possibly have direct experience of more than a fraction of the group, the ability to use national symbols to objectify group solidarity is essential to arousing group identification. Third, if group symbols facilitate in-group identification and magnify social identity ideals, they should also augment group members' attempts to positively distinguish in-groups from out-groups in an effort to enhance self-esteem. Finally, key symbols such as flags, dress or national anthems represent the group as a whole or in the abstract, thereby communicating 'groupness' itself, the shared in-group identity. Emile Durkheim asserted the following:

> The soldier who dies for his flag dies for his country, but as a matter of fact, in his own consciousness, it is the flag that has the first place.[64]

During the past few years Mas'ud Barzani, the KDP leader and president of Kurdistan, kept the Iraqi flag off of public buildings in the Kurdistan region. He was particularly concerned that Kurdistan's flag as the symbol of Kurdish unity not be diluted or confused with another competing symbol, especially one that had been a symbol of oppression for the Kurds.[65] National flags, food and anthems, emblems, national flowers and animals, all symbolize a nation's uniqueness, sovereignty, dignity and patriotism.[66]

For ethnic nationalists the ethnic group constitutes an individual's primary sense of belonging. Thus, an individual's deepest sense of loyalty derives from the ties of common ancestors and kinship, distinct language and culture, the unique historical legacy of the group, shared traditions, customs, norms and values and attachment to a particular territory. Ethnic nationalists seek political autonomy to preserve, protect and defend their collective identity from the encroachment of competing cultures to ensure the continued survival of the collective identity. The offspring of this development is a world increasingly characterized by the binary division of 'us' versus 'them'.

When ethnic groups seek aspirations of national sovereignty, political and ethnic tensions escalate, resulting in intense social conflict. Smith views the Kurds of Iraq as an *ethnicity* that 'opted to remain autonomous ... within a larger state, given the political obstacles to national unity, let alone full independence'.[67] The Kurds *qua* Kurds possess all the attributes of Smith's six dimensions that qualify a group as an ethnic community.

In the pre-modern era society was predominantly composed of peasants and their relations with the 'landowners' or *Aghas* who ruled over them. Having long since lost the semi-state principalities with which they had in some ways identified, the Kurdish nomads and peasantry suffered the loss of their princes and *Agha* elites, which were expediently absorbed by the Ottoman gentry. Thus, the source of their discontent was not a class of people that spoke the same language or shared the same religion and customs, but foreign oppressors, which is how they came to be seen. At the early stage of the Ottoman Empire the Ottomans and the Safavids were foreigners. Having lost virtually all its upper principalities by the nineteenth century, except for the religious status of the *Sheikhs* or *Aghas*, the Kurds were composed of backward peasants. This reality served to both hamper and enhance the development of Kurdish ethnic consciousness rather than a national one.[68]

However, the lingering memory of greatness with which no Kurd was currently associated, fuelled anxiety and discontent. When the conditions were right, it sparked ethnic awareness. The Ottoman reforms in the late eighteenth century provided the infrastructure which allowed the rebirth of the Kurdish intelligentsia in Kurdistan and thereby set the process of nationalization in motion. Even when all the aforementioned elements of proto-nationalism were present in a given society, this did not necessarily guarantee the development of national sentiment and nation. However, Eric Hobsbawm suggests that in places where proto-nationalism existed, the task of nationalism was simplified exceedingly, as proto-national sentiments could be mobilized behind a modern cause or modern state.[69]

Yet Hobsbawm, like the other contemporary and modernist scholars of nationalism, views the historical evidence of nationalism as emerging from the sharing of language, territory, ethnicity, religion and historical-political attributes. But he labels it as 'proto-nationalism' and offers an insightful discussion of such groups, terming them 'proto-nations.' These communities, that share some type of common traits like language or religion, but attach no political connotations to that fact, are very different from the full-fledged nations they sometimes grow into.[70] Though Hobsbawm's idea of proto-nationalism applies to the Kurdish case before the 1990s, especially during the pre-modern era, after the 1990s the model is insufficient.[71]

Hobsbawm uses the term 'proto-nationalism' to describe an ethnic group's development towards nationalism. Proto-nations live across large areas and even in diaspora. They feel that they belong together because of their mutual ethnicity; but they lack a common polity. Where proto-nationalism exists, it is possible to mobilize the existing national symbols to create a modern state.[72] Smith stated that 'nations according to Hobsbawm owe much to "invented traditions", which are the product of social engineering'. They are created to 'serve the interests of the ruling elites by channelling the engineers of the newly enfranchised masses'.[73]

Language, Imagination and Imagined Communities

One of the most celebrated and influential contributions to the debate on nationalism has been Benedict Anderson's *Imagined Communities*. For the last twenty-five years his definition of nation has been the dominant one for students of nationalism. Treating it in cognitive, anthropological and spiritual terms[74] Anderson's description of the nation as an 'imagined community' is useful and important because it emphasizes the symbolic artificiality of national identity. He characterizes nations, as well as all other communities that are larger than primordial villages of face-to-face contact, as imagined communities and argues that communities need to be distinguished from one another not by their authenticity but by the way in which they are imagined.[75] For Anderson this community is an imagined—not imaginary—one.

Nation is an imagined political community, and imagined as both inherently limited and sovereign. ... It is *imagined* because the members of even the smallest nation will never know most of their fellow-members, meet them, or even hear of them, yet in the minds of each lives the image of their communion.[76]

Anderson argues that the nation is to be imagined as a unique entity in terms of time and space, but does 'not rely upon a continuous act of imagination' for its existence. It should be pointed out, however, that nationality, nation-ness and nationalism for Anderson are essentially 'particular cultural artefacts created towards the end of the eighteenth century'.[77] Anderson refers to Watson's definition as it elaborates what he wants to explain. Hugh Seton-Watson writes:

A nation exists when a significant number of people in a community consider themselves to form a nation, or behave as if they form one.[78]

Anderson considers that only if the nation is imagined to have an identity, may its people claim to have one. National identity can be similarly conceived as 'imagined' if it provides an 'imaginary unity' against other possible unities. A nation is a 'community of people, whose members are bound together by a sense of solidarity, a common culture and a national consciousness'.[79]

What needs to be explored is what particular kind of imagination emerged to permit 'national imagination', and what it is that 'makes the shrunken imaginings of recent history (scarcely more than two centuries) generate such colossal sacrifices'.[80] Anderson, like Smith, devotes more attention to the cultural construction of nationalism, or as he puts it, 'the cultural roots of nationalism'.[81] He advises how nationalism must be understood:

Nationalism has to be understood by aligning it, not with self-consciously held political ideologies, but with the large cultural system that preceded it, out of which, as well as against which, it came into being.[82]

The 'two relevant cultural systems' for Anderson are (1) the religious community and (2) the dynastic realm.[83] The religious community was imagined through the medium of sacred languages and written scripts, which fragmented, pluralized and regionalized in later years following the demise of Latin. Dynastic realms were the only political system that people 'as subjects rather than citizens' thought of belonging to.[84]

Nations were imagined in a very particular way, as passing through an uneventful linear time line. In explaining Anderson's ideas, Smith points out that 'the decline of cosmic religions and monarchies [happened] at the points when new conceptions of time and 'print capitalism' made it possible to imagine nations moving through linear time'.[85]

This is a distinctly modern type of imagination, Anderson observes. The technical preconditions were provided by the novel and the newspaper. Print capitalism had thus been central to the rise of nationalism. The capitalist publishing industry, driven by a restless search for markets, assembled the multiplicity of pre-modern vernaculars into a much smaller number of print communities, each of which prefigured a modern nation.[86]

Anderson argues that historically speaking, the possibility for the communities to imagine themselves as a nation only occurred when the 'three fundamental cultural conceptions' of fraternity, power and time collapsed during the rise of capitalism in the late eighteenth century. These three crucial cultural conceptions are: (1) the identification of 'a particular script-language', such as the identification of Latin in Christendom and the *Ummah* in the Islamic world, with access to religious truth; (2) the belief that society was organized in a natural hierarchy, at the summit of which were 'monarchs who were persons apart from other human beings'; and (3) a view of the inseparability of cosmology and history, which rendered 'the origin of the world and of men essentially identical'.[87]

Accordingly, the interconnected decline of these three meant that human beings required 'a new way of linking fraternity, power and time meaningfully together'.[88] For Anderson the emergence of the printing press, or 'print capitalism', related very much to the rise of nationalism. What mattered to Anderson was the advent of print culture rather than industry *per se*. As Montserrat Guibernau stated, it was not until the end of the fifteenth century when the printing press had been established in Europe. By the seventeenth century, according to Febvre, language had been established in modern forms.[89]

Consequently, Latin decreased as an instrument for reading and communication among the elite intellectuals, monarchs, clergy and the public. The reading of vernacular print-languages and literature, mainly newspapers, journals and books, portrayed the imagined political community and became the basis of national consciousness.[90]

Anderson is quite correct in his suggestion that print capitalism provides the new institutional space for the growth and development of the modern national language.[91] However, in pursuing these lines of arguments in relation to Iraqi Kurdistan, one might find good examples where it was at the initiative of the Ottoman Empire and later the British rule in Iraq that the first printed books were produced in Kurdish. This happens at the end of the seventeenth century when Ahmadi Khani printed his *Mam u Zin* in Kurdish. The crucial movement in the development of the modern Kurdish language came, however, in the 1970s, when the Kurdish intellectual elites in Iraq made it a cultural and political project to provide its mother tongue with the necessary linguistic equipment to enable it to become an adequate language for modern culture.

After the 1990s an entire institutional network of printing presses, publishing houses, newspapers, magazines and literary societies was created outside the purview of the previous Iraqi state. It was through this venue that a new approach and modern standardized language were given shape.

The Kurds of Iraq imagined their community to be a territorial political entity. This can be seen clearly in the recent skirmish for their rights to be written into the future constitution of Iraq. As to publication of newspapers, books and media, Anderson's argument fits Kurdistan's case very well. After the 1990s the means of new technological communications played a significant role in Kurdish national aspirations.

There is no single universal theory of nationalism. This is due to the concept's diverse interpretations and uses. However, there are three approaches that most of the theories of nationalism can fit into for the most part. They are (1) modernism, (2) ethno-symbolism and (3) social constructivism. The modernist view emphasizes nationalism as an invention and sees the process as a modern and recent political phenomenon (Gellner: industrialization and modernization; Hobsbawm: the invention of tradition; and Anderson: the printed word, language and imagination). Our concern has been to focus on the main points of their treatment of nationalism theory, rather than the historiographical details. However, Gellner and Anderson and probably Hobsbawm to some extent belong in different ways to the school which concentrates on the arguments that nations and nationalisms, especially in the West, are constructed through a political process and this happens in the modern period through the mobilization of groups seeking recognition of their political rights or through cultural policies of established states. The nation, for modernists like Hobsbawm and Gellner, is not only recent, but it is novel and a product of the processes of modernization.[92]

Ethno-symbolism is adopted by those who oppose a purely modern origin of nations approach (a group sometimes misleadingly called 'primordialists') and argue that modern nations have strong connections with pre-modern ethnic communities. The principal proponent of this view is Smith who considers his theoretical framework to be 'an internal critique and expansion of modernism'.[93] While not discarding the forces of modernity, Smith argues that nations are not freely invented. Nation-building is constrained by the *ethnie*.

Social constructivism constitutes an important part of the latest wave of nationalism literature. Constructivists, in contrast to modernists and ethno-symbolists, tend to be sceptical about grand theorizing. They argue that there is no one type of 'nation-ness'. 'Nation-ness' is a socially constructed discourse. National identity varies across time and sections of the population.

It seems that the theoretical explanation for the origins and development of nations that best fits the Kurdish case is that proposed by Anthony Smith and the historical ethno-symbolist school of thought. Smith's paradigm provides a thorough explanatory framework for understanding Kurdish nationalism and is preferred to alternative theories because (1) it stresses 'subjective' memories, values, myths and sentiments, which can be seen clearly in the Kurdish case; (2) it recognizes the impact that 'old' cultural identities and ethnic ties have on the growth of nations and national identities; and lastly, (3) it clarifies the importance of collective passions and deep-seated loyalties.

Smith rightly judges nation-formation to be a long-term process subject to a great variety of influences: political, economic, social and emotional, as conditions in respective communities evolve and the elites are continually called upon to adjust their means and goals accordingly to maintain their power positions and to keep the populace thinking towards nationhood.

4

MAKING SENSE OF
KURDISH HISTORY:
TERRITORY, LANGUAGE AND
PROTO-NATIONALISM

Anthony Smith's ethnic historicism may be viewed as a rediscovery and repossession of a group's communal history. Assessing the cultural and territorial springboard of ethnic nationalism requires a clear understanding of the origins of a nation's roots.[1] Smith argues that to understand a nation's roots and its continuing appeal, 'we must trace them ... to their underlying ethnic and territorial contexts'.[2]

The nation of Kurdistan has always been assessed as a territorial community. A study of Kurdistan as a territory, its ancient history and proto-national identity reveals the importance of language to the national identity in Kurdistan. Kurdistan's political culture from the twelfth through the nineteenth century is considered to answer the fundamental question as to whether there existed a Kurdish nationalism in the modern sense of the term during that period.

Territory, Ancient History and Proto-National Identity
Difficulties in the periodization of Kurdish history pale in comparison to the task of its political-cultural analyses. The historical background of Kurdistan from ancient until modern times is reviewed to gain some perspective as to how Kurdish nationalism emerged and developed over time. By analysing the manner in which Kurdish nationalism has constructed and reconstructed the nation in terms of territory, one can better understand how the demands of Kurdish nationalism for political recognition based on linguistic differences ultimately rely on territorial premises. It is clear that what underlies Kurdish national identity is a 'sense of place' rather than a 'sense of tribe and blood'.[3]

Kurdish-ness is based on living in a common territory. Thus, territory is one of the main elements of nationalism for the Kurds. Territorially the perceptions of Kurdistan and Kurdish national identity have existed long before their neighbouring nations existed and they remain central to the Kurds' sense of 'imagined' national identity.[4] The territorial concept of the nation is difficult to conceive of outside the realization of sovereign statehood.[5] But it is important to clarify that the ethnic concept of the nation for the Kurds plays a key role by way of the territorial idea of 'homeland.'

Control over a given territory is a key claim of nationalism. In order to justify the claims that are made in the name of a nation, the nation itself must be defined in terms of the territory. For the Kurds generally, the sense of territoriality contributes a great deal to the Kurdish sense of national identity.

Kurds and Kurdistan in the Pre-Modern Era

The reconstruction of the early history of the Kurds is not an easy task. Smith suggests two types of pre-modern ethnic community. The first type is lateral and extensive, which is characterized as an aristocratic type of *ethnie* including the clerical and scribal strata along with some of the wealthier urban merchants. In this type of ethnic community the culture is stratified and the elite strata are weakly diffused. Apart from the court and bureaucrats, only nobles, gentry and clergy had access to the Great Traditions. This united them loosely, while dividing them from the masses, particularly in the countryside, which remained embedded in folk culture.

The second is the urban-based vertical and intensive *ethnie*. It is also called 'demotic' *ethnie* in which a single ethnic culture permeates most strata of the population, even if its base remains urban and outlying rural areas exhibit local variants of the culture. In this type of ethnic community the indigenous culture cannot remain the preserve of any class, even if its producers and transmitters come from particular strata and institutions.[6] Pertaining to the Kurds, Smith refers to the Medes' tribal confederation (ca.1100 BC) as lateral ties of ethnicity which persisted over many years before suffering dilution and dissolution, or alternatively, transformation into demotic *ethnie* and incipient nations.[7]

There were also many 'Kurdish Kingdoms' and city-states in Kurdistan before the arrival of the unifying Medes, such as the kingdoms of *Kummuhu, Melidi, Gurgum, Ungi (Unqi), Kamanu, Kasku, Nairi, Shupria, Urkish, Mushku, Mardu, Kardu* and, most importantly, *Manna* and *Qutil*. These are presently known primarily through their Mesopotamian names, with their native names still waiting to be discovered.[8]

This second type of *ethnie*, the vertical-demotic one, emphasizes the ethnic bond that unites a people against the 'stranger' or 'enemy'. This signifies a marked emphasis upon sharp boundaries with bans on religious syncretism, cultural assimilation and even inter-marriage. This type of *ethnie* falls into discrete sub-types: (1) *city-state amphictyonies*, (2) *frontier ethnies*, (3) *tribal confederations* and (4) *diasporas* and *sects*.[9] The Kurds represent one instance of a premodern *ethnie* which fits clearly into Smith's second and third sub-types.

Mehrdad Izady believes that the Kurds can be traced back more than 50,000 years. From the fifth century BC to the sixth century AD would be 'the homogenization and consolidation of modern Kurdish national identity' and the term 'Kurds' was established during this time.[10]

The Kurdish population occupies the territorial limits of the Zagros Mountains. It has been these inhospitable mountains that have provided a geographical 'buffer' from the political interests of the great empires of the past. The failure of the Persian, Arab and Ottoman Empires of the past 1,000 years to subdue the people of the Zagros Mountains has left a cultural space in which the Kurdish language and culture have evolved.[11]

British Scholar G. R. Driver concludes that the Kurds belong to Aryan stock. Their land was called land of *Kar-da* or *Kyrtii*. The earliest account of the Kurd comes from the Sumerian clay tablet in the third millennium BC on which the name of the land called *Kar-da* or *Qar-da* is inscribed.[12] Some scholars trace Kurdish history (the Medes) to *Madai*, a son of Japheth who was one of the three sons of Noah, also in the third millennium BC.[13] 'The Medes migrated south of the Caspian Sea and north of the Tigris River. This region has been predominately Kurdish since antiquity and includes the mountains of Ararat in eastern Turkey where Noah's Ark allegedly rested as the flood waters receded (Genesis 8:4).'[14] Biblical maps show the ancient Medes inhabiting the areas where the Kurds still live today.[15]

This land, south of Lake Van in eastern Turkey, was inhabited by the people of 'Su' who were connected with the *Qur-ti-e*, a group of mountain dwellers. It is with the name of *Qur-ti-e* that Driver makes his first etymological connection. He further argues that the second derivation, an early version of the word 'Kurd' is perhaps encountered in Xenophon's epic *Anabasis* in reference to the *Karduchi* or *Kardukhi*.[16]

Xenophon (430–352 BC), a student of Socrates who became a historian and army commander, describes the retreat of the Greek army of 'Ten Thousand' (401–400 BC) from the warlike *Karduchi* or *Kardukhi* living east of *Botan* which was to become a Kurdish emirate of the Ottoman Empire.

The name of *Khardukhi* has subsequently been found on the left bank of the Tigris River near Mount *Djudi*.[17]

Jemal Rashid Ahmad, the Kurdish historian who specializes in the ancient history of the Kurds, confirms that Driver's account is the most reputable that can be relied upon.[18] Ghassemlou wrote that 'the Kurds are generally regarded as descendants of the *Medes* and the conquest of *Niniveh* in 612 BC by *Kyaxar*, King of the *Medes*, marks the beginning of their history.'[19]

Martin van Bruinessen has rightly pointed out that 'Kurdish ethnicity is much older than Kurdish nationalism'.[20] Many historical sources assert that the term 'Kurdistan', which means the 'land of the Kurds', first appeared in the twelfth century (AD 1150) when the Turkish Seljuk prince Sanjar (*Saandjar*) created a province with that name. This province included the *vilayets* of *Sinjar, Sharazur, Dinawer* and *Kermanshah*.[21]

Kurdish medieval history from the sixth to the sixteenth century represents an important period of Kurdish Islamic history. The seventh to the ninth centuries mark the re-emergence of Kurdish political power. Powerful Kurdish dynasties were established that defended the Middle Eastern heartland against outside invaders, such as the Crusaders, and produced a 'golden age' of Kurdish culture, during which the Kurds excelled in the fields of history, philosophy, music, architecture, mathematics and astronomy.[22] By the beginning of the thirteenth century the Kurdish period of Islamic history had ended and that's when four 'Turkish centuries' began.[23]

Boris James argues that the medieval era of the Kurds did not attract many scholars in comparison with the focus scholars have paid to Armenian history, for example. Vladimir Minorsky wrote a large tome, but after him no one else seemed interested. According to James, there are many reasons for this lack of attention and interest. First are political or ideological reasons: the Kurds are not interesting; the Islamic period isn't interesting because Islam has undermined the Kurdish national destiny. Second, the alleged paucity of sources available and the fact that those sources are written by non-Kurdish people or from a non-Kurdish perspective might pose a central problem in apprehending Kurdish reality during the Middle Ages. A third reason is that the use and the value of the term, 'Kurd', reveal a problem of categorization.[24] Vasili Nikitine quoting Vladimir Minorsky says, 'Very early in the Arab historiography, the word Kurd became a synonym for nomad.'[25] Martin van Bruinessen says, 'Medieval Arab geographers used the term "Kurd" (in its Arabic plural form *Akrad*), to denote all nomadic or semi-nomadic tribes that were neither Arab nor Turkish'.[26]

Accordingly, 'Kurds', as an identifier of a distinct people was in use as early as AD 1150, although it did not necessarily imply a national identity.

In recent times, however, the term has come to include a distinct ethnic or national identity. By the end of the sixteenth century there existed a clear awareness of Kurdish ethnic identity.[27] More than three decades ago Cecil John Edmonds, a British diplomat and expert on the Kurds, defined Kurdistan as: 'the territory inhabited by the Kurds as a more or less homogeneous community constituting a majority of the population, which is divided between Persia, Turkey, Iraq and Syria'.[28]

Some Arab geographers and historians of the Middle Ages have tried to trace Kurdish ethnicity to the Arabs. Tenth-century Arab geographer Mohammad Bin Hawqal and twelfth-century al-Masudi were two.[29] More recently, scholars such as Hakan Ozoglu have attempted to trace the Kurds to the Turkish or Arab tribes.[30] Even during the *Ba'thist* era this claim was occasionally announced via some chauvinist Arab writers such as the former Syrian secret police officer, Munthir al-Muselli and the Egyptian writer, Muhammad Rashid al-Feel.[31]

The essentialist approach declares that the Kurds descended from the Medes. There is clear and distinct evidence that Kurdish identity is differentiated from the Arabs, Turks or Persians.

On Kurdish Language and National Identity: The Centrality of Language

If one wants to understand the evolution of national consciousness, the role of language must be considered not only as an instrument of communication, but also as the basis for national identity. There is a general agreement among scholars on the importance of language for national identity and nationalism. Language offers an essential ethnic boundary and it is the defining element of national identity.

Language also provides a way of expressing a difference, which applies to the dominant state as well as the subordinated nation(s). The policies that impose a language are inherent in nation states and stateless nations and they form a basic element in the representation of collective identity. The state-mandated education system works through its operations and mechanisms to impose the state language.[32] In countries where there is only one language this obviously does not lead to conflict. But in those states that are multilingual, it may invite conflict. Conflicts relating to languages and cultures prove to be some of the most distinctive battles relating to the identities of ethnic groups and nations.

Contrary to much of what has been written about the language(s) of the Kurds, one thing is clear from the start. In Iraqi Kurdistan there is *one* Kurdish language—not multiple languages as many Western observers erroneously believe. What's more, there are only two dialects. The theoretical dimension of language should be considered as a vital element in the process of consolidating national identity before considering how many languages and dialects the Kurds speak.

Theorists of nationalism have assessed the vitality of language in consolidating national identity. For Benedict Anderson the most important thing about language is its capacity for generating 'imagined communities' to build particular solidarities.[33] The vernacular languages in particular are used in many different ways to win the minds of those who speak or understand them. As Anderson puts it, 'The choice of language appears as gradual, unselfconscious, pragmatic ... development.'[34]

While Gellner argues that language is the tool of trade for humanist intellectuals, Vico understood language to be more than a tool of culture; it *was* culture.[35] Development of a common vernacular from several local dialects marks a new ethnic group on the horizon, just as the vernacular's further standardization, codification and dissemination in printed form lays the foundation for modern nation-building.[36]

Nationalism is closely related to language and often conflated with it. 'Why is language so important in the definition of Kurdish identity?' One answer is historical: 'It is, over hundreds of years, together with Kurdistan's political culture, that which has been the sign of Kurdish identification.' Indeed, Kurdish nationalists define a 'Kurd' as whoever is born, lives and speaks Kurdish. Another answer is political: 'It is the easiest way to expand and reproduce the Kurdish population without resorting to criteria of territorial sovereignty that would then necessitate collision with the territoriality of the Iraqi state.' Yet, an additional and more fundamental answer may be linked to what language represents, as a system of codes, crystallizing historically a cultural configuration that allows for symbolic sharing without the worshipping of icons other than those emerging in the communication of everyday life.[37]

Most scholars agree that the modern Kurdish language belongs to the Iranian language group and it has almost been considered a branch of the Indo-European family of languages.[38] Elsewhere it has been argued that the Kurds speak and write in one language and that is Kurdish. But two major dialects exist in Kurdistan: Sorani and Kirmanj. Kirmanj is referred to in Iraqi Kurdistan as 'Bahdinani' or 'Badini'.[39] If one doesn't know the Kurdish language from the inside, it can be confusing. The disagreement among scholars in categorizing and classifying the Kurdish language and its dialects can be at times amusing.

The majority of these 'specialized' and 'non-specialized' scholars mistakenly classify the Kurdish dialects as languages. Or they view their classifications as variants of one another. Martin van Bruinessen categorizes the language into three dialects: *Kurmanji*, *Sorani* and the third as the sub-dialects of *Sine'i* (*Sanandaji*), *Kermanshahi* and *Leki*, but it was categorized under different terminology and geographical places.[40] Hassan Arfa's classification has been: *Zaza*, *Kirmanji* and *Gurani*.[41] David McDowall divides the Kurdish language into two major languages or dialects: *Kirmanji* and *Sorani*. He asserts that another three languages exist in various places in Kurdistan: *Kermanshahi*, *Zaza* and *Gurani*.[42] Kreyenbroek argues that there is no one language or dialect. For him there are five different dialects: *Kermanshahi*, *Zaza*, *Gurani*, *Kurmanji* and *Sorani*.[43] Nader Entessar classifies it as three languages rather than dialects: *Kurdi*, *Kurmanji* and *Zaza*.[44] He contends that the failure to adopt a *lingua franca* has not only hindered inter-Kurdish communication, but it has also reduced the importance of language as a symbol of ethnic identity for the Kurds.[45]

Entessar puts *Gurani* and *Suleimani* into the same dialect group. However, whether identified as the dialect 'spoken mostly by the Kurds of *Kermanshah*',[46] or used as a label for the *Hawrami* dialect, *Gurani* cannot be placed in the same group with *Suleimani*. 'North and South *Kurmanji*' (better known as *Sorani*), which he puts in one group, also belong to two dialect groups. Entessar fails to mention that *Sorani* is the most developed standard variety of Kurdish. He locates *Zaza* (*Dimili*) speakers in 'the Iranian province of Western Azerbaijan and central Turkey'.[47]

Gareth Stansfield posits that in Kurdistan generally there exists a Kurdish group of languages, which subdivides into four major groupings: (1) *Kurmanji* (*Bahdinani*), spoken in Turkey, Iran and Iraq; (2) *Sorani*, mostly spoken in Iran and Iraq; (3) *Sanandaj*, *Kermanshahi* and *Liki*, spoken mostly in Iran; and (4) *Zaza* and *Gurani* mostly spoken in Iran.[48]

Kurdish nationalists such as Hajar Abdurrahman, Hemen Mokryani (from Iranian Kurdistan), Aladdin Sajadi, Jamal Nabaz and Ferhad Shakely, emphasize the role of language as a vital factor for consolidating Kurdish national identity. Thus, for the Kurds the Kurdish language is extremely important as a symbol of who they are and it has been a crucial protector of *Kurdishness*. This has been evident since the creation of Iraq by the British in 1921. The Kurdish language since then has been formalized as a language of two formal dialects, written in two separate scripts and a number of very significant sub-dialects of each.

However, even with these linguistic rifts, all of the dialects of Kurdish remain true to their claim to be 'the Kurdish language'. It is quite certain that up to World War One, the *Kirmanji* dialect was favoured. But since the 1960s the *Sorani* dialect has become dominant among the Kurds of

Iran and Iraqi Kurdistan.[49] The problem of the lack of a unified tongue is exacerbated by the fact there is also no unified Kurdish script. In Iran and Iraq a modified version of the Perso-Arabic alphabet has been used and in Turkey a version of the Latin alphabet has been used.[50]

The Kurdish cultural revival of the early 1930s and 40s and afterward until the mid-70s in Iraqi Kurdistan was not so much concerned with converting the Kurdish language into one with modern literary prestige; rather it provided the means for the grounding of many elements of national identity in the national homeland itself, which consequently became the source of that national identity.

Such territorial premises still inform the way Kurdish nationalism approaches the status of the Kurdish language and its role as the principal element of national identity differentiation. The central point here is that the limited literature on the Kurdish language demonstrates that there is no single unified standard language in Kurdistan. Certainly the development of written Kurdish in the last fifty years has resulted in two distinct dialects that are written in prevailing scripts: *Sorani* and *Kirmanji*.

There are two other sub-dialects that are similar to each other, as well as to ancient Persian, yet geographically separate from each other and they are *Zaza* and *Gurani*. Unlike *Sorani* and *Kirmanji* these sub-dialects of Kurdish have little written tradition. In actuality, the two dialects are generally used in Turkey's Kurdistan, rather than in Iraqi Kurdistan.

Nevertheless the Kurdish 'languages' still assist in boundary maintenance of Kurdish identity from 'the other'. In the Kurdish case language divisions have come to reflect the repeated divisions of Kurdistan, both past and present. This is most likely the reason why it is so salient an issue within Kurdish factionalism today.

Historically speaking, the Kurds were isolated mountain tribes, often nomadic for political and economic reasons. As a result the dialects of the Kurdish language have a very limited written tradition.

Kreyenbroek asserts that Kurdish as a written language emerged by the end of the nineteenth-century Ottoman Empire.[51] On the contrary, Baba Tahiri Hamadani (935–1010), Malay Ciziri (1407–81), Bisarani (1641–1702) and Ahmadi Khani (1650–1706) were earlier poets who wrote in Kurdish. These poets wrote in *Hawrami* (*Hawramani* and *Luri* dialects), whereas Nali (1798–1855), Salim (1800–66) and Mawlawi (1806–82) wrote in the *Sorani* dialects.[52] Khani, wrote *Mam u Zin* in Kurdish at the end of the seventeenth century.[53]

The Kurdish nation represents a 'minority' national group in the states where they reside. The vast majority of them are bilingual. The linguistic situation in Iraqi Kurdistan is actually less complex than it would appear from the above classification. It is much less problematic than the case of Turkey, Syria, Russia or even Iran. Nevertheless, unlike many Western observers' viewpoints, the speakers of these two dialects (*Bahdinani* and *Sorani*) in Iraqi Kurdistan can be orally understood by each other in a limited fashion.

While an educated person may read or speak both dialects, in Iraqi Kurdistan the *Sorani* dialect is dominant in both speaking and print. This has been the case since the 1930s. It is also probably the case that the choice of a particular dialect to serve as the official written language for the Kurds would give a measure of stability to the language. Although this would not solve the differences between the dialects, it would lead to a narrowing of the range of possibilities and facilitate communication through print. Comparing Kurdish with the historical development of languages in Europe and in France in particular, it was several centuries before French, a corrupt form of Latin, became the official language of the French courts of justice in 1539.[54]

Hobsbawm teaches us that for the masses, spoken languages do not advance as rapidly as they do in print. By the Revolution of 1789, 50 per cent of the people of France did not speak French at all and only 12 to 13 per cent spoke it correctly. In the north and south of France, nobody spoke French.[55] Similarly, only 2.5 per cent of the inhabitants of Italy spoke Italian in 1860.[56] Therefore, it must not be thought for a moment that by not having a unified language, Kurdish nationalism is undermined.

The specificity of the Kurds' locale and the presence of particular political and historical factors after the 1990s have made Kurdish instead of Arabic the major and first language of communication in Iraqi Kurdistan. This has helped to consolidate Kurdish national identity, especially for the young educated generation that has little appreciation or understanding of the Arab-Iraqi culture and language. In other words, since the 1990s the Kurdish language has become increasingly and more accurately a self-marker for the Kurds. The Arabic language has come to be viewed as a clear cultural and/or ethnic marker that can be mapped out to determine where the political frontiers and boundaries are.

Recently the KRG Parliament declared a strategy to implement the writing of Kurdish in Latin as a unified script. This project began in 2008 at the primary educational levels in Kurdistan.

The Kurds and Kurdistan from the Twelfth
to the Nineteenth Centuries

From the twelfth to the nineteenth centuries there were no nationalist movements among the Kurds. The historical readings of Kurdistan's social and political culture during these seven centuries assert that tribal and religious affiliations, rather than national consciousness, characterized both Kurdish society and politics. From the twelfth to the eighteenth century the early tribes and communities of Kurdistan were brought under the territorial authority of the sophisticated Kurdish principalities, whose methods of administration, political affairs, arts of war and practical abilities were imposed upon them. During the rule of these principalities, (*Mirnisheenakan* or *Emirates*), the loyalty of the Kurds was primarily oriented toward religion (Islam) and to the protectors of the Ottoman (versus the Safavid) dynasty. It certainly was not oriented toward nationality or national identity. However, the Kurdish principalities had some features of statehood and the Kurdish Prince (*Mir*) was responsible for running his tribal and administrative affairs autonomously.[57]

Historically speaking, the Kurds continued to enjoy a good deal of autonomy under the Ottomans and Safavids until the early sixteenth century, when tensions arose between the two empires. As a result of war, on 23 August 1514 Kurdistan was divided between the two empires for the first time. The divisions were formalized in 1639 when a treaty of *Zuhab* was signed between the Ottoman and Safavid authorities.[58]

One cause of tension was sectarian antagonism. The Ottomans were *Sunni* and the Safavids were *Shi'ite*. Since many Kurds were also *Sunni*, the Ottoman Sultan Selim used the Kurds against the Safavids, while focusing his imperialistic schemes on Eastern Europe. In return for their military support, the Kurds were given relief from paying taxes and they continued to have freedom in their internal affairs. The Ottomans formed sixteen autonomous Kurdish emirates or principalities, which were basically tribal confederacies. These continued until the mid-nineteenth century.[59]

As indicated, tribalism and religious affiliation were the most important determinants in the formation of Kurdish political culture. Since the time the Kurdish provinces were split between the Ottoman and Persian empires in the sixteenth century, strong tribal chieftains successfully fought to retain some measure of local autonomy against the central authorities. Tribalism was by and large one of the biggest obstacles in all of the Ottoman centralization efforts in the *Tanzimat* years. It was also the main reason for the failure of the Kurdish nationalist movement to gain any momentum at the grassroots level in the late Ottoman Empire.[60]

The Persians also allowed the Kurds under their jurisdiction to have independence until the mid-nineteenth century. By this time both empires began centralizing their governments, while subjugating the Kurdish principalities and leaving the Kurds to face an uncertain future.[61] This led to many uprisings, which continue to the present day. Thus, the Kurds survived in ancient times as a people and they continue to survive as a distinct nation.

In 1597 the Kurdish Prince Amir (*Mir*) Sharafkhan, the ruler or prince of Bitlis, wrote the first historical book on Kurdistan, *Sharafnama*. This book was not a history of Kurdistan *per se*, but it was about the Kurdish rulers of Kurdistan.[62] Sharafkhan clearly distinguishes the Kurds from the Turks and elaborates upon the urban aristocratic, tribal and peasant divisions within Kurdish society. Furthermore, he addresses the oppression that the Kurds faced by the Turkish suppression of their Kurdish pride and identity.[63]

Ahmadi Khani's (1650–1707) and Haji Kaderi Koyi's (1817–96) ideas about nationality were nothing like their contemporary European nationalist concepts. Ahmadi Khani was perhaps the greatest Kurdish poet and scholar and was widely respected in the past and by contemporaries for his excellently written works, which were all odes to the Kurdish nation. Khani believed that loyalty to Islam did not mean that there was no national identity or Islam would be opposed to national interests.[64] Bruinessen views Khani to be a precursor of Kurdish nationalism because Khani was aware of and very proud of his Kurdish national identity.[65]

Khani called on the Kurds to remain loyal to their identity and ethnicity. One of Ahmadi Khani's well known works was *Mam u Zin*, written in 1644–45. It called upon the Kurds to unite and establish an independent Kurdish state, to be liberated from the Turks and Persians and to find a Kurdish king, a Kurdish crown, Kurdish currency and to improve Kurdish culture. He also blamed the Kurdish princes for being dependent on the Turks and Persians. Khani excluded the poor as well as the Kurdish intellectuals from blame, as they had no power.[66]

Hassanpour asserts that Sharafkhan and later Ahmadi Khani and Haji Kaderi Koyi's writings lack a philosophical or theoretical account of nationalism or the nature of political power in Kurdistan.[67] However, Hassanpour designates *Mam u Zin* as the historical origin of Kurdish nationalism. Haji Kaderi Koyi, a more modern writer, was influenced by Khani's *Mam u Zin*. Many Kurdish nationalists regard Koyi as the father of Kurdish nationalism.[68]

The Kurdish principalities in both empires cultivated literature and the arts to a considerable degree. Small educated Kurdish elites gradually sprang up. In the nineteenth century, the same drive toward national identity that was spreading among the Arabs also influenced the Kurdish elites, but for the most part the several small Kurdish rebellions against the Ottomans were prompted by a sense of injustice on the part of the local tribal leaders. These rebellions were promptly suppressed by the Ottoman government and, as they threatened the weakening empire, led to the imposition of direct Turkish rule on the previously autonomous Kurdish principalities.[69]

As a result of the Ottoman and Persian empires' policies of direct rule, by the mid-nineteenth century the autonomous privileges had been eliminated. One can argue that during the long era of the seventeenth, eighteenth and nineteenth centuries, Kurdistan experienced no original Kurdish nationalism.

It was during the eighteenth and nineteenth centuries, when the modern era reached the boundaries of the Ottoman Empire, that the Kurdish intellectual elite became inspired to present themselves as a group distinct from the Turks, Arabs and Persians. In the 1930s and 40s the urban secular Kurdish elite of Turkey began participating in Kurdish nationalist movements, well ahead of the Kurds of Iraq.

Robert Olson's seminal work on the emergence of Kurdish nationalism connects the establishment of the relatively autonomous Kurdish tribes within the Ottoman Empire to the emergent Kurdish movements that culminated in the Sheikh Said Rebellion of 1925.[70] These autonomous Kurdish tribes based their identities and imageries upon a style of nationalism that appeared almost to be in the mode of the twentieth century. In other words, the eventual collapse of the Ottoman Empire happened at the same time the Kurdish tribes were waking up to the reality of their distinct identity.

Janet Klein argues that during the late Ottoman period (1908–9) this movement 'was neither unified nor linear.'[71] She asserts that the Kurdish nationalist movement of that time, which was represented by the educated Kurds in Istanbul, was not a threat to the empire.[72] Klein concludes that from 1910–25 'Kurdish nationalism emerged as one possible future political arrangement for the Kurds', but it certainly was neither a 'cause nor direct result of imperial disintegration'. It was only 'one of several *responses* to it and particularly to the state-building aftermath'.[73] This was definitely not the case in Iraq during the first two decades of the twentieth century.

Kurdish Proto-National Identity and the Rise of the 'Imagined Community'

Hobsbawm and Anderson posit that at the end of nineteenth century and beginning of the twentieth, a myriad of cultural, social and political experiences and values, preserved in both written form and collective memory, would serve as 'proto-national bonds'. These cultural elements would be passed down to later generations and eventually regenerate a people emerging from the darkest period of their existence. At a time when people began to speak in terms of nations and nationalism, the Kurds, and in particular the Kurds of Iraq, would harken to their past experience and these proto-national bonds. Drawing on Smith's paradigm, these links to a past identity, together with a more modern outlook on politics, culture, religion, language and self-worth, would inform the Kurds' quest for freedom and define them as a people.

Kurdish proto-national bonds may be separated into the categories of culture/religion or 'holy icons', language and political experience, though in actuality they tend to overlap one another. Before identifying examples of proto-nationalism, the following question must be asked: In what ways would a tribal or peasant Kurd in the late nineteenth century identify with an ancestor from any given social stratum or era of Kurdish history? If a peasant or tribal Kurd were to look back on Kurdistan, he would find several things of meaning and value: a rich variety of Kurdish rituals and the existence of two major dialects and written and spoken Kurdish (the dialects of which varied depending on region). It is possible to say that all of these examples would represent an essential part of his or her identity and distinguish the Kurdish peasant from others.

As for those aspects which no longer represented a viable part of a peasant's daily existence, they would remain deep in the collective memory through folklore and the oral tradition and less so through such works as *Mam u Zin* and *Sharafnama* that were studied by literate, educated members of their nationalist intelligentsia. This becomes evident in later references in the populist press (in the 1880s) to the 'glorious legacy' of Kurdistan.[74]

This legacy includes such details as the important role of a diverse social stratum, towns, as well as the not so pleasant aspects, such as life under the Ottoman Empire and the self-defeating practice of internal rivalry. The peasants would most likely have lacked the leadership necessary to provide the national movement with its initial momentum and to encourage their fellows to educate and better understand themselves for the sake of the common good. In proposing the theory of proto-nationalism, it is apparent that Hobsbawm was inspired by Benedict Anderson's notion of the 'imagined community' of nation.

The problem before us derives from the fact that the modern nation, either as a state or as a body of people aspiring to form such a state, differs in size, scale and natures from the actual communities with which human beings have identified over most of history, and makes quite different demands on them. It is, in Anderson's useful phrase, an 'imagined community,' and no doubt this can be made to fill the emotional void left by the retreat or disintegration, or the unavailability of *real* human communities and networks, but the question still remains why, having lost real communities, people should wish to imagine this particular type of replacement.[75]

This is where Hobsbawm introduces the theory of proto-nationalism. He proposes that prior to the entrance of modernity societies were characterized by proto-national bonds, or variants of feelings of collective belonging. With the decline or loss of certain cultural conceptions (age-old imagined communities), individuals, already in possession of a proto-national identity, found a suitable replacement in the imagined community of 'nation'. As Hakan Ozoglu states, the term 'Kurdish proto-nationalism' is problematic since it designates that Kurdish movements in the pre-World War One period were destined to become nationalist.[76]

5

THE HISTORICAL AND SOCIO-POLITICAL CONDITIONS FOR THE DEVELOPMENT OF KURDISH NATIONALISM: 1921–91

It was in Iraq that Kurdish nationalism first became a mass movement. Iraq is the only state which recognizes the existence of the Kurds as a distinct component of its population. Iraq's Constitution explicitly mentions the Kurds as one of the country's two nationalities. Accordingly, the Kurds have enjoyed more cultural rights in Iraq than do the Kurds of Turkey, Iran or Syria.

Losing the Game of State Formation

Most historians and political scientists view the early years of the twentieth century as the key starting point for conceptualizing Kurdish modern political history. The new country of Iraq was formed from the Ottoman provinces (*vilayet* or *wilaya*) of Baghdad, Basra and Mosul (populated mainly by Kurds) with its oil fields. Northeast of Baghdad the province of Mosul has significant geopolitical value because of Kirkuk's oil.[1] The disposition of Mosul caused many skirmishes among the powers involved, but the British, who were to administer the new Iraq, prevailed and in 1925 Mosul was attached to Iraq. The Kurds had no voice in the discussions and Turkey (Kemal Ataturk) was decidedly displeased.[2]

Between 1918 and 1929 the British policy towards the Kurds was to encourage Kurdish nationalism, but not independence. From 1918 to 1923 British colonial officers had no clear policy or approach toward the Kurds or the Mesopotamian region. Many observers felt that the British policy in Kurdistan was vague and amorphous. British policy was not only fluid, but it also varied according to the perceptions and interests of decision makers.

This was due to the inconsistency between the India Office and the Foreign Office.[3] One problem facing the British officers and decision makers in the application of such policies was knowing exactly what the Kurds wanted.

Major E. M. Noel, the first British officer who negotiated with the Kurdish leadership, was sympathetic to Kurdish aspirations for self-government and independence. Lord Toynbee of the Foreign Office also had a clear interest in the idea of creating a Kurdish state. The India Office, however, suggested that it was ineffective to limit the Kurds to a single state due to the 'prohibitive racial and geographical difficulties.'[4] A number of British colonial civil servants opposed Major Noel and wanted to interject the Mosul *vilayet* into the newly created country of Iraq. The Kurds opposed the idea of incorporating the Mosul province into Iraq and revolted against their rulers. Sheikh Mahmud Barzinji, the first influential Kurdish leader who became the governor (*Hukmdar*) of the Suleimaniya division in December 1918, led the Kurdish revolts in the early 1920s.[5] In March 1919 Sir Arnold Wilson, the Acting Civil Commissioner, decided to 'gradually curtail' Sheikh Mahmud's power and replace him with Major E. B. Soane (who disliked Sheikh Mahmud) instead of Noel as Political Officer in Suleimaniya.[6]

As the mandated power, the British were sympathetic to Kurdish aspirations and wanted to establish one or more autonomous Kurdish provinces within the sovereign state of Iraq. They encouraged Sheikh Mahmud to run such a Kurdish government, but when he declared himself the King of Kurdistan and challenged British authority, they suppressed his government and exiled him to India.[7] Sheikh Mahmud led a second revolt in April 1931, when he called for a 'united Kurdistan'. The British defeated him again and the Iraqi government kept him under house arrest until his death in 1956.[8]

British policymakers seem to have concluded that the best way to exploit the oil fields in and around Mosul and Kirkuk was by creating a single state, 'the Kingdom of Iraq', which would include the Kurdish areas in question. By 1925 the British declared that 'it forms no part of the policy of His Majesty's Government to encourage or accept any responsibility for the formation of any autonomous or independent Kurdish state'.[9]

Rebellion in Kurdistan

In the unstable aftermath of World War One, the Kurds (along with the Armenians and the people of Hejaz) came close to attaining their national aspirations when they were promised by the Great Powers (Great Britain and France) the opportunity to form a Kurdish national state.[10] This promise was stated orally by US President Woodrow Wilson in his Fourteen Point Programme for World Peace speech to the League of Nations[11] and it is also written in section three, articles 62, 63 and 64 of the Treaty of Sèvres. It was signed by the Constantinople (Ottoman) Government and by the Allied Powers on 10 August 1920.[12] Under Article 64 the Kurds would be granted independence within a year. However, of all the signatory countries, only Greece ratified the Treaty and the provision for Kurdish autonomy never became a reality.[13] There were several concerns, such as fears over the Soviet Union's undue influence over newly formed states and Britain's concern that there was no obvious choice of a Kurdish leader who could be counted on to put Kurdish national concerns above tribal interests, that kept Kurdish independence an elusive dream.[14]

The Treaty provided that the province of Mosul could join Kurdistan, if the majority of its inhabitants voted for independence. This was the first time in Kurdish history that the need to resolve their problem was acknowledged internationally.[15]

The Treaty of Sèvres redrew the political map of the Middle East largely in accordance with European interests. The Ottoman Empire was dismantled under the pretext of punishment for their participation in the war on the part of the Central Powers and, in its stead, several new states were formed, including Turkey and the Kingdom of Iraq. The humiliating conditions of the 1920 Treaty, combined with continued encroachments on Turkish sovereignty after the war, led to Ataturk's overthrowing the Turkish Administration that signed the Treaty. 'He led a war of independence on behalf of non-Arab Muslims of the Ottoman Empire against the French, Greeks and Armenians, who staked competing claims for parts of the former Ottoman territories.'[16] In 1922 the newly established Grand National Assembly abolished the Ottoman Sultanate and established the modern Turkish Republic with its strong sense of Turkish nationalism under Mustafa Kemal Ataturk.[17]

It was at the Cairo Conference in 1921 and largely at the urging of Major Noel and Winston Churchill, that the delegates reached an agreement regarding the Kurdish state. The Kurdish state, which would function as a 'buffer zone', would be established in the north of Mesopotamia. Nevertheless, both Percy Cox and Ms. Gertrude Bell held the minority view that Kurdistan should be included in Iraq.[18]

The Treaty of Sèvres was rejected on 24 July 1923 and the Treaty of Lausanne was signed instead in which the Republic of Turkey was recognized and the idea of creating a Kurdish national state was abandoned. The Treaty of Sèvres was now meaningless.[19]

The Sèvres–Lausanne period was a watershed in the Kurds' political history. These unfulfilled promises and lost opportunities led many Kurds to feel that they were 'expendable tools in the hands of the great powers'.[20] In 1925 the League of Nations awarded the *vilayet* of Mosul to Iraq under the British mandate because the British stated that Mosul's oil was necessary to ensure the economic viability of Iraq.[21]

Thus, the Treaty of Lausanne ratified what had been accomplished by Mustafa Kemal Ataturk through force of arms.[22] The Treaty, ratified by Turkey and the allied powers to finally settle the distribution of territory, failed to mention or refer to the Kurds by name. The question of Kurdish autonomy was no longer an agenda item.[23] Kurdistan was split between Iraq, Syria, Turkey and Iran on 5 June 1926.[24] The Kurds of Iraq became citizens of an Arab state which was the Kingdom of Iraq. Kurdish nationalism and national identity for the Iraq Kurds from this point forward would be dealt with according to the changes in Iraq's political system and culture.

The history of Kurdish nationalism of the first three decades of the twentieth century in Iraq is mainly the history of Kurdish tribal nationalist movements, which challenged the Ottoman, British and Iraqi authorities. British policy at this time was to 'retribalize' Kurdish social relations as a means of securing administrative control.[25] Gareth Stansfield has rightly asserted that 'tribal militancy' in the Kurdish rebellions played a cardinal role in the mobilization of the Kurdish political institution. When studied closely, these rebellions may be viewed as a balance between tribal and nationalist interests.[26]

By the mid-1920s a small number of educated and a growing number of professional classes in the Kurdish towns were beginning to show interest in Kurdish national identity. All of the revolts and uprisings, which occurred during the first three decades of the twentieth century, may be characterized as tribal, religious and proto-nationalist movements. These ambitious and fragmented uprisings were aimed at asserting ethnicity as a marker of national identity as well as a way of life.[27]

These uprisings and revolts were fragmented because of the tribal or religious leadership on one hand and the undeveloped rural structure of Kurdish society on the other. Exploring the nature of Kurdish nationalism at this time Cecil John Edmonds (1889–1979) questioned the purity of a nationalism that was used to cloak the ambitions of certain leaders or the intolerance of tribesman of any type of order and administration.[28] On the motives of Sheikh Mahmud, Michael Gunter comments:

> It would be a mistake, however, to see the activities of the Sheikh as exercises of Kurdish nationalism. At the height of his appeal, he never exceeded the primordial bounds of tribalism.[29]

And McDowall continues in this vein:

> It is tempting retrospectively to clothe Sheikh Mahmud in the garb
> of modern nationalist ideas.... It is significant that Sheikh Mahmud
> did not waste his time appealing to nationalist sentiment. He was a
> sayyid, and the language his constituency understood was the language
> of Islam. In 1919 he appealed for a *jihad*, not a national liberation
> struggle. Furthermore, his style was to use kin and tribal allies and
> his aim was the establishment of a personal fiefdom. Sheikh Mahmud
> offered Kurdish liberation from British rule, but not from himself.[30]

Gunter feels that real Kurdish nationalist aspirations were expressed
in September 1930 when the educated middle class demonstrators of
Suleimaniya went to the streets and held a strike with no direction or guidance from a tribal or religious leader.[31] It is important to note that the religious and tribal rebellions that broke out during the 1920s and 30s remain
efficacious symbols for many Kurdish nationalists even today. These rebellions have become an important part of the Kurdish nationalist narrative
and myth and they have served as an inspiration and model for subsequent
rebellions. They also opened up the Kurdish nationalist movement to the
lower strata of Kurdish society for the first time.

The ability of the *Sheikhs* to achieve significant political integration was
limited by substantive divisions that sometimes resulted from their religious
character. The power of the *Sheikhs* derived not only from their charismatic
talents, but also from their personal wealth and the regional land base which
they had secured when the 1858 Ottoman Land Code allowed them title to
large tracts. So while they articulated their demands in terms of legitimacy
and protection for the Kurdish nation, they were often just as concerned
with securing or preserving the legitimacy and protection of their own
regional power bases.

According to McDowall Kurdish opinion, particularly outside of
Suleimaniya, was not entirely behind Sheikh Mahmud, the self-declared
King of Kurdistan, whose lofty ambitions were generally distrusted.

> Nothing perhaps, expressed Kurdish disarray more than the effort of the
> British to establish whether their proposal that their protégé, the *Emir*
> Faisal, should become King of all Iraq was acceptable to the Kurdish
> population. Mosul and Arbil voted in favour, Kirkuk voted for a delay
> on its decision (decided in 1923 in favour of Faisal's Iraq), though the
> interesting fact is that its Kurds asked for a separate Kurdish province

but only on condition that they were not incorporated with the Kurds of Suleimaniya. Only the population of the latter voted unconditionally against Faisal or any inclusion in Iraq.[32]

The most significant violent opposition to external rule in Iraq emerged from Barzan, which was led first by *Sufi Sheikh* Ahmad Barzani and later by his brothers Muhammad Sadiq and Mulla Mustafa. Mustafa Barzani was essentially a charismatic national leader; his conversion to Kurdish nationalism was gradual and due largely to the violent means by which the Iraq movement attempted to suppress his regional autonomy.[33]

The Meeting of Tribalism and Nationalism: 1930s–58

The reassertion of tribal power was the backlash to the British administration's explicit strategy to secure tribal loyalty. The British essentially revived the indirect rule policies of the earlier Ottoman administrations. They removed uncooperative *Aghas* and replaced them with others who were often, as one officer remarked, 'small men of no account until we made them powerful and rich'.[34] Judging by the remarks of British colonial officials, the revival of a dependent class of local landlords was the result of a calculated policy from the British Foreign Office.

> Settled agriculture and extended civilization have tended to disintegrate the tribe and to weaken the influence of the Sheikhs. To restore and continue the power of the tribal Sheikhs is not the least interesting of the problems in land administration which the Baghdad '*vilayet*' presents…. We must recognize that it is primarily our business not to give rights to those who have them not, but to secure their rights to those who have them.[35]

In Iraq the landlord class became essentially parasitic to the rural economy, moving to the towns and villages while keeping the growing numbers of sharecroppers tied to the land. Most villages were owned by single families and any remaining collective or tribal land was quickly converted into large private estates. By 1958 one per cent of the landowners owned 55 per cent of all private land in Iraq.[36]

As outlined, the *Sheikhs* in Kurdistan had provided the opportunity for the integration of more diverse elements of Kurdish society in the nationalist struggle and the tribal tradition supplied the military strength. The integration of these elements into a modern nationalist movement with objectives that transcended class and regional allegiances, however, began with the emergence of urban nationalist organizations. Kurdish urban nationalism began in the towns and cities of Kurdistan.

Traditionally the Kurdish intelligentsia developed in *Madrasa* (Islamic religious schools). From the late seventeenth to the early twentieth century, these schools provided leaders who promoted Kurdish ethnic interests. However, from the mid-twentieth century the educational landscape of Kurdistan changed and those who were educated in Istanbul, Tehran, Baghdad, Damascus and other major cities became the dominant forces in Kurdistan. These individuals and groups (with few exceptions) looked down upon Kurdish culture, traditions and way of life.[37] Those who had the good fortune to study abroad, whether East or West, tended to keep with other Middle Eastern groups instead of joining the host countries' mainstream. This did not help Kurdistan at all. There was no other country that had so many self-loathing intellectuals.

It should not be surprising to find that apart from the reading circles in the mosques, the majority of the Kurds in Iraqi Kurdistan were largely illiterate until the twentieth century. From the 1930s the urban educated strata began to involve themselves in Kurdish nationalism. The formation of nationalist organizations in the urban centres of Kurdistan and Baghdad gave the Kurdish educated politically active elites some sort of legitimacy that increased the sense of *Kurdayati* as a way of thinking. Nevertheless, during the years between the formation of Iraq and its independence in 1932, very few steps were taken on behalf of the Kurds.[38]

Unlike the constitutions of the states of Turkey, Iran or Syria, the Iraqi Provisional Constitution of 1921 affirmed that Iraq was composed of two national groups, the Arabs and Kurds. Arabic and Kurdish languages had equal status. Seeking Iraq's admission to the League of Nations, the British tried to ensure minority groups' rights in Iraq.[39] After 1925 the initial Iraqi local language law provided for limited teaching of Kurdish in schools within Kurdish speaking areas and for the publication of Kurdish language books. There was also limited Kurdish representation in government.[40]

This stimulated Kurdish aspirations among the educated elite. During the 1930s and 40s many journals and underground groups organized among the Kurdish educated strata in both Erbil and Suleimaniya. The Kurds had been granted limited cultural rights and Iraqi Kurdistan had become the centre of Kurdish cultural life since the late 1920s.[41] The Iraqi government certainly did not favour these developments in Kurdistan. During the early state formation period, the Kurds still qualified as a 'non-imagined' community.[42] Nevertheless, this would change in the ensuing years.

Political Developments in Iraq and Kurdistan

In the 1930s and even more so in the 40s, two main currents of ideologies emerged which affected Kurdish nationalism. One was communist and socialist ideas; the other was pan-Arab nationalism.[43] The Kurds reacted against the emergence of Arab nationalism and many intellectuals were affected by the socialist ideas of the Iraqi Communist Party, which had been founded in 1934. Among them there were intellectuals like Ibrahim Ahmad, Jalal Talabani, Hamza Abdulla and Salih al-Haidari. However, the 1930s had witnessed the emergence of Kurdish cultural, political and nationalist activities. Several Kurdish political organizations had organized their movements in the towns and urban centres such as Erbil, Suleimaniya, Kirkuk, Kifri, Kalar and Khanaqin. Baghdad also had been the base for many Kurdish cultural and national movements. The organizations that developed were *Komalay Lawan* (a youth organization, announced in Baghdad in 1930), *Komalay Brayati* (Brotherhood Organization, 1938–43 in Suleimaniya), *Shorish* (Revolution) and *Rizgari Kurd* (Kurdish Liberation, 1945).

The most significant and effective of the movements were *Darkar* (Woodcutters), in Suleimaniya, and *Hiwa* (Hope), in Erbil. *Hiwa* played a key role in solidifying the Kurdish nationalist sentiment.[44] By the time of the Second World War, a much more diverse cross-section of the Kurdish population was involved in nationalist and other opposition movements in Iraq. Thus a new urban class of political activists was coalescing. The Iraqi Communist Party (ICP) initially attracted the support of many urban Kurds. Although this support dropped off when the party abandoned its commitment to Kurdish independence, it continued to have a Kurdish wing named *Azadi* (Freedom). In 1940 a new urban Kurdish nationalist party *Hiwa* (Hope) was formed that gathered together the disparate activist elements that had formed in several Kurdish cities.

Hiwa also moved quickly to link up with the emerging nationalist coalition centred in the city of Mahabad in Iran. While the party's nationalist rhetoric was attractive to middle-class intellectuals, it was less attractive to rural *Aghas* and landlords (and the peasants they controlled). It was quickly suppressed after the defeat of the first Barzani rebellion. In *Hiwa*'s place emerged a party called *Rizgari Kurd* (Kurdish Liberation) which launched a formal appeal to the UN for the independence of a united Kurdistan. This agenda brought it into ideological conflict with the Iraqi Communist Party, which regarded the Kurdish issue as a minority problem within the Iraqi state.[45]

The notable and prominent Kurdish political activists of this time were Ibrahim Ahmad from Suleimaniya and Salih al-Haidari from Erbil.[46] The new Iraqi government, which under the Anglo-Iraqi treaty of 1930 was granted independence, ignored the question of Kurdish autonomy and barely tolerated Kurdish nationalist interests. Demonstrations and strikes were organized to protest the monarchical ruling elites' treatment of the Kurds.

The most influential Kurdish leader to emerge from the unrest of the 1930s was Mustafa Barzani. By the mid-40s he had influence over a relatively large area of Kurdistan. He became the leader of the Kurdish nationalist movement. In 1943 he fled from exile in Suleimaniya and escaped to Barzan where he reorganized his position at the expense of rival tribes and the Iraqi government. He requested autonomy for the Kurdish areas of Kirkuk, Suleimaniya, Erbil, Dohuk and Khanaqin. The *Hiwa* assisted him in a revolt.

Barzani was a fascinating character and his career highlighted the internal contradictions of Kurdish nationalism.[47] In 1945 the Iraqi army forces, assisted by Royal Air Force bombers, forced Barzani and his followers to retreat to Iranian Kurdistan. In Mahabad he joined the Iranian Kurdish nationalist movement, which was in the midst of its struggle for a Kurdish republic. Barzani and his followers played an important role in the defence of Mahabad before retreating to the Soviet Union.

Barzani directed the armed forces in defending the first Kurdish Republic proclaimed in Mahabad by Qazi Mohammed on 22 January 1946.[48] The Mahabad Republic lasted only for eleven months. Their leaders were captured and later hanged by the Iranian army in *Chwar Chera* Square in Mahabad city. After his escape with his followers, Barzani lived the next eleven years in exile in the Soviet Union.[49] On 16 August 1946 the Kurdish Democratic Party was announced in Baghdad at the first congress held there and Barzani was selected as its president-in-exile. In the third congress of 1953 the name was changed to the Kurdistan Democratic Party.[50]

The hegemony of Barzani in the mid-1940s over the Kurdish movement ended with the secular nationalists and urban-educated Kurds cooperating with the Iraqi Communist Party. When Barzani was forced to leave Iranian Kurdistan and seek refuge in Stalin's Soviet Union in 1946, the relationship with the left generally, and the Communists specifically, developed and re-emerged under the leadership of Ibrahim Ahmad.[51] Thus, the Kurdish nationalist movement for the next decade was less effective in terms of tribal and nationalist desires and geared more towards class-based politics. This was the case until the 1960s when Kurdish nationalism re-appeared.[52]

During the 1940s–50s British policies in Iraq were still in effect. Iraqi society was heterogeneous, being a mixture of *Shi'i* and *Sunni* Arabs, Kurds,

Chaldo-Assyrians (or Aramaeans), Armenians, Turkmens and a small minority of Jews. Instead of neutralizing ethnic and religious differences, the British heightened them by elevating *Sunni* Arabs to high positions of power in the government and introducing the politics of ethnicity which antagonized the Kurds and *Shi'is*.[53] The acting leader of the KDP and the Kurdish nationalist movement during 1953–8 was Ibrahim Ahmad. The KDP and Kurdish nationalist ideology moved towards Iraqiness (*Iraqchiyeti*) under Ahmad's leadership and with the cooperation of his son-in-law Jalal Talabani and the other leftist Kurds.

Ahmad's approach and attitudes were to harmonize Kurdish nationalism with Arab leftist nationalist groups, rather than to differentiate the Kurdish ethnic and national identity from that of Arabs.[54] The tensions that characterized the Kurdish nationalist movement during the period 1930–58 formed a hard-line sort of cooperation between tribal nationalist leadership and urban intellectual leftists. Both sides tried to outmanoeuver and take advantage of the other. Consequently, after 1958 it was Barzani's achievements and charisma that played a leading role in Kurdish nationalism, more than the urban intellectual leftists.[55]

The political instability in Iraq during this period made the Kurds an important player in Iraq's internal politics, especially during the 1950s and 60s. This was the time for consolidating Kurdish national identity.

The Kurdish Nationalist Movement in the Republican Era: 1958–68
From 1958 to 1968 many *coups d'état* failed in Iraq and there were four changes of political regimes. During Qasim's era, Iraq witnessed political instability, ideological clashes and military authoritarianism.[56] On 14 July 1958 the Hashemite monarchy and the government of Prime Minster Nuri Sa'id were overthrown. The political parties that had been underground until then, such as the ICP and KDP, wholeheartedly supported the new republican government of Abdul Karim Qasim and the Free Officers.[57]

In Article 3 of the first Provisional Constitution announced on 27 July 1958 the Kurds were named as part of the state and their national rights were 'guaranteed'. But for the Kurds, Article 2 was complicated and self-contradicting as it stated that 'Iraq constitutes part of the Arab nation'.[58] This reflected an ambiguity in defining Iraq's national identity and at the same time demonstrated the attempt to reconcile Arab national identity and its pan-Arab tendencies with a territorial Iraqi national identity.[59]

The post-revolutionary era may be characterized as chaotic since Qasim and his leftist supporters were asserting the 'Iraqi-first' identity tied to *wataniya* nationalism. The second person in the government, Abdel Salam

Arif, was anti-leftist, claiming that Nasserite Arab nationalism amalgamated with Islamic Arabness (*Uruba* in Arabic). Qasim, however, never belonged to any political party or organization. His official state discourse was to create a sense of Iraqiness based on Arab–Kurdish fraternity.[60]

On 6 October of that year Barzani returned to Iraq as a hero from the Soviet Union.[61] Perhaps these two factors were most persuasive in making the Kurds support Qasim and his regime.[62] Accordingly, the Kurds were allowed to broadcast in Kurdish and to publish books and periodicals. Elementary schools in Kurdish-speaking areas were allowed to use Kurdish as the medium of instruction. Kurdish departments were also established in some of the Iraqi universities.

Qasim and his political system recognized Kurdish ethnic and national identity and affirmed the partnership between the Kurds and Arabs.[63] This enabled Barzani to consolidate his power over the KDP and Kurdish nationalism alike. The relations of the Kurds with Qasim did not last long and soon disintegrated. By 1960 concessions to the Kurds had been withdrawn. Like most of those who ruled Iraq, Qasim began to fear that the Kurdish demand for autonomy would lead to independence.[64]

The significant events to underline are these: (1) in July 1959 the Kurds and the Communists were used by Qasim to suppress anti-Qasim insurgents in Mosul and Kirkuk.[65] These two outbreaks of insurgency were led by Arab nationalist Free Officers, namely *Abdel Wahab al-Shawaf* and *Nathem al-Tubuychuli* (locally called the *al-Shawaf* movement or *Harakat al-Shawaf*). (2) During 1960–1 Kurdish demands for cultural, national and economic recognition and needs for security, health and education were sent to the government by KDP members in Baghdad. This was after Barzani had left Baghdad and gone to stay in Barzan. These demands were ignored and Qasim began to attack Barzani through old tribal enemies (the *Zebari*, *Surchi* and *Herki* tribes). Many members of the KDP were arrested. Later the *Khabat* newspaper (KDP's political voice) was closed in Baghdad.[66]

Smith's description of the Kurds as a 'proto-nation' fits the situation during this time:

> Where disaffected *ethnies* become alienated enough to resort to terror and revolt, their ethnic nationalism may become the vehicle for a new national identity that draws many members of the community involved in the conflict into a new type of politicised vernacular culture and creates a different kind of participant society. In these cases the movement itself is the prototype and harbinger of a new society and culture. Its cells, schools, guerrilla units, welfare associations, self-help groups,

women's societies and labour unions, as well as its songs, flags, dress, poetry, sports, arts and crafts all presage and create the nucleus of the future ethnic nation and its political identity, even where secession is prevented and the community fails to obtain its own state.[67]

Kurdish 'vernacular mobilization' was vital to demoting the Kurds' ethnic nationalism.[68] Historically speaking, the revolt against Qasim began after the Iraqi Army attacked Barzan. The Kurdish Revolution thus began in March 1961 and continued until September 1961 when Barzani controlled all of the Kurdistan mountain regions.[69] The revolution was moderate; it sought to secure autonomy and had an advanced social agenda, which involved nearly all classes of Kurdish society. It was the KDP which gave the movement a solid political, military and administrative structure.[70] This continued until 1962. The *Ba'th* Party overthrew Qasim on 8 February 1963 and the Iraqi Army under Abdel Salam Arif overthrew the Party itself nine months later.

On 13 April 1966 Abdel Salam Arif was killed in a helicopter crash during a sandstorm while returning from Qurna to Basra. The nationalist Army Officers appointed his brother, Abdel Rahman Arif, to replace him, but the Arab *Ba'th* Socialist Party resumed power on 17–30 July 1968 under the presidency of Ahmad Hasan al-Bakr and Saddam Hussein, his relative, became the vice president.[71]

Many Iraqi observers characterized Abdel Rahman Arif as weak and not as aggressive as his younger brother, Abdel Salam, was. With this high degree of political instability in Iraq, it is not surprising that so little could be achieved in terms of substantial demands of a Kurdish national movement. It seems that during the five years of Qasim's rule (1958–63) the Kurds managed to consolidate and develop their cultural rights more than their national rights and, as a consequence, the demands for autonomy were put aside.

During both brothers' terms of rule, Abdel Salam and Abdel Rahman, (1963–6 and 1966–8), Kurdish demands were apparently received in a friendly manner and promises were given without real consideration. In reality, however, the Kurds' demands were answered by the attacks of the Army on Kurdistan. It is striking that under the rule of Arif the second in 1966, the new cabinet had a moderate, civilian prime minister, a British-educated academic and lawyer, Abdel Rahman al-Bazzaz.

Al-Bazzaz had tried to establish peace with the Kurds within a democratic system in Iraq. After two weeks of negotiations with the Kurds, al-Bazzaz reached an agreement known as the June 1996 accord, or the 'al-Bazzaz Declaration,' which included a fifteen-point offer to resolve the Kurdish demands for autonomy and national recognition of their rights.

However, the Nasserite national Officers, the *Ba'thist*s and even the Communists had rejected the agreement. In August of that year while al-Bazzaz was in the Soviet Union, this group agreed to replace him by resignation and nationalist Army Officer Naji Talib succeeded him.[72]

One of the most remarkable evolutionary developments in the Kurdish national movement was the replacement of the local tribal *Agha* or *Sheikh*, who played a significant role prior to the 1940s and 50s, by the secular urban educated strata. For several reasons however, Barzani was an exception. By the 1960s even the role of religious groups and their authorities had declined. It was the KDP under the influence of the secular urban educated politicians that played a major role in the Kurdish nationalist movement.

Kurdish Nationalist Mobilization in the *Ba'th* Era: 1968–90

After the 1960s Kurdish political mobilization made a radical departure from the mainstream of tribalism and religious affiliation. The Kurdish nationalist movement grew stronger and more powerful in terms of party organization and military prowess. The Arab *Ba'th* Socialist Party returned to power for the second time, but in different circumstances; they came to power through a *coup d'état* against Abdel Rahman Arif.[73]

The Iraqi state was weak before the *Ba'thist*s consolidated their power. One key point should be made about the *Ba'th* Party. At the early stage of their rule, the affirmative consolidation of power and the stability of the regime were their main ends.[74] After 17 July Ahmad Hassan al-Bakir and Saddam Hussein were very concerned with getting rid of the powerful pan-Arab nationalist Army officers, (the non-*Ba'thist* clique of palace officers). Among this group was Colonel Ibrahim Abdel Rahman al-Dawud, Commander of the Republican Guard; Colonel Abdel Razak al-Nayef, Head of Military Intelligence; Colonel Sa'adun Gedan, Commander of the Armoured Brigade of the Guard; and later *Ba'thist* Army officers such as Hardan Abdel Gafur al-Tikriti, Commander of the Air Force and Salih Mahdi Ammash, Minister of the Interior.[75]

The problem was how to impose a solid form of unity and a shared Iraqi identity on Iraq's multiethnic and sectarian groups. The Kurdish question for the new regime was the most complex and difficult problem.[76] The *Ba'th* hegemony over the state and society was not sufficiently consolidated and they failed to crush the Kurdish revolts of 1969. Consequently, negotiations with the Kurdish nationalist leadership culminated in the Agreement of 11 March 1970.

The Agreement of 11 March 1970

'Any *ethnie* that aspires to nationhood must become politicised and stake out claims in the competition for power and influence in the state arena', states Smith.[77] This is, in fact, what happened in the early 1970s between Iraq's new regime and the Kurdish national movement. The Kurdish movement's political demand was 'democracy for Iraq and autonomy for Kurdistan.'[78]

In July 1970 the fledgling regime announced conditions that if agreed to would enable the ICP and the KDP to join a 'Progressive National Front'. Barzani refused the proposal and the ICP joined the Front.[79] The civilian faction of the new Revolutionary Command Council (RCC), dominated by Saddam Hussein and President Ahmad Hasan al-Bakr, offered to negotiate a solution which would grant the Kurds a large measure of autonomy. Though a contentious issue in *Ba'th* Party circles, their strategy of offering autonomy was necessitated by the fact that Iran had increased the level of military support to Barzani, including heavy weapons and air support. According to Stephen Pelletiere, Kurdish relations with the Shah of Iran and Israel helped to consolidate Barzani's power over the KDP and Kurdish nationalism.[80]

Saddam Hussein travelled to Kurdistan and met with Barzani. He gave Barzani a couple of blank sheets of paper and asked him to write down the Kurds' demands. Saddam took back the details to discuss with the Revolution's Command Council (RCC), which ultimately led to the March Agreement.[81] Because of this strategic subordination of Kurdish to Arab Iraqi identity, Saddam Hussein was able to justify granting wide-ranging autonomy to the Kurds in 1970, while insisting that they were still an integral part of Iraq.

The 13 articles of the agreement provided for full recognition of Kurdish nationality; autonomy within four years; a Kurdish Vice-President of the Republic; five Kurdish Ministers in the Cabinet; the concession to make Kurdish an official language along with Arabic; to allow for the formation of Kurdish political parties and cultural organizations; the integration of the *peshmarga* into the border guard and Army units; and a census and plebiscite to determine the status of Kirkuk.[82]

This agreement further consolidated Kurdish national identity and led to the legislation of the KDP. It was also to provide for a census, which would serve as the basis for settling the territorial boundaries of Kurdistan. The latter, however, never came about due to the disagreement over the Kirkuk region and its demography in which the Kurds had a majority of citizens. The government refused to consider allowing Kirkuk to be included in the territory of the Kurdish region. The *Ba'th* ruling party was fully aware that the majority of Kirkuk's citizens were Kurdish. Meanwhile, the government undertook its Arabization policy in the provinces of Mosul, Kirkuk and Khanaqin by deporting the Failis to Iran and replacing them with Arabs from the surrounding tribes of Mosul and the *Shi'is* in the south.[83]

Not surprisingly, while the Kurds firmly referred to the 'March Proclamation' as an 'agreement' (*Ittifaq* in Arabic), the Iraq government's media deliberately insisted on calling it a 'March Proclamation' (*Bayan Athar* in Arabic) to demonstrate that it was a unilateral offer from a sovereign state to its subjects, not an agreement between equals. This distinction is crucial because for the Kurds the guarantee of protection within the Iraqi state depended upon recognition as equals to the Arabs and as nations. Their place within Iraq was not automatic or given, but depended upon a voluntary union (*Ittihad Ikhtiyari* in Arabic).[84]

The use of this language always infuriated the *Ba'th*, who found it treasonous and a threat to the territorial integrity of the Arab Nation. More importantly, the insistence that the rights that the Kurds enjoyed had been granted them by the unitary sovereign state implied that these rights could be unilaterally withdrawn as well. Although partial implementation of the less contentious aspects of the March Agreement began in 1970–1, the more important issues, involving recognition of the Kurds' 'national rights', the acceptance of Barzani's candidate for vice-president, the teaching of the Kurdish language in schools and the territorial issues, were continually delayed. Following the assassination attempts of Idris Barzani in Baghdad in 1970 and of Barzani himself in 1971–2, the relation between the Kurds and the central government deteriorated. The negotiations between the Kurdish leadership and the Iraqi government during the long period of 1973 until spring of 1974 resulted in deadlock.[85]

What the *Ba'th* regime had in mind in the years following the *coup d'état* was the imposition of hegemonic power over the state. They would reinforce the legitimacy of *Ba'th* Party rule throughout Iraq, rather than seriously consider Kurdish national and political demands. They were successful in achieving this end.

The Algiers Agreement: 1974–5 and the Kurdish Revolution

The war had begun in 1974. Baghdad had unilaterally announced a new Autonomy Law (*Qanun al-Hukm al-Thati* in Arabic) that gave the Kurds fewer national rights than the 1970 agreement warranted. It also gave them a much more restricted definition and territorial extension of autonomy. Barzani, overconfident and miscalculating Iranian and US support, rejected the offer and demanded a larger territorial area as well as a share of Iraq's oil revenues proportionate to the size of the Kurdish population.[86] Meanwhile the Iraqi government, in an attempt to weaken and collapse the Kurdish struggle, offered Iran a revision of the agreement governing the demarcation of the disputed *Shat al-Arab* waterway. As a result, Iran and the US withdrew their support for the Kurds, resulting in the collapse of the Kurdish revolt. The negotiations relating to the issue of *Shat al-Arab* took place between Tehran (the Shah) and Baghdad (Saddam) in Algiers on 6 March 1975 at the Organization of Petroleum Exporting Countries (OPEC) meeting.[87]

In exchange for its withdrawal of support for the Kurds Tehran demanded that Iraq recognize the *Shat al-Arab* as an international waterway. Iraq agreed to this substantial territorial concession and within a very short period, the Iranians withdrew their support for the Kurds. Iraq gave the Kurds two weeks to surrender and Iran threatened to assist in the military suppression of the resistance if it persisted.[88] On 23 March 1975 Barzani announced that he was ending the struggle and he and his family sought refuge in Iran. Over the next two weeks the movement completely collapsed with over 100,000 Kurds seeking refuge across the border. Some of those refugees eventually found their way to the US, including Mustafa Barzani, who needed medical treatment. He came to the US in 1977 and died there in 1979.[89]

It was both the Shah's action and the Algiers Agreement that shattered Kurdish political aspirations and which ultimately led to the collapse of the Kurdish nationalist revolt. The collapse of the Kurdish revolutionary movement, which started in September 1961 and lasted for the next four-teen years under the leadership of Barzani, was from all accounts a trau-matic watershed experience for many Kurds in Iraq and in the other parts of Greater Kurdistan.

It was after the collapse of the Kurdish movement in 1975 that Jalal Talabani disagreed with the decision of the Kurdistan Democratic Party, specifically Barzani, that continuing resistance against the Iraqi government would be ineffectual. Talabani formed a new party, the Patriotic Union of Kurdistan (PUK).

The leadership of the Kurdish movement was thus split and the PUK, with Jalal Talabani at its head, dominated Kurdish national aspirations until 1983. After 1975 two coherent policies were practised by the government of Iraq to secure its hold over Kurdistan. The first was the ill-fated and discrim-inatory Arabization of Kurdistan policy and the second was the Ba'thization of Iraqi society policy, including Kurdistan. With the cooperation of security forces, the Iraqi army created a security belt along the Iranian and Turkish borders. Villages that fell within the belt were systematically destroyed.[90]

Internal Displacement

The UN Guiding Principles on Internal Displacement (the 'Guiding Principles')[91] represent the 'benchmark for national, international and non-state actors in their interactions with the internally displaced, providing guidelines in relation to each stage of the phenomenon of internal displacement, as well as providing a framework for the consideration of issues of responsibility.'[92] '"Internally displaced persons" includes any person or group who involuntarily left their home ... in order to protect themselves from the consequences of armed conflict.'[93] It does not have to be across a state border, it can be forced removal to another village, town or locale. Saddam Hussein's Arabization policy amounted to the attempt to eliminate Kurdish national identity by forcibly assimilating them into the official myth of a distinctive, unifying Iraqi territorial identity. This strategy began in the oil-rich and well-known Kurdish areas of Kirkuk, Sinjar, Ain-Zala and Khanaqin.[94] About 200,000 Kurdish families were forcibly deported to villages and towns belonging to Imara and Naseriya cities and suburbs in the south. In addition, numerous Kurdish villages, cities and small towns were renamed. Kirkuk, for instance, became *Al-Tamim* which means 'nationalization' in Arabic. Toz, with its majority population of Kurds, was attached to Tikrit and renamed Salahaddin. In Bahdinan the Arabization policy affected Zebar, Barzan, Atrush and Zakho.[95]

Eventually nearly half a million Kurds had been displaced from their homes and forbidden to return.[96] The systematic and organized Arabization policy in these sensitive areas led the *Ba'th* to remap the province of Kirkuk, Suleimaniya and Erbil by cutting or detaching Kurdish inhabited districts and attaching them to the provinces of Salahaddin and Mosul in a way which trapped the Kurds between the Arab tribal areas of Kirkuk and Erbil.

Consequently, much smaller areas became Kurdish and the Arabs were moved into the excluded Kurdish areas to dilute the Kurdish populations. On 18 November 1975 the towns of Kalar and Chamchamal were both detached from Kirkuk and attached to Suleimaniya as an integral part of the 'Autonomous Region'. Further on, Kifri was attached to the Diyala Province.[97] The Ministry of Northern Affairs was abolished. Kurdish schools were closed. The Kurdish Language Department at the University of Baghdad was shut down and national and cultural activities that were not consistent with *Ba'th* interests were banned.[98]

When the *Ba'th* proceeded with the Autonomy Law after 1974, a Legislative and Executive Council was established in Erbil. Many Kurdish figures that had previously split from the Central Committee of the KDP were appointed to the Executive Council, which was headed by Hashim Aqrawi.[99] Erbil became the capital and administrative centre for the autonomous region.

Following the 1975 disaster the Kurdish national movement split into three factions as new political discourses arose: the Patriotic Union of Kurdistan (PUK); the Kurdistan Democratic Party 'Provisional Leadership' (KDP-PL, *Qiyaday Mu'akata* in Kurdish); and the Democratic Party of Kurdistan 'Preparatory Committee'.[100]

Militant Kurdish Nationalism: 1976–90

While in Damascus on 1 June 1975 and after the collapse of the movement, Jalal Talabani (known and called by the Kurds as *Mam Jalal*) formed his left-wing elements into an umbrella organization later known as the Patriotic Union of Kurdistan. It consisted of three major groups: the *Komala*, led by a young left-wing nationalist named Nawshirwan Mustafa; the *Bezutnaway Socialist* (Socialist Movement*)*, a less extreme brand of socialist ideologues; and *Hezi gishti* (General Force), led by Jalal Talabani from Syria until his return to Kurdistan in 1977.[101]

The formation of the PUK was a result of the political vacuum of 1975.[102] Talabani and his comrades in the PUK were critical of Barzani's leadership, as it was considered to be 'tribal.'[103] While the KDP-PL, led by Idris Barzani (Mustafa Barzani's son), remained ineffective in Iran especially during 1978–9, both Sami Abdul Rahman and Mahmud Uthman split from the KDP-PL and established their own political organizations. The PUK, however, had continued its limited fighting against the Iraqi Army via guerrilla warfare from Kurdistan.

In the last years of the 1970s many left-wing political organizations and parties had been formed in Iraqi Kurdistan. In 1976 Mahmud Uthman formed the Popular Alliance of Socialist Kurdistan (PASOK); in 1979 following a disagreement with Jalal Talabani, Rasul Mamand formed the Kurdistan Socialist Party of Iraq (KSPI), with Mahmud Uthman joining the party later. In 1981 Sami Abdul Rahman founded the Kurdistan Popular Democratic Party (KPDP).[104] These small political parties were ineffective on Kurdistan's political landscape. They lacked deep roots, a social base and historical perspective.[105]

In 1968 and for the following ten years, Saddam was a prominent figure in the Iraqi state. However, he implicitly disliked the expression, 'Mr. Vice President' (*al Sayid al-Na'ib* in Arabic), and on 16 July 1979 took the Presidency of Iraq from his relative, al-Bakr, in a silent coup on the pretext of the latter's 'poor health'.[106]

Saddam had already organized his civilian and army secret police agencies by the time he took power. He controlled the Army by arranging for the promotion of officers who were from his home town of Tikrit and by establishing *Ba'th* Party control over it. These controls over the Armed Forces consolidated his position as the Head of State and the Army alike. He controlled the apparatus of the government in the same way.[107] The *Ba'th*, with its many security service associates, behaved in clandestine and conspiratorial ways. Their relatively privileged members served as the eyes and ears of the Regime. At the end of the 1970s and early 80s, Saddam's authoritarian political regime was solid and his loyal Republican Army was strong. Saddam had appointed many members of his extended family to key posts in various security apparatuses of the state.[108] Ultimately these appointments enabled him to act as omnipotent ruler and increased his psychological tendencies towards dictatorial rule.

The 1978–9 revolution in Iran led to the overthrow of the Shah's regime and brought the *Shi'i* Islamists to power. This change of events startled Saddam and alarmed his secular *Ba'thist* regime. It was as if they feared that a similar scenario could happen in Iraq. Interpreting the post-revolutionary chaos as an opportunity to grab power, Saddam ordered the invasion of *Qasr Shirin* in September 1980, thus beginning the Iran–Iraq War.[109]

Kurdish nationalism's strategies and tactics had changed. The KDP for the most part stayed in Iran during the Iran–Iraq war which spanned 1980–8. During the mid-1980s, however, the political climate in Iraqi Kurdistan grew extremely complex due to the divisions within the political organizations and parties, on one hand and their differing goals and infighting, on the other.[110]

From the start of the Iranian revolution the KDP, under the leadership of Idris Barzani, allied itself with the Iranian government. The PUK found itself in a more critical situation because it faced the Iranian army on one side and the KDP and Iraqi forces on the other. Consequently, the PUK had to cooperate with the Kurdistan Democratic Party of Iran (KDPI), led by Abdul Rahman Ghassemlou, who was receiving support from the Iraqi government against Iran. By 1984 Talabani openly negotiated with the Iraqi government in Baghdad and by early 1985 the talks had broken down.[111] After the failure of the PUK's negotiation attempt with Baghdad in 1985, the Arabization and deportation of the Kurds resumed.

The Regime announced a dirty plan for the resettlement of 500,000 Kurdish families via the destruction of their villages. They would be internally displaced and installed in settlements (*mujam'ats* in Arabic) located close to the main roads and military bases in order to give the governmental authorities greater capacity to control them.[112]

The deteriorated situation and the open conflict between the KDP-PL and the PUK led to violence and skirmishes in the years following 1976. The traumatic events that took place during 1976–87 played a significant role in the inability of the Kurdish movement to unite. This weakened the already fragmented nationalist movement in the mid-1980s. This is not to say that Kurdish pride in Kurdistan and the national identity of the Kurds was fragmented, however.[113]

Thus, following the appointment of Saddam's cousin, Ali Hassan al-Majid (known as 'Chemical Ali' to the Kurds), as the head of the Iraqi State Security Services and the chief of the *Ba'th* Party's Bureau for Northern Affairs in March 1987, the ruthless systematic *Anfal* campaign started (1987–8). The use of chemical weapons in *Halabja* on 16 March 1988 allowed the Iraqi Army including members of Republican Guard to have access to the pro-government Kurdish forces (*Jash*, which means 'small donkey' in Kurdish). This allowed them to regain control of almost all the Kurdish territories and inflict a severe setback for the Kurds. It was during Ali Hassan al-Majid's time that the ethnic cleansing of Kirkuk became more systematic. These ruthless strategies of Arabization and deportations continued during the 1980s–90s in clear violation of the 'UN Guiding Principles'.[114] The most striking aspect of this strategy was the process of building the camps for the deported villagers and the transfer of the Kurds to these camps (*Mujam'ats*). In 1989 in clear violation of international law the government prevented the Kurds of Kirkuk and its surrounding areas from buying or building houses unless they agreed to change their nationality to 'Arab'.[115]

From 1988 to 2003 the *Ba'th* regime engaged in the ethnic cleansing of Kirkuk under a policy called 'nationality correction' which was aimed at changing the language and ethnicity of all inhabitants of the city to Arab and Arabic respectively. If non-Arabs refused to change their nationality, they were deported and their land, property and belongings confiscated. Arabs from the south were brought in to replace them and provided with strong material incentives to stay and entrench themselves into the affairs of the city.[116]

These policies of displacement and disfranchisement of the Kurds from the rural areas of Kurdistan were strategically designed by Saddam Hussein to increase their dependence on the state. It is clear that the Arabization of Kurdistan 'territorialized' Kurdish national identity, while linking Kurdish demands more specifically to the geopolitically significant Kurdish areas of Kirkuk and Khanaqin. Consequently, the central issue behind Kurdish autonomy centred on the original ethnic makeup of Kirkuk and its demo-graphic structure rather than the political or cultural rights of the Kurds.[117]

It is estimated that 100,000 innocent Kurds were killed due to the *Anfal* campaign. Halabja lost 5,000 in one chemical attack. In later years, however, Halabja, a small town near the Iranian border south of Suleimaniya, would draw international attention to the oppression of the Iraqi Kurds and become a national symbol that would further politicize *Kurdishness* and strengthen Kurdish national consciousness.[118]

Anfal marks one of the most brutal acts of genocide in modern Iraqi history. It had a profound demographic, economic and psychological impact on the Iraqi Kurds.[119] In May 1988 despite the tensions, disagreements and infighting, different Kurdish political parties made an umbrella organization representing the Kurdish national movement to resolve their differences and present a united Iraqi Kurdistan Front (IKF: *Baray Kurdistani Iraqi* in Kurdish) which was locally called the 'KF'.[120] The participating factions included the Kurdistan Democratic Party (KDP); the Patriotic Union of Kurdistan (PUK); and six other small political parties including the Kurdistan Popular Democratic Party (KPDP) led by Sami Abdurrahman; the Kurdistan Socialist Party (KSP or PASOK in Kurdish) led by Mahmud Uthman; the Iraqi Communist Party (ICP) led by Aziz Mohammad since 1964; the Kurdistan Toilers' Party (KTP); and the Assyrian Democratic Party (ADM). The Iran–Iraq war ended on 18 August 1988 with Saddam Hussein's armed forces more powerful than ever. Between that time and the Iraqi occupation of Kuwait on 2 August 1990, the Kurds via the Kurdistan Front ceased guerrilla activity in the Kurdish areas and concentrated on advancing their cause politically from exile in Iran.[121]

The Kurdistan Front's aim was the right of self-determination for the Kurds and democracy for Iraq. The KF had a significant role in promoting Kurdish aspirations in the latter days of the March uprising of 1991.

6

RECONSTRUCTING AND CONSOLIDATING NATIONAL IDENTITY: 1991–2008

Due to the decline of *Ba'th* hegemony and the disappearance of its dominant authoritative apparatus, Kurdistan underwent a great transformation in its political culture after 1992. After 1997 this transformation led the young educated Kurds to take on another feature of their identity. This new generation views themselves as *Kurdistani* rather than Iraqi. In the post-1990s the notion of *Kurdistanism* (*Kurdistaniyeti*) appears as an alternative descriptor to that of 'Iraqi Kurd'. *Kurdistanism* means the promotion of Kurdistan in its civic and traditional ethnic conceptions. It is also a term that captures the territorial and political imagination of young *Kurdistanis* and consolidates the essence of Kurdish national identity. In formal KRG discourse *Kurdistani* identity is the civic expression of the *status quo* of Kurdistan and has been since the 1990s. It also means sharing the experience of the non-Kurdish minorities with the Kurds during the 1990s era.

Contemporary scholarship views nationalism as a product of modernization. Kurdistan has not experienced a 'normal' or 'proper' period of modernization until very recently. Because of that Kurdistan did not have a sense of nationalism until well into the twentieth century. Modern Kurdish national identity is a twentieth-century phenomenon, indeed.

The real history of the consolidation of Kurdish national identity and nation-building in Iraqi Kurdistan began after March 1991 and the election of 1992. This period effectively put an end to the tyranny of the *Ba'thist* regime in Kurdistan. This is even more evident in post-1998 Kurdistan. One cannot help but notice that the Kurds have been entering a new era of nation-building since the 1990s.

The *Rapareen* of March 1991: Causes and Consequences

Two very important developments took place in the early 1990s. The first was Iraq's invasion and occupation of Kuwait on 2 August 1990, an event that caused a deep regional and international crisis and ended the goal of a unified Arab defence and sense of Arab unity.[1] The second development was the subsequent 'safe haven' for the Kurds created by the US-led Allied forces after the failed uprising in Kurdistan. The invasion of Kuwait and what followed brought new political hope to Kurdish national aspirations, especially after 15 February 1991 when President Bush called on the Iraqi people to overthrow the Dictator.[2]

For the first time in Iraq's contemporary history, and even before the ceasefire on 2 March 1991, the oppressed *Shi'a* in the south rebelled. But the most significant event was the defeat of the Iraqi Army in Operation Desert Storm.[3] During the first week of March a spontaneous widespread uprising took place in Kurdistan.[4] Military bases, Security and *Ba'th* Party Headquarters in the Kurdish towns and cities were attacked and overthrown by the Kurdish masses with the support of *Peshmarga* led by the Kurdistan Front (and the *Jash* units later).[5]

Unlike the uprising in the south, which varied from place to place, the revolt in the north began on 4 March in the small town of Ranya north-east of Kurdistan. Suleimaniya and Erbil followed on 6 and 7 March respectively. The uprising continued and on 11 March the people of Dohuk and Zakho rebelled. On 21 March the city of Kirkuk, especially in the north, was under the control of Kurdish Front forces. The southern part of the city, which was mostly inhabited by Arab army officers and security police personnel, remained under the control of the government until 29 March when Saddam Hussein gathered his Republican Guard, marched back into the territory and retook Kirkuk on 30 March. Immediately after, all the major Kurdish cities were under his control.[6]

The *Peshmarga* forces of the Kurdistan Front had joined in towards the latter part of the uprising. They were able to offer strategy and direction especially during the fighting inside Kirkuk city. The Kurdistan Front had given amnesty to all of the *Jash* units and asked them to cooperate with the KF. The response of the *Jash* units was positive and they cooperated in the rebellion.

As the Republican Guard proceeded to take over, well over two million Kurds fled in unprecedented numbers to the Turkish and Iranian borders. Iran accepted the Kurdish refugees, but Turkey refused them entrance. Refugees on the Turkish border were stranded on mountainsides exposed to the winter weather. Because trucks could not reach them, there was a desperate lack of food to sustain them and materials to shelter them. However, Turkey allowed foreign journalists into the area and the world watched as hundreds of Kurds died.[7]

Western governments (principally those of the Unites States, the United Kingdom and France) responded by dispatching supplies through Turkey and by direct airdrops to the refugees. The UN Security Council passed Resolution 688 on 5 April. This was a historic resolution as it was the first time the Kurds were ever mentioned by name.[8]

On 8 April 1991 at a European Community meeting in Luxembourg, Britain's Prime Minister John Major presented a proposal for a UN-protected Kurdish enclave. The other European leaders endorsed the plan and a week later it was endorsed by the United States as well. 'Operation Provide Comfort' is the name given to the safe haven for the Kurds that was implemented by the United States and its Gulf War Allies in 1991. Under the Operation Provide Comfort umbrella, Allied Western troops on the ground persuaded the Kurds to descend from the mountains into the plains where camps were set up with relief supplies as an added inducement. Allied troops were also sent into Dohuk to maintain a presence so that the Kurdish refugees who had fled to that area could go back to their homes. And the area of Iraq above the 36th parallel, which includes Erbil, Mosul, Zakho and Dohuk, was declared a 'no-fly zone'. Any Iraqi plane flying above the parallel would be subject to reprisal.[9] More than a million Kurdish refugees who had fled to Turkey and Iran began returning to their towns and cities in May 1991.

By mid-July the system had been put in place and the Western troops withdrew from northern Iraq to bases in Silopi, just across the southeastern Turkish border. They left a small staff, the Military Coordination Centre in Zakho, to oversee continuing relief efforts and to act as a stabilizing force. The no-fly zone was regularly patrolled by aircraft from the United States, Great Britain, France and Turkey.[10]

Operation Provide Comfort was not the only source of help to the Kurds. There were several other relief programmes supported by different countries and agencies and a number of initiatives aimed at strengthening opposition to the Iraqi government and Saddam Hussein. At this stage the Americans apparently did not want Saddam to be toppled by external forces, or they were favouring a military coup from within Iraq. Later in 1991 Kurdish leaders joined the Iraqi National Congress (INC), a US-backed opposition group and allowed it a presence in Iraqi Kurdish territory from which to operate against Baghdad. Meanwhile the Iraqi opposition, including Kurdish Front representatives, had meetings in Damascus and Beirut that aimed to develop an Iraqi united front, which had the goal of overthrowing Saddam Hussein and setting up a coalition government for Iraq.

After the failure of the *Rapareen* many Iraqi Kurds found themselves in ambiguous administrative and political predicaments, being neither fully inside nor fully outside of the Iraqi state framework in the unprotected safe-haven zone in north Iraq. The intent of the safe-haven, or no-fly zones in southern and northern Iraq, was to protect the *Shi'a* and the Kurds from revenge attacks by Hussein's Army. The US–UK coalition flew warplanes over these zones (without Security Council authorization) to prevent Hussein's airforce from using military aircraft to attack the Kurds and *Shi'a*. In April of that year negotiations began with the central government, which continued until August. They finally and completely broke down in January 1992.[11]

The negotiations between the Iraqi government and the KF failed because KF representatives asked the Iraqi authorities to sign the agreement under the observation of the UN or to be protected internationally.[12] Baghdad refused. As a result, the central government withdrew its military forces and administrative services from Kurdistan and on 23 October 1991 imposed an economic sanction on the region. As a result Kurdistan suffered great economic hardship due to the double embargo imposed by Saddam and the UN. Decision-making processes were the most important issue that the KF faced. The KF proposed a general election to fill the political vacuum created by the withdrawal of Iraqi governmental institutions.[13]

The 19 May 1992 Elections and the 1992–8 Power-Sharing System

The no-fly zone is considered to have ended on 19 March 2003 when Operation Iraqi Freedom and the 'shock-and-awe' campaign began. Despite economic privations resulting from massive population displacements, the cessation of most government-supplied rations from Baghdad and the devastating impact of intra-communal conflict between the PUK and KDP in 1996, the Kurds in the three northern governorates of Erbil, Suleimaniya and Dohuk established democratically elected administrations while founding a number of civil society and human rights organizations. The National Assembly was legally established following the 19 May 1992 elections.

The Unity Party of Kurdistan (UPK) was founded after the 1992 elections under the leadership of Sami Abdul Rahman. It was a merger of three other parties: the Kurdistan Popular Democratic Party (KPDP), founded in 1981 by Sami Abdul Rahman; the Kurdistan Socialist Party of Iraq (KSPI), founded by Rasul Mamand in 1979 after a falling out with the PUK; and the Popular Alliance of Socialist Kurdistan (PASOK), founded in 1976. The UPK was dissolved when it joined the KDP in 1993 during the latter Eleventh Congress. This greatly affected the balance of power in *Kurdistani* party politics. As a result the KDP was temporarily renamed the United Kurdistan Democratic Party (UKDP).[14]

The National Assembly was established with two major parties, the KDP and the PUK, holding the balance of power between them. This was later called the '50/50 power sharing system'. The remaining five seats were allocated to the Christian Assyrians and Islamic movement representatives. In actuality the KDP and the PUK won 50.22 per cent and 49.78 per cent of the vote respectively. The top leader for Kurdistan was not chosen because the final vote left Mas'ud Barzani and Jalal Talabani too close to call at 466,819 to 441,057.[15]

The London-based Electoral Reform Society pronounced the process 'free and fair' with 'no evidence of substantial fraud that would have significantly affected the result'.[16] Neither Mas'ud Barzani nor Jalal Talabani had held positions within the governmental or administrative legal system. Due to the political violence between KDP and PUK groups, as well as the fragmentation and polarization of society during 1993–4, the *Peshmarga* intervened to forestall the erosion of party authority. With the establishment of the first cabinet of the Parliament on 4 June 1992, 105 members were announced with the speaker from the KDP and his deputy from the PUK. A month later on 4 July 1992 a regional government was formed with the prime minster from the PUK and his deputy from the KDP. On 4 October 1992 the Kurdistan Parliament proclaimed Kurdistan to be a federal state within Iraq. Not surprisingly, the Iraqi government recognized neither the election nor the federalism. Iraq's Arab leaders feared that Kurdish demands for a federation masked a quest for full independence, a concern shared by neighbouring states with large Kurdish populations (Turkey, Iran and Syria).

Power-sharing is an important means by which conflict can be mitigated or even avoided. In the high stakes of Kurdish politics an agreement is of little use if in the end it produces losers as well as winners. The sincerity of a pledge to cease fighting must always be doubted if losing an election means that a disputant is worse off than had he continued the war. Power-sharing, on the other hand, creates conditions where all the parties are at least partial winners. It reduces the perception that an election is a zero-sum game, where losing at the ballot box necessarily entails losing (perhaps permanently) everything and endangering the survival of an ethnic group.

The formula for power-sharing in Kurdistan, namely 50–50, was applied at all levels of the administration in all the ministries of the region. This system in later months brought tension and conflict between the two sides. Add to this the pre-existing chaos within the Islamic Movement in Kurdistan (IMK), which ended in a skirmish in December 1993. Unfortunately this division of power developed into violent conflict, as was seen in May 1994.[17]

There was disagreement between the KDP and the PUK over sources of income from border trade with Turkey. The KDP benefited more and the PUK felt squeezed out of power and starved of finances. This conflict led to civil war.[18] Thus in early 1994 the uneasy power-sharing arrangement between the KDP and PUK collapsed and armed clashes broke out over territorial control and the sharing of revenues. The Kurdistan Regional Government had no role in these events as the two parties were the two main political players in Kurdistan's political arena. Instead of uniting the *de facto* state, which was established in the early 1990s, the two parties divided Kurdistan into two administrative regions. This became evident after the internal fighting of 1996 ended with the hegemony of the PUK over Erbil city and its surrounding towns.

Due to continued skirmishes state rebuilding was compromised. The fight for political hegemony between the KDP and the PUK continued during 1993–96. This incapacitated the government, which was represented in Parliament, and continued discord made it difficult, if not impossible, to kick-start a coherent process of state rebuilding. Skirmishes and internal fighting were endured, on and off, until 17 September 1998 when the two parties signed a cease-fire agreement in Washington.[19]

Since then the political balance between the two sides has been maintained and the region has witnessed great stability, albeit little cooperation. After 1996 the governmental and administrative division between the two parties deepened. That is not to say that the division of the political system created two different political cultures. The Kurds did not confuse political identity with the national. Initially the multi-party election of 1992 and the establishment of the KRG that followed was the most important event in the history of the modern Kurdish national movement.[20] The divided political and administrative systems that emerged in August 1996 allowed the two sides to administer Kurdistan without internal competition.[21] The KDP was allocated administration of Erbil and Dohuk, while the PUK was allocated governance over Suleimaniya, Derbandikhan and the towns that belonged to Kirkuk. Gareth Stansfield has rightly called the current political system 'a consociational type of political and administrative system'.[22]

Administering and governing the region was not an easy task for the two parties. That is why it took them nearly ten years to proclaim unity, at least publicly. It was only in 2006 when the two parties announced the unification of the two administrations that any sort of unity occurred. Despite all the political crises and fragmentations, the Kurds still viewed Iraqi Kurdistan as a single entity. That is remarkable.

Political Power Structures, Power-Sharing and Kurdish National Identity: 1998–2008

The analysis of power structures and groupings within the leadership apparatus of Iraqi Kurdistan illustrates that the parties are characterized by central leadership structures governing a politics of diffusion. This arrangement ensures that pluralistic demands are controlled within a hegemonic structure.

Power-sharing would ideally work as a catalyst for peaceful cooperation among contending parties after a deal is signed. A central feature of the 17 September 1998 Washington Agreement between the KDP and the PUK was agreeing to a cease-fire. The requirement was that power be shared among the competing political groups in the transitional institutions of government. Both parties agreed to establish an arrangement of measures for the sharing of power that would foster a sense of security in a post-1996 skirmish environment (May 1994–October 96) that would make the return to armed conflict less likely. The KDP and the PUK have controlled most of the economic activity and communication networks as well as the *Peshmarga*, which is used to defend their territories and impose order. The causes for the fighting were manifold, including historical enmity between the two parties' political elites and the dissatisfaction of both parties over the power-sharing formula enacted in Parliament and the Cabinet which was established in 1992. Kurdistan had two executive jurisdictions, two premiers, two cabinets and two army forces.

Ten years have passed since the formal ending of the three-year period of skirmishes in Kurdistan. There has been no internal fighting since 1997 and the movement is toward reconciliation and even cooperation.[23] Significant political achievements have been directed to supporting the region's transition towards a lasting democratic peace. The establishment of a unified Kurdistan Regional Government, the unification of a Kurdistan Parliament, selection and appointment of a Kurdistan president and the unification of *Peshmarga* forces in Kurdistan, are some of the signs that indicate the health and maturity of Kurdish national politics. The process of normalization that has been achieved by the KDP and the PUK gained US support in 1998 under the terms of the Washington Agreement. While remaining highly wary of each other, the KDP and the PUK have worked in an increasingly cooperative manner since 2000. As a result, they coordinate their two governments' activities and have undertaken a range of normalization and confidence-building measures. These activities stepped up when it became clear that the US intended to remove the *Ba'th* regime.[24]

Since 2001 the KDP and PUK have gained prominence within the Iraqi opposition. From the US's perspective, they control a swathe of Iraqi territory that could prove crucial in the event of an invasion. The removal of the *Ba'th* regime in 2003 heralded a new period of consolidation and prosperity for the Kurds.[25] The Kurds entered post-Saddam national politics on an equal footing with Iraqi Arabs for the first time by participating in a US-led occupation administration, the Coalition Provisional Authority (CPA). Holding several seats on an advisory 'Iraq Governing Council' (IGC), which was appointed in July 2003, were Barzani, Talabani and three independent Kurds.

Hoshyar Zebari formally became Foreign Minister over the objection of many Arab Iraqi figures in the transitional government that assumed authority on 28 June 2004. This government operated under the 8 March 2004 'Transitional Administrative Law' (TAL), which was a provisional constitution that laid out a political transition process as well as citizens' rights. The Kurds maintained their autonomous Kurdistan Regional Government (KRG) with power to alter the application of some national laws. Another provision allowed the Kurds to continue to field the *Peshmarga* at 75,000 strong. The TAL did not give the Kurds control of Kirkuk province, however. They set up a process to resettle the Kurds that were expelled from Kirkuk by Saddam. Despite opposition from Iraq's *Shi'ite* leaders, the Kurds succeeded in inserting a provision into the TAL that allowed any three provinces to vote down, by a two-thirds majority, a permanent constitution. (The Kurds constitute an overwhelming majority in Dohuk, Erbil and Suleimaniya provinces, assuring them of veto power, which they did not use in the referendum that adopted the Constitution on 15 October 2005.[26])

While the power-sharing system aims to manage joint governance at the national level, it is designed to manage the potential outbreak of conflict between the KDP and the PUK. The function of power-sharing is a mechanism for resolving the commitment problem in a context of serious mistrust and vulnerability. In the absence of a strong civic culture and society in Kurdistan the *Kurdistanis* may not reject parties advocating order and economic advancement.

While the main function of power-sharing is to end violence, it does not necessarily facilitate the building of democracy. Here, power-sharing denotes all types of sharing and dividing of power between former foes with less emphasis on democratic representation and elections. Though power-sharing can be compatible with democracy, it is sometimes constructed as an alternative to competitive elections.[27]

Following the Washington Agreement the two parties have increased cooperation, normalized political relations, improved the economic sector of the region and organized joint committees of their representatives with the UN and NGOs. Both parties participated in the opening of the National Assembly in October 2002. As democracy in a unified Iraq takes root, it remains to be seen whether the two parties and their leaders will face competition from new actors with new agendas in Iraqi Kurdistan.[28]

Under Iraq's Constitution the KRG has a large measure of political autonomy within its own regional boundaries, including primary legislative, budgetary and administrative authority.[29] The KRG drafted a constitution and presented it to the National Assembly this past summer (2009). As the supreme authority of the KRG, the Parliament is weak but gradually it is growing stronger. In 2007 for the first time the Parliament exercised its prerogative to call in Cabinet ministers for questioning and they did this on about a dozen occasions. In early 2008 Parliament received a detailed current government budget with just enough lead time to allow some real debate.[30]

Beyond any formal institutional structures the Parliament and the Executive are under a form of joint management by the KDP and the PUK. Organized political opposition is tolerated and visibly represented in both main branches of government. But it is also effectively marginalized precisely because the two major parties have put aside ferocious past conflicts in favour of a kind of political cease-fire over the KRG as a whole. In fact the KRG actually provides major funding for both dominant parties, along with minor funding for other parties in a way that helps preserve the existing political balance.[31] Following the elections of 2005, 39 seats were each held by the KDP and PUK, 15 are held by the two Islamic parties, 5 by the Chaldo-Assyrian Christians, 4 by the Turkmens, 3 by the communists, 2 by the socialists, 1 by the Toilers' Party and 1 place is shared by smaller parties. A third of Parliament's seats (29) now belongs to women.[32] In analysing the internal structures of the KDP and the PUK, Gareth Stansfield has concluded:

> Structurally, and officially, the two parties exhibit few differences from each other. Both of their internal organisations are similar, and both have similar structures of authority. However, when the power

structures of both parties are assessed, it is clear that they are somewhat
different with the KDP being characterised by a strong central leadership and democratic central tendencies. While there are divisions
apparent within the leadership of the KDP, they are being managed
in a subtle manner by Massoud, and the stability of the party should
remain. With the PUK, the central leadership possesses strong person-
alities with their own support bases and, while they are all loyal to
Talabani, the decision-making process within the PUK is animated
by these divisions. Perhaps most importantly, however, both parties
exhibit strong patrimonial tendencies within their leadership structures, with both Massoud and Talabani manoeuvring themselves
into positions where they remain in command of their organisations,
while attempting to encourage more democratic processes within their
respective parties.[33]

Considering the small parties in Kurdistan, efforts towards power-sharing
or inclusion go a long way toward the overall reduction of conflict. It seems
that power-sharing is a sort of ideal, whereby the most prominent political
parties and leaders share the most important political posts equally. The
diluted version of power-sharing was brought about by distributing lesser
posts or seats to small ethnic groups or parties that were almost guaranteed
to cooperate or follow the KDP's and PUK's political agenda.

After several months of negotiating, on 7 May 2006 the KDP and
the PUK agreed to reunify the Kurdish Regional Government under
the premiership of KDP heir apparent Nechirvan Barzani. Since then
the investment law of Kurdistan has been altered to allow for 100 per
cent foreign ownership of companies operating inside the region, thereby
encouraging a flood of investment. The KRG has embarked on a public
relations initiative to show Iraq, the Middle East and especially the US,
that it not only exists but is a consolidated, economically vibrant entity
that can no longer be ignored. This political and economic advancement
has been more than matched by socio-cultural developments within the
Iraqi Kurdish population. Autonomy from Baghdad has invigorated the
Kurdish sense of nationhood. With a national narrative previously built
around catastrophic events such as *Anfal*, the Kurds can now point to a
more positive development in the form of their autonomy and governmental institutions. The popular discourse in Kurdistan among young
educated Kurds has rapidly become dominated by notions of *Kurdistani*
identity, nationalism and even the moral right to statehood possessed by
all Kurds.[34]

The Notion of *Kurdistanism* (*Kurdistaniyeti*) as a New Form of Asserting National Identity: 1998–2008

The Kurds have governed their region for nearly two decades. The region has been in a zone in transition and is progressively improving. Since 1998 Kurdistan has witnessed peace and progress with the support of UN agencies which were forced to assist the local offices in administrative areas through the Oil for Food Programme (SCR 986).[35]

The previous Iraqi government had no choice but to accept the deal on 20 May 1996, which allowed the central government in Baghdad to export $2 billion in petroleum and petroleum products over a six month period. Accordingly, $200–300 million, or 13 per cent of the worth of the income was to be allocated to the Kurds. The programme was renewed every six months. However, by December 1999, the ceiling on Iraqi exports was lifted by the UN Secretary-General.[36] In the long run the Oil for Food Programme (OFFP) provided a mechanism for settling disputes and resolving many conflicts between the PUK and KDP. It improved living standards in Kurdistan considerably. These economic developments were matched by the normalization of political relations between the KDP and the PUK as evidenced after the Washington Agreement.[37]

Considering the internal development in Kurdistan, the education sector has improved significantly. During the last eighteen years the Kurdistan Regional Government has built more than three thousand schools. Higher education has been expanded by establishing and institutionalizing new universities such as Suleimani, Dohuk (both established in 1992), Koya (established in 2003), the University of Kurdistan-Hawler (established in 2006 where the programmes, teaching, research and communication are all conducted in English) and the American University of Iraq-Suleimaniya (established in 2007).

Numerous publication houses have been established in the major cities of Kurdistan. Numerous television and satellite channels have been broadcasting throughout Kurdistan. Kurdish authorities have established their own standing police and military colleges. Many aspects of Kurdish culture have focused on Kurdish national discourses such as literature, folklore, art and music. Arabic is no longer dominant in the Kurdish educational system and in the collective memories of the young educated generation.

In the post-1990s era Kurdish children have been brought up without having to learn Arabic history or language.[38] English, rather than Arabic, has become this generation's 'world language'. These socio-political transformations combined with inclusive cultural traits have played a key role in fostering Kurdish national identity and strengthening *Kurdistaniyeti* among the young generation. Children who were five years of age in 1991 are 23-year-old adults in 2009. They have no knowledge of Arabic or of Iraq's history and politics. They consider themselves to be *Kurdistani* rather than Iraqi. For this generation the separation from Iraq's politics and culture has aided in the process of identity construction, especially in the aftermath of Saddam's removal from power.[39] For the Kurds in Kurdistan and elsewhere, independence is the ultimate dream. During the first two months of 2004 the referendum movement in Kurdistan collected 1,700,000 signatures of those who were demanding a vote on whether Kurdistan should remain part of Iraq. This represented approximately two-thirds of Kurdistan's adults who weighed in on the issue.[40]

Following the early days of the invasion, the United States appointed General Jay Garner as the temporary ruler for Iraq. After three weeks Ambassador Paul Bremer replaced him and later established the Coalition Provisional Authority (CPA) to govern Iraq.

Government authority was transferred to an Iraqi Interim Government in June 2004 and a permanent government was elected in October 2005.[41] The unsuccessful strategy of the US was to hold Iraq together by establishing a strong central government. Most political scientists and observers believe that a strong unitary state in Iraq is impossible without a federal system. Some have suggested what has been called a three-state solution.[42] It seems that partitioning Iraq into three federal regions would be a reasonable way to treat the pathologies under which Iraq struggles.

Following the election of January 2005 the KDP and the PUK united to form an alliance with several smaller parties in order to push the government to draft a permanent constitution. The Kurdish alliance has 53 deputies in the new Iraqi parliament, while the Kurdish Islamic Union has five. Jalal Talabani was elected President of the new Iraqi administration on 6 April 2005 and Mas'ud Barzani became President of the Kurdistan Regional Government. Unlike the rest of Iraq, the Kurdistan region witnessed an economic boom after 2003, even greater than the boom of 1998 in terms of property development, roads, supermarkets and urban planning.

On 21 January 2006 the two major parties in Kurdistan reached an agreement to form a unified government and administration. This unified regional government is planning to implement many policies to develop Kurdistan's own natural resources, water, minerals, oil and the hydroelectric power industry within a secure legal environment, which in the long run will encourage investment in and diversification of the regional economy.[43] In recent years the KRG has appeared to carry more political weight with the US and the international community than ever before.

PART TWO

7

NATIONALISM AND NATIONAL IDENTITY AMONGST UNIVERSITY STUDENTS

The new generation's conception of national identity and its attitude towards Iraq are different from those of their parents and grandparents. For university students it is *Kurdistanism* (*Kurdistaniyeti*) rather than Iraqiness (*Iraqchiyati* in Kurdish) which is the main focus of national aspirations. The subjects of this study are young educated Kurdish university students predominantly in the 18–25 age group that live in all parts of Iraqi Kurdistan. The 1990s in Iraqi Kurdistan demarcates a significant change in the attitudes of the thinking in the region and these students testify to an awareness of the deep differences. Since the term 'Kurd' is most often understood as ethnicity, it is necessary to realize that some Kurds, especially the young educated ones, understand their own Kurdish-ness in another way: they are *Kurdistani*.

The purpose of my research was to obtain data on the perception of modern students towards their national identity. My data indicate that national identity is undergoing transition. How it is changing and in what direction it might be heading was a major concern.

Why University Students?

Universities have played a central role in social movements around the world in the last two centuries. In the US the students at Kent State University come to mind during the protest against the Vietnam war. In China Tiananmen Square comes to mind when thinking of students that put their lives on the line to make political statements about national policies. These youthful social movements have impacted governments and have been known to change the course of history. This generation of young educated Kurds have grown up and been politically socialized during the

1990s. Their ages fall between 18–25 years old for the most part. They were never taught or educated in the Arab Iraqi school system; hence they lack the knowledge of Arabic or even extensive knowledge in Iraq's geography and history. They did not witness the important political developments of Iraq that enabled Iraqi Kurdistan to be self-governing. The hypothesis was that they do not consider themselves as Iraqi as much as they consider themselves to be *Kurdistani* or Iraqi Kurds.

The Method

The survey instrument was designed to cover students' perceptions toward their national identity and their attitudes toward Kurdistan and Iraq. The questionnaire consisted of 49 closed or objective questions divided into eight sections. Other questions used Likert scales to measure the intensity of respondents' feelings on particular topics. Respondents were selected as follows, 200 from Salahaddin University, 150 from Suleimani University and since Dohuk University was much smaller in size and number than Salahaddin and Suleimani universities, only 100 questionnaires were distributed there: 50 to the College of Arts and 50 to the College of Science.

The questionnaire was distributed to two colleges at each university: the College of Arts and College of Science. Sophomores and juniors were selected within each college. Random stratified sampling techniques were used to assure that the profile of the sample matched the profile of the population of students from which they were drawn. The following variables were measured: place of residency, urban/rural background, gender, age, marital status, fathers' and mothers' educational status, fathers' and mothers' occupational status, family income and social status. The interviews were carried out during March–June 2007. Since the respondents were Kurdish speakers, the questionnaire was presented in the Sorani (Kurdish) dialect. The response rate of the survey was 100 per cent since the respective course tutors at each university supported the research project and allocated about 40 minutes of class time for the completion of the questionnaires. Fifteen qualitative in-depth interviews (five from each university) were conducted with students who had explicitly expressed their interest in the topic after they had returned the questionnaires. These interviews related to the way in which they perceive their identity, how they thought of politics in Kurdistan and how they viewed politics in Iraq. Descriptive analyses were conducted to provide a meaningful summary of the distribution for each variable in the study.

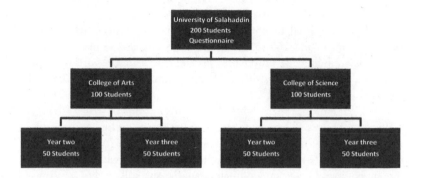

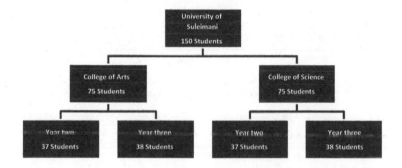

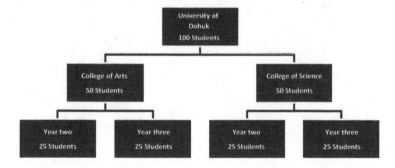

Diagram 7.1 Respondents' Colleges and their Year of Study at Three Universities

Respondent Demographics
Gender Distribution

The sample consisted of 450 male and female students: 281 (62.4 per cent) were males and 169 (37.5 per cent) were females. Since more males in Kurdistan attend the universities than females, the proportion of male and female respondents in this study approximated the proportions who attended the universities.

Table 7.1 indicates that slightly higher proportions of males attend the Colleges of Science (52 per cent versus 46 per cent) and higher proportions of females attend the Colleges of Arts (54 per cent versus 48 per cent). While the differences are not great, the results do fall in line with traditional sex role stereotypes. Higher rates of males than females still tend to be attracted to the 'hard sciences', and the opposite tends to hold true for females and the 'soft sciences'. These are stereotypical gender role formations which take time to be socialized out of.

Table 7.1 Respondents' Gender by College of Study

Gender	Colleges of Arts		Colleges of Science		Total N	%
Female	91	(54%)	78	(46%)	169	100%
Male	134	(48%)	147	(52%)	281	100%
Total	225	(50%)	225	(50%)	450	100%

Source: 2007 Field Survey

Place of Family Residence

Figure 7.1 displays the place of respondents' family residence. The majority (N = 328) of the respondents (73 per cent) came from urban backgrounds, which is not surprising. The cities of Erbil, Suleimaniya and Dohuk are regarded as urban centres. The suburbs of these cities are administrative rural areas called *Nahya* and *Qaza*. They are socially and economically regarded as 'rural' and may be considered as villages. Figure 7.1 illustrates that 122 respondents (27 per cent) came from rural areas: 51 (11.5 per cent) from the suburbs and 71 (15.5 per cent) from villages. It is more difficult for students from rural areas to attend the universities in the 'big cities' than it is for students in the urban centres. It takes more effort for governments to attract rural or village young people to the universities. Considering the historical backwardness of Kurdistan in terms of education, it should not be surprising that only 27 per cent of this sample came from rural or village backgrounds.

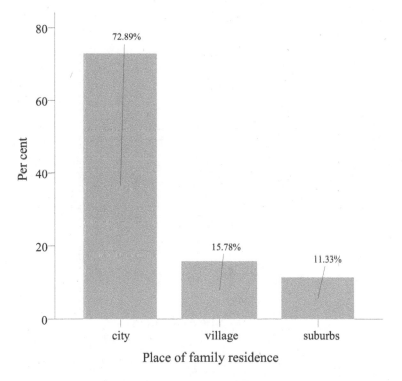

Figure 7.1 Respondents by Place of Family Residence

Place of Birth

Figure 7.2 indicates that the majority of respondents were born in the cities Erbil, Suleimaniya and Dohuk (380: 84.4 per cent), whereas 71 respondents (15.6 per cent) were born in the rural areas of Kurdistan. This is not surprising since the universities are located in the three governates or provinces of Kurdistan, which are the three largest cities in the Iraqi Kurdistan region. When comparing Figure 7.1 with Figure 7.2, it is evident that 27 per cent now live in the rural regions, but only 15.6 per cent were born there. This means that 11.4 per cent of our sample have moved to the rural areas for one reason or another, which is surprising. With the move to modernity and industrialism, one would expect the populace to move to the cities for jobs and education.

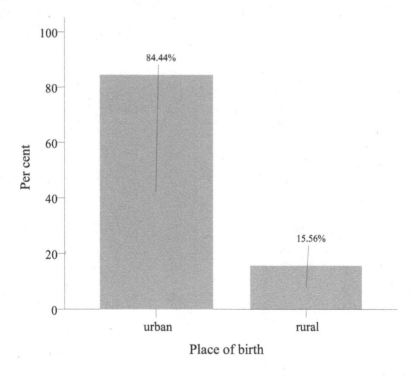

Figure 7.2 Respondents by Place of Birth (Urban/Rural)

The Age of the Respondents

Age varies slightly among our respondents as would be expected among university students. Figure 7.3 shows that the majority of the respondents (361: 80 per cent) were between the ages of 18–21 and are categorized as the 'young generation'. The next age group, 22–25, consists of 73 respondents or 16 per cent of the sample. In the 26–29 age group there were 16 students or four per cent of the sample. This means that the majority of the respondents were born in the early 1990s, specifically 1991–3.

Table 7.2 indicates that the pattern of living in cities and villages is very similar by sex of the respondent. The proportion of males who live in the suburbs, however, is about twice as high as that of females, but the numbers are small and insignificant for the purposes of this study.

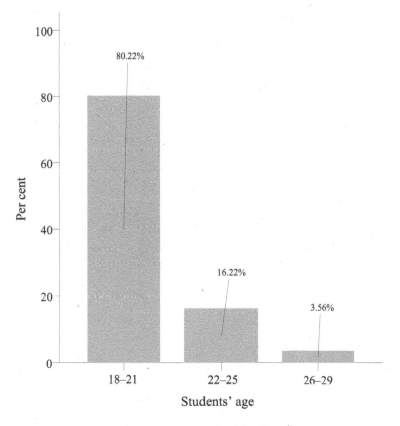

Figure 7.3 Respondents by Age

Table 7.2 Place of Family Residence by Gender

Family Residence	Female		Male		Total	
City	127	75.1%	201	71.5%	328	72.9%
Village	29	17.2%	42	14.9%	71	15.8%
Suburbs	13	7.7%	38	13.5%	51	11.3%
Total	169	100%	281	100%	450	100%

Source: 2007 Field Survey

Family Profiles: Parents' Occupations and Educational Levels
Fathers' Occupations

Figure 7.4 indicates that 60.2 per cent of the respondents' fathers (N = 271), worked in the governmental sector. The second-largest category was the private sector where 26.8 per cent of the fathers worked (N = 121). Only 10.8 per cent (N = 49) indicated that their fathers were retired. Two per cent (N = 7) indicated that their fathers were unemployed.

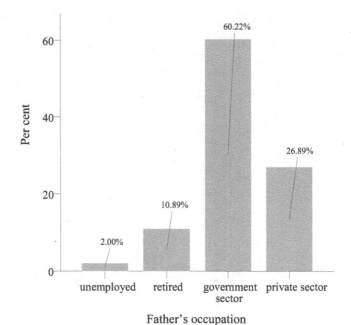

Figure 7.4 Respondents' Fathers' Occupations

Fathers' Educational Levels

Figure 7.5 indicates that 54.2 per cent of the fathers (N = 244) completed preparatory school (high school) ; 15.1 per cent (N = 68) were university graduates; eight per cent (N = 36) had primary education experience and 11.3 per cent (N = 51) were illiterate. A total of 26.44 per cent (N = 129) of the fathers either graduated from or had some university educational experience.

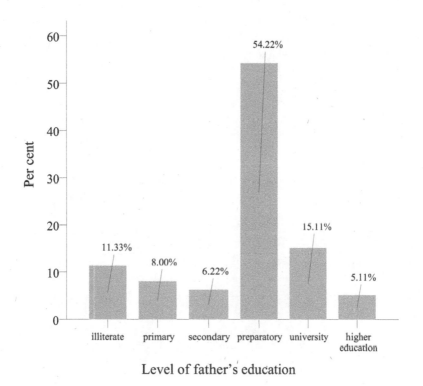

Figure 7.5 Respondents' Fathers' Educational Levels

Mothers' Employment

Figure 7.6 indicates that 60 per cent of the respondents' mothers (270) were not economically active, meaning that they were stay-at-home mothers and wives. Forty per cent (N = 180) of the respondents' mothers worked outside the home. Out of this number 59 per cent (N = 106) worked in the governmental sector and 41 per cent (N = 74) worked in the private sector. When you compare these mothers' figures with the fathers' figures, the comparisons are 59:60 per cent (mothers to fathers respectively) worked in the governmental sector and 41:27 per cent (mothers to fathers respectively) worked in the private sector. The difference in the private sector is made up by the 11 per cent of male respondents' fathers who were retired and the two per cent who were unemployed.

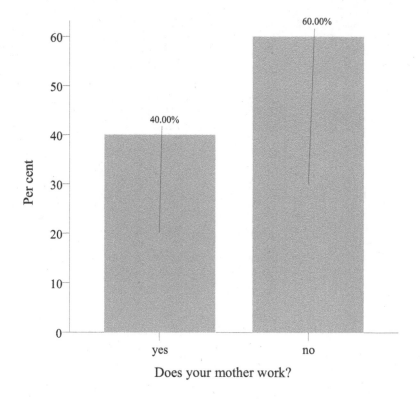

Figure 7.6 Respondents' Mothers' Employment

Mothers' Educational Levels

Figure 7.7 illustrates that 56.2 per cent of the respondents' mothers (N = 253) had achieved a primary education; 14.4 per cent (N = 65) had achived a secondary education and 29.3 per cent of the mothers were illiterate (N = 132). In Kurdistan it is usually thought that Kurdish women are gifted with more opportunities than Arab women. Their participation in economic activity is generally thought to be higher than that of Arab women due to the relative 'open-mindedness' of the Kurds towards women generally. However, to achieve gender equity, Kurdistan has a good way to go in educating its women and employing them at proficient levels. In recent years numerous civil society organizations have been established in Iraqi Kurdistan to encourage women's rights and development. The University of Salahaddin is working this year to establish a Gender Studies programme as is the University of Dohuk, and Suleimania.

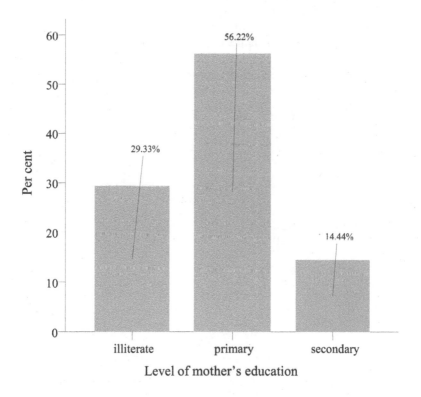

Figure 7.7 Respondents' Mothers' Educational Levels

Feminist activities are ongoing in Kurdistan, whereas activism appears to be lagging in Iraq proper. What is noticed when comparing data of fathers' and mothers' educational levels is that eight per cent of the fathers had only a primary education compared to 56.2 per cent of the mothers. Of course, 54 per cent of the fathers had finished high school and 26.4 per cent of the fathers had some university education. The illiteracy rate of fathers was at 11.3 per cent, but the illiteracy rate of mothers was at 29.3 per cent. This indicates a severe lag in women's educational levels compared to that of men. The Kurdistan educational system must overcome these shortcomings and ensure that all of the people of Kurdistan have the opportunity to attain an adequate education. Obviously, educating Kurdistan's parents as to the need of giving their daughters a thorough education is also necessary.

Respondents' Family Social Status

Family background and social status are important for understanding respondents' attitudes toward nationality and national pride. Two variables, one objective and the other subjective, were taken into account to classify respondents' family social status: the family's monthly income (objective) and the social class that respondents categorized themselves in (subjective). In addition, the size of the family and type of dwelling in which the respondents live are objective indicators which may be useful for determining a family's social status.

Respondents' Monthly Family Income

Figure 7.8 demonstrates that 74.2 per cent (N = 334) of the respondents' families earned more than 500,000 Iraqi dinars per month;[1] 20.2 per cent (N = 91) had a monthly income of 301,000–500,000 dinars per month; 2.7 per cent (N = 22) had the lowest family income at 200,000–300,000 Iraqi dinars per month. While it is difficult to say what an 'adequate standard of living' is, based on the majority of the population's lifestyle in Iraqi Kurdistan, in 2007 500,000 or above dinars per month reflected what could be considered 'middle' class living in Kurdistan. 'Upper class' categorization would depend on how high incomes went beyond 500,000. Since respondents were not asked specifically how much their families earned beyond '500,000 dinars per month', we cannot tell from the data what upper class means in this context.

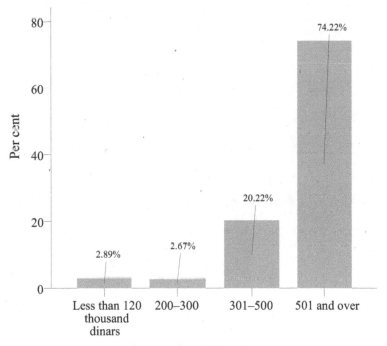

What is your monthly family income?

Figure 7.8 Respondents' Monthly Family Income

Respondent' 'Class Stratification

The key to defining a class system, as compared to other systems of social differentiation like castes, is the relative freedom people have to move between the socio-economic strata. Such mobility in Kurdistan today applies mainly to style of living and the educational system. Figure 7.9 indicates that 65.5 per cent of the respondents (N = 295) consider themselves 'middle class'; 6.8 per cent (N = 31) consider themselves 'working class' and 27.5 per cent (N = 124) saw themselves as belonging to the upper class. Due to the lack of general income data available in Kurdistan, reported figures of the incomes of respondents' families cannot be compared with official figures. Therefore, the assessment as to where the lines of demarcation may be drawn, if at all, between the various classes is uncertain.

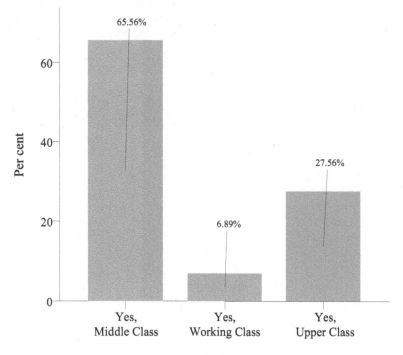

Figure 7.9 Respondents' Opinions of their Social Classes

Figure 7.10 indicates that 79 per cent of male and 66.3 per cent of the female students reported their monthly family income levels at more than 500,000 Iraqi dinars per month; 25.4 per cent of female and 17.15 per cent of male respondents reported incomes between 300,000 and 500,000 dinars per month; 1.8 per cent of male and 4.7 per cent of female respondents indicated family incomes at less than 120,000 dinars per month. This is shocking when considering the sizes of the families that these students reportedly come from. Most of the respondents confirm that they live in large extended families. It is clear that there are many families in Kurdistan that are barely getting along financially.

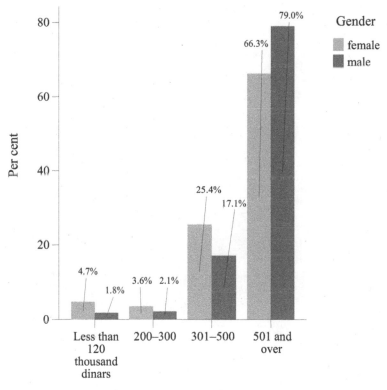

What is your monthly family income?

Figure 7.10 Respondents' Monthly Family Income by Gender

Respondents' Style of Dwelling

Figure 7.11 indicates that 65.3 per cent of the participants (N = 294) lived in villas. Villas are large houses on relatively large parcels of land. Repondents' families who lived in apartments or 'flats' amounted to 18.6 per cent (N = 84); those living in 'an old house' constituted 16 per cent (N = 72). These figures are indicative of the style and social status of respondents' family backgrounds. Apartments would be smaller and cheaper; houses could be run-down and decrepit depending on the location; 'villas' would be middle-class or upper-class nicer homes.

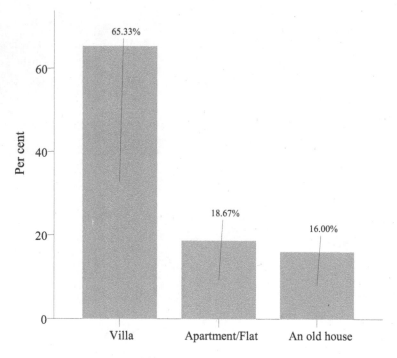

What kind of house do you live in?

Figure 7.11 Respondents' Style of Dwelling

Respondents' Family Size

Figure 7.12 demonstrates that the size of the family in Kurdish society is still considerably large. Almost 59 per cent of the respondents (N = 265) have 5–7 family members living in their households; almost 24 per cent (N = 107) indicated that the size of their family was 8–10 members. These figures reflect the fact that the Kurdish family in Iraqi Kurdistan may still be characterized as an extended family. Only 17.3 per cent (N = 78) reported living in nuclear family arrangements (2–4 members).

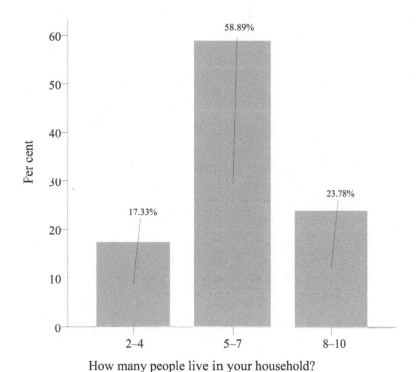

How many people live in your household?

Figure 7.12 Respondents' Family Size

Family Decision-Making

Respondents were asked who was responsible for making decisions in the family. Figure 7.13 indicates that for 80 per cent of the respondents' families, decisions were made by the father. Only 9.8 per cent indicated that the mother took responsibility for family decision-making. Those who chose 'all the family' category for making decisions made up 10.2 per cent of the sample. This category meant that all of the members of the family weighed in on decisions that were to be made.

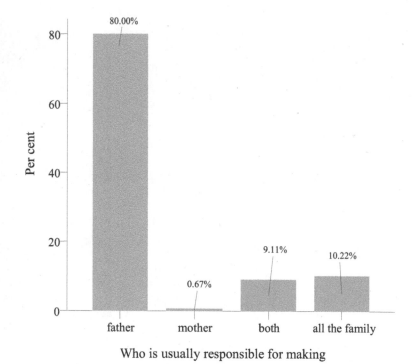

Who is usually responsible for making
decisions in your family?

Figure 7.13 Parental Responsibilities for Family Decision-Making

Freedom to Talk to Parents about Personal or Family Issues

When asked if they felt free to talk about their personal matters or family issues at home 83.6 per cent indicated that they did. But surprisingly, the student respondents overwhelmingly preferred to talk to their fathers (86.5 per cent) rather than their mothers (2.9 per cent). See Figures 7.14 and 7.15. The difference between which parent to talk to, at 86.6 per cent, is so great that it must be interpreted to mean that a serious problem exists in the home relating to confidence in the mother. This is just the opposite of what one might expect in the West, where sons and daughters, if they talk to their parents at all, may be more likely to confide in their mothers. Why such a low percentage of respondents were willing to talk to their mothers is a baffling finding. Perhaps her low educational level or status as illiterate make her a less likely candidate to trust. The relatively educated child might be embarrassed or ashamed of a mother who coudn't read, speak correctly and is less educated than he or she. But, again, in a traditional society one

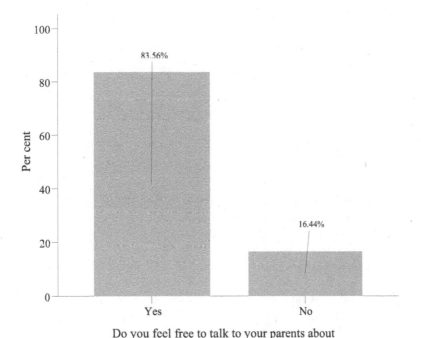

Do you feel free to talk to your parents about
your or your family's affairs?

Figure 7.14 Openly Talking to Parents about Personal and Family Issues

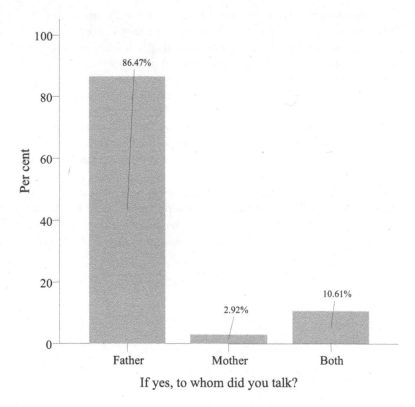

Figure 7.15 Respondents' Choice of Parent to Talk to

would hope that respect toward the mother, which would be taught in the home, school or mosque would compensate for any lack of education or literacy. It can at least be said, as in the West, that the fact that the mother makes less money than the father makes her less valued as well. This seems to be a universal phenomenon. But that still does not explain the huge and wide range of difference in the choice of parent that student respondents would speak to about personal or family issues.

How religious values (or lack thereof) might diminish the mother's status in the home is worthy of future exploration. Religion, *per se*, might mirror her traditionally low status in the community at large. These are serious issues that should be looked into.

Discussion

Of the 450 undergraduate university students from Salahaddin, Suleimaniya and Dohuk universities 62 per cent, or approximately two-thirds, were male and one-third (38 per cent) were female. Most were single (94.4 per cent) and ages ranged from 18 to 33 years old, with 80 per cent of respondents in the 18–21-year-old category. This sample's responses presented few surprises—except for the fact that so few of the respondents chose to address their mothers about personal and family issues. The young educated generation of the post-1990s in Iraqi Kurdistan came predominantly from the major cities, were mostly from the middle class (61.6 per cent) and tended to live in extended families (58.8 per cent). The parents of the participants had high levels of illiteracy compared to international standards (11.3 per cent for the fathers and 29.3 per cent for the mothers). Yet in this part of the world among Middle Eastern populations, these numbers would be considered 'normal' or perhaps even 'low'. The majority of parents who were employed worked in the governmental sector (60.2 per cent for the fathers and 59 per cent for the mothers) indicating that the government is most probably the largest employer in the urban areas of Kurdistan. Three-quarters (74.2 per cent) of the population earned more than 500,000 Iraqi dinars per month and most of them live in villas (65.3 per cent).

The Kurdish family in Iraqi Kurdistan is still male-orientated and men still dominate the action in the home by making the major decisions (80 per cent). The vast majority of the students (83.5 per cent) asserted that it was the father that they most talked to regarding their own personal and family affairs. Only 2.9 per cent preferred to discuss matters with their mothers, which is an astonishing finding. More research needs to be carried out to find out why mothers attract such a low confidence rating and have such a low standing in the home—the most important domain to her, traditionally speaking. It may be due to either her low educational level, her status of illiteracy, or the fact that the socio-religious-cultural complex of Kurdistan and the Middle East in general, tends to devalue women overall.

With more research and further development towards a viable civil and democratic society, one would hope that women will come to be valued more and achieve more parity in terms of education and socio-economic status with men. It is also hoped that with movement towards civic and democratic values, the status of women in society at large will rise and women will be more empowered to contribute—and receive—in the family setting in a way that will make family life more fulfilling, as well as her participation in social roles and society at large. Women's contributions are needed in the greater community to help Iraqi Kurdistan's overall productivity to rise. A nation cannot thrive and compete in the global marketplace when 50 per cent of its population are ignored, devalued, oppressed, or denied their rightful place as full participants in the public arena, whether it be commercial, educational, religious, civic, the arts, media, government, or the family.

8

TOWARD AN UNDERSTANDING OF MODERN KURDISH NATIONALISM AND NATIONAL IDENTITY

How do young Kurds identify themselves? What does it mean to be *Kurdistani* or Iraqi? To what extent is Kurdish identity linked with Kurdistan and *Kurdistanism*? Which identity is predominant to the Kurds in Kurdistan: national, tribal, Islamic or local? The *Kurdistani* conception is problematized by asking and seeking answers to these questions.

I have proposed that the young educated generation be identified as *Kurdistani* Kurds rather than Iraqi Kurds or Iraqis. This would be due to the fact that in the 1990s Iraqi Kurdistan witnessed the consolidation of *Kurdistanism* (*Kurdistaniyeti*).

Kurdistani and Iraqi National Identification

Identity is a concept which is constructed in social and historical contexts by the creation of marked 'differences' between the self and the other. Distinguishing oneself and/or one's group from outsiders serves to strengthen or reinforce the individuals or groups who identify themselves with that particular identity. In response to questions such as 'How do you view yourself?' or 'What do you consider your national identity to be?' a glimpse of both positive and negative attitudes toward Kurdistan and Iraq may be obtained. It may be noted that these kinds of issues have not been addressed in the literature until now.

Figure 8.1 presents the results to the question of national identification of students. There are 73.1 per cent (N = 329) that see themselves as *Kurdistani* and only 17.3 per cent (N = 78) who consider themselves as simply 'Kurds'. This 'proof' underlines and informs the kind of political consciousness that was expected among the educated young people in Iraqi Kurdistan. Only 5.1 per cent of the respondents (N = 23) regarded themselves as *'Kurdistanis but not Iraqis'*. Those who identified as 'Kurdistani', 'Kurds', 'Kurdistanis but not Iraqis' or 'Iraqi Kurd' total 96.8 per cent. A total of three per cent identified as 'more Iraqi than Kurd' (2.2 per cent) and 'Iraqi not Kurd' (0.89 per cent). This self-definition question is a crucial one. Although national identity is a dynamic phenomenon that can change over time, it has some rooted or stable characteristics that tend to resist change and thereby provide the self-schema of a long-lasting identity.

Smith points out six main factors that play a role in the formation of a group's national self-schema: a collective proper name, a myth of common ancestry, shared historical memories, one or more differentiating elements of a common culture, an association with a specific 'homeland,' and a sense of solidarity of significant sectors of the population.[1]

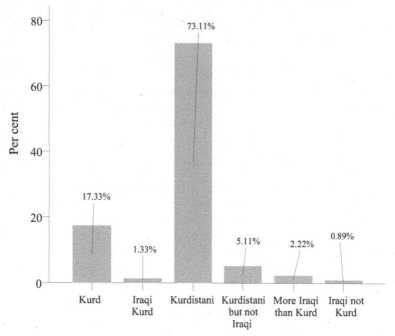

How do you view yourself, or what do you consider
your national identity to be?

Figure 8.1 Respondents' National Identification

In the internalizing process one of these factors usually stands out and plays a noticeably more prominent role than the others in shaping and informing the nature of a group's identity. Each group is different and may have a different factor play the most prominent role. For instance, if the nation emphasizes the myth of common ancestry as a factor in its national self-schema, then ethnic nationalism will likely be the basic or most important tenet of national identity. Alternatively, if the community emphasizes the homeland as the most important factor in its national self-schema, then civic nationalism will likely be the basic tenet of national identity. Thus, a nation's identity reflects its unique historical and cultural background, as well as the current political situation of the nation in question. In Iraqi Kurdistan, the national identity of young educated Kurds consists of both the ethnic and civic tenets of nationalism.

Table 8.1 indicates that 18.5 per cent of males (N = 52) and 15.4 per cent females (N = 26) identify as 'Kurd'. This is not a great proportional difference between the sexes. Slightly more males (209: 74.4 per cent) than females (120: 71 per cent) identify as *Kurdistani*. What was noticed is that a higher proportion of males than females identify as 'Kurd', 'Kurdistani', or 'Iraqi Kurd'. However, applying the chi-square test on the different reporting measures between females and males, there was no statistical significance regarding their national identification by category. A very small number of respondents, (10: 2.2 per cent), saw themselves as 'more Iraqi than Kurd' and only 2 students (0.9 per cent) saw themselves as 'Iraqi and not Kurd' There is one likely interpretation for this finding. It would be expected that those who viewed themselves as 'more Iraqi than Kurd' or 'Iraqi and not Kurd' reflect the attitude of the non-Kurdish minority in Kurdistan. They might be Turkmen, Chaldo-Assyrian, or Arabs who do not consider themselves Kurds or *Kurdistani*, but rather 'Iraqi' to some degree.

Correlation coefficients were run to see if fathers' educational level would be correlated with student respondents' national identification. Surprisingly, they were not, but other things were.

Table 8.2 shows that the level of fathers' education is highly correlated with level of mothers' education at the .01 level. This may be interpreted to mean that the educated are marrying the educated or that those that value education marry those with like values and they pursue their education later. Or lastly, the partners reinforce educational values in the family, causing mothers (probably) to attain a somewhat higher level of education after they are married. Also fathers' education is highly correlated (.05 level) with the place of family residence, but mothers' educational level is not. This may be interpreted to mean that it is the fathers' educational level that

Table 8.1 Respondents' National Identification by Gender
Question: *What do you consider your national identity to be?*

Self-Identification	Female Resp.	Male Resp.	Total
'Kurd'	26	52	78
	15.4%	18.5%	17.3%
'Iraqi Kurd'	2	4	6
	1.2%	1.4%	1.3%
'Kurdistani'	120	209	329
	71.0%	74.4%	73.1%
'Kurdistani, but not Iraqi'	11	12	23
	6.5%	4.3%	5.1%
'More Iraqi than Kurd'	7	3	10
	4.1%	1.1%	2.2%
'Iraqi, not Kurd'	3	1	4
	1.8%	0.4%	0.9%
Total number	169	281	450
Total per cent	100%	100%	100%

Source: 2007 Field Survey

determines where the family will live. Due to the recognized high correlation among socio-economic status variables, in all likelihood it is the fathers' occupation, income and education taken together that determines where the family lives in a way that mothers' income, education and occupational status does not. These findings coincide with the fact that it is the father that is dominant in the home, not the mother. It is respondents' fathers' education (income and job) that determines family's place of residence, not the mothers' education income or job. The levels of parents' education was expected to influence the way students self-identified because fathers' and mothers' educational backgrounds were expected to impact their children's political socialization and values in the home.

But there was no correlation between the national identity of respondents and either parent's educational levels. It may be that there were too many categories for respondents to identify with, thus diffusing the results. Had the categories been collapsed, different results may have been found. For example, if the *'Kurdistani'* and *'Kurdistani,* but not Iraqi' categories were collapsed; the categories 'Kurd' and 'Iraqi Kurd' were collapsed; and 'Iraqi,

Table 8.2 Correlation Coefficients for Gender, National Identity, Family Residency and Parents' Educational Levels

Correlation Variable Coefficient		Gender	Place of Family Residence	Considering National Identity	Level of Father's Education	Level of Mother's Education
Gender	Correlation Coefficient	1.000	.052	−.094*	.046	.088
	Sig. (2-tail)	N/A	.275	.046	.327	.061
Place of Family Residence	Correlation Coefficient	.052	1.000	.022	.110*	−.020
	Sig. (2-tail)	.275	N/A	.645	.020	.667
How do you view yourself, or what do you consider your national identity to be?	Correlation Coefficient	−.094*	.022	1.000	.033	−.003
	Sig. (2-tail)	.046	.645	N/A	.490	.949
Level of Father's Education	Correlation Coefficient	.046	.110*	.033	1.000	.127**
	Sig. (2-tail)	.327	.020	.490	N/A	.007
Level of Mother's Education	Correlation Coefficient	.088	−.020	−.003	.127**	1.000
	Sig. (2-tail)	.061	.667	.949	.007	N/A

Source: 2007 Field Survey
* Correlation is significant at the 0.05 level (2-tailed).
** Correlation is significant at the 0.01 level (2-tailed).

not Kurd' and 'More Iraqi than Kurd' were collapsed; the findings might then have proved to be significantly correlated.

Had those same national identification categories been collapsed, a significant relationship with place of residence and respondents' national identity might also have been found. Figure 8.2 bears out that most of the respondents were from the city. Urbanized people are more oriented towards national pride and national identity than villagers or rural based people are. As it was, however, the numerous identification possibilities appear to have diffused the results and no significant correlations showed up between place of residence and respondents' national identity.

Gender is significantly related to national identity in the sample and this result was maintained despite the fact that there was an unwieldy number of ways to self-identify politically. This significant negative correlation can be interpreted here to mean that being male is positively correlated with the Kurd or *Kurdistani* identification and being female is negatively correlated with *Kurdistani* or Kurdish identification (at the .05 level). It is evident that being socialized to a strong degree of Kurdish identity is considered to be more important for males than for females. As mentioned, this is worthy of further research to discover the underlying dynamics that cause females to be overlooked in the socializing strategies that enable males to identify more strongly with the Kurdish national cause.

The percentages in Figure 8.2 indicate that 76.9 per cent of respondents whose families reside in the cities consider themselves to be *Kurdistani*, whereas those whose families are from rural areas: villages (15.8 per cent)

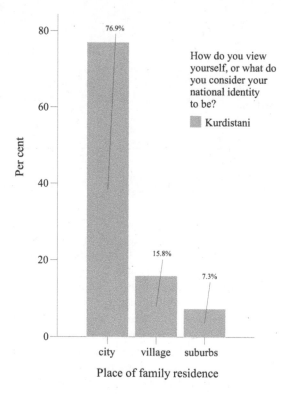

Figure 8.2 Kurdistani National Identification by Place of Family Residence

and suburbs (7.3 per cent), do not consider themselves as *Kurdistani* to the same extent. It may be deduced that people who reside in the rural areas are more concerned about their way of life and how to survive, than about their national identification. Also, they are out of mainstream political thinking that mingling in the large cities brings, such as interaction and involvement with social movements. Ideas and new thoughts tend to develop in the urban areas, rather than the rural regions that are subject to less stimulation. Also, you will recall that many had extremely low income levels. One may surmise that these less-well-off respondents were from the rural areas overall. Perhaps the economic difficulties that these respondents faced also had an impact on their political/national identification. While this wasn't tested specifically, it is a subject worth looking into.

Respondents were asked about the major factors that consolidate national identity. They were given six choices to select from. Table 8.3 reflects these data. The majority of respondents, 35.8 per cent, (N = 161) indicated that the factor that most consolidated Kurdish national identity was the national factor. The second major factor to consolidate Kurdish national identity was the territorial factor (109: 24.2 per cent).

Table 8.3 Opinions on the Major Factors that Consolidate National Identity

Question: *What are the major factors which consolidate Kurdish national identity?*

Factors that consolidate national identity	Valid	
	N	%
National Factor	161	35.8
Political Factor	86	19.1
Economic Factor	2	0.4
Linguistic Factor	89	19.8
Territorial Factor	109	24.2
Educational Factor	3	0.7
Total	450	100

Source: 2007 Field Survey

The linguistic factor was the third most mentioned factor (89: 19.8 per cent). The political factor drew 19.1 per cent (N = 86) of the respondents and the educational and economic factors were not as important, as the data shows that only 0.7 per cent (N = 3) of the respondents chose this factor and 0.4 per cent of the respondents (N = 2) selected the economic factor. These data reveal that for the Kurds, the national, territorial and linguistic factors were most crucial in consolidating Kurdish national identity. This is not surprising considering the deep sentiments the Kurds have to their 'cause', their 'nation', their ancient land and the language and dialects that only their nation speaks as a national language.

Attitudes, Pride, Attachment and Loyalty toward Kurdistan and Iraq

Other important aspects of the sense of belonging to a group or nation are one's ethnicity, a feeling of concern for one's culture, a sense of 'nationhood', and the experience of exclusion, contrast, or separateness from other groups. Figure 8.3 reflects the strength of loyalty and attachment to Kurdistan as a whole. The data indicate that 87.1 per cent of the respondents feel that they are very closely attached and loyal to Kurdistan; 7.5 per cent confirmed that they feel 'fairly close' and loyal to Kurdistan; and 4.8 per cent declared that they are 'not very close' or loyal to Kurdistan. Only 0.44 per cent felt that they were 'not at all close' to Kurdistan. These results reveal that a strong majority of young educated Kurds feel that they are very closely attached to Kurdistan and they are loyal to it. This is a robust finding.

In contrast, when students were asked the same question about Iraq, 69.7 per cent indicated that they did 'not feel very closely attached or loyal' to Iraq; 12.8 per cent indicated that they do 'not feel closely attached or loyal' to Iraq 'at all' and 13.3 per cent of the respondents indicated that they are 'very close, loyal, or attached to Iraq' as a whole (see Figure 8.4). These results give us 92.5 per cent of the respondents who either 'are not' or 'are not at all' closely attached or loyal to Iraq. It is quite clear from the sample that for the vast majority of the students, attachment and loyalty to Kurdistan is much stronger than loyalty and attachment to Iraq. It may be that the Iraqi identification factor reflects identification with the *state* which this generation has very little or no connection to.

In the in-depth interviews with students on the subject of attachment to Kurdistan and Iraq, there was a clear sense of scepticism towards Iraq that revealed a lack of a strong emotional bond or overall attachment. The following quote from Anthony Smith, while applied to Europe, offers an illustrative example of how this kind of scepticism may apply to students' perceptions of Iraq:

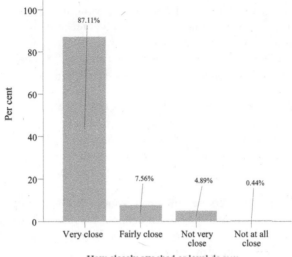

Figure 8.3 Attachment and Loyalty to Kurdistan as a Whole

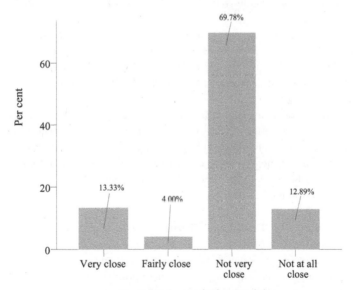

Figure 8.4 Attachment and Loyalty to Iraq as a Whole

Without shared memories and meanings, without common symbols and myths, without shrines and ceremonies and monuments, except the bitter reminders of recent holocausts and wars, who will feel European in the depth of their being, and who will willingly sacrifice themselves for so abstract an ideal? In short, who will die for Europe?[2]

Of course, these students would only have heard of the 'recent holocausts and wars' as they were not around to witness *Anfal* or the chemical attacks of Saddam Hussein against their people. Nonetheless, it is sure that they have heard about it and their primary socializing agents, i.e., their parents, have shared their bitterness and stories of disappointment and survival with their children.

The qualitative interviews provided some additional support for the widely shared consensus that attachment to the nation is the ideal core concept of national ideology and 'political "love" gives palpable expression to the abstraction of the nation.'[3] The following three statements from respondents are representative of the opinions expressed in this regard:

'I love Kurdistan and I'm willing to give my life to it. I don't have this sort of feeling toward Iraq.' (Male student from Salahaddin University)

'Kurdistan for me is my fatherland and I don't have any feeling towards Iraq.' (Male student from Salahaddin University)

'I'm willing to give my life to Kurdistan, but I'm not prepared to do that for Iraq.' (Male student from Salahaddin University)

When you compare Figure 8.3 to Figure 8.4, it is evident that not only were respondents' attachments and loyalty to Kurdistan far more positive than their attachments and loyalty to Iraq, but the relationship to Iraq appears to be strongly *negative* compared to the positive attachments and loyalty expressed toward Kurdistan. This can be expected since the respondents are identifying as newly forged *Kurdistanis*.

Pride as a *Kurdistani* versus Iraqi

The notion of *Kurdistanyati* (i.e., *Kurdistani*) is a new concept that reflects the contemporary national identification among the young educated generation in Iraqi Kurdistan. The strength of respondents' pride was measured by asking students 'How proud are you of being a *Kurdistani?*' From Figure 8.5 and Table 8.4 we can observe that the majority or 88.9 per cent of respondents are very proud of being *Kurdistani* (N = 400). Those who were

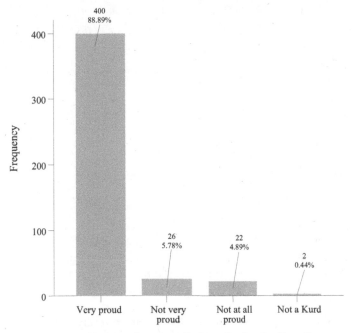

Figure 8.5 Pride as a *Kurdistani*

not proud of this identification represented only 5.8 per cent (N = 26) of the total sample. Only 4.9 per cent (N = 22) of the students declared that they were not proud of being *Kurdistani* 'at all'. Not surprisingly, only two of the respondents, or four per cent, were not Kurds.

In comparing this data to that in Figure 8.6 and Table 8.5, it is evident that the feeling of pride towards Iraq among the respondents is, once again, quite negative. This finding is likely due to the hegemony of Kurdish nationalist culture in this area for nearly two decades. This would encompass all the years of upbringing that most of these respondents can remember.

It might also explain their lack of knowing about Iraqi politics and culture on one hand and the Kurdification of the educational and political institutions in Kurdistan on the other. Thus, the terms 'Kurdistan', '*Kurdistani*', and '*Kurdistaniyeti*' all appeal to young educated urbanites and students in the broadest sense. These terms would be used in the speech of the younger generation as well. Qualitative evidence provides insight into how respondents feel pride as *Kurdistanis*.

Table 8.4 Strength of Pride as a *Kurdistani*
Question: *How proud are you of being a Kurdistani?*

Strength of Pride	N	%
Very Proud	400	88.9
Not Very Proud	26	5.8
Not at all Proud	22	4.9
Not a Kurd	2	0.4
Total	450	100.0

Source: 2007 Field Survey

Figure 8.6 and Table 8.5 reveal that most of the students (76 per cent) do not see themselves as Iraqis and 7.8 per cent are 'not very proud' of being Iraqis. What's more, 3.6 per cent have declared that they are 'not proud' to be Iraqis 'at all'. Only 12.7 per cent of the sample affirmed their pride as Iraqis. The mean was 3.43 and the standard deviation was 1.078. These findings provide additional strong evidence that university students in the Kurdistan region of Iraq mainly identify as *Kurdistani* and definitely not Iraqi. Almost all of the interviewees acknowledged that respondents do not see any elements of a shared culture (the fourth dimension of Smith's ethnic community) with Iraq or Iraqi culture. It seems that they do not distinguish between *Kurdistanism* and *Kurdistaniyeti* either. The two concepts, from their perspective, have the same meaning. These findings reflect Kurdistan's contemporary political and national culture.

Table 8.5 Respondents' Strength of Pride as an Iraqi
Question: *How proud are you of being an Iraqi?*

Strength of Pride	N	%
Very Proud	57	12.7
Not Very Proud	35	7.8
Not at all Proud	16	3.6
Not Iraqi	342	76.0
Total	450	100.0

Source: 2007 Field Survey

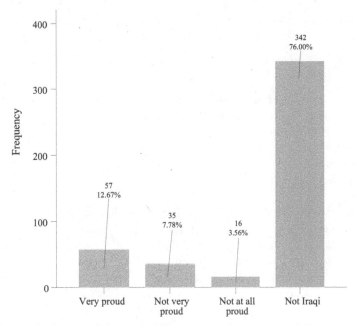

Figure 8.6 Strength of Pride as an Iraqi

Moreover, the very Kurdification of Kurdistan's culture has revealed itself in the controversy between the KRG and the Iraqi authorities in Baghdad over the former's unwillingness to fly the Iraqi flag over KRG public buildings. In addressing the role of national symbols being conveyed in taken-for-granted ways in so much of the life of a political community, Smith says the following:

> …flags, anthems, parades, coinage, capital cities, oaths, folk costumes, museums of folklore, war memorials, ceremonies of remembrance for the national dead, passports, frontiers—as well as more hidden aspects, such as national recreation, the countryside, popular heroines, fairy tales, forms of etiquette, styles of architecture, arts and crafts, modes of town planning, legal procedures, educational practices and military codes—all those distinctive customs, mores, styles and ways of acting and feeling that are shared by the members of a community of historical culture.[4]

Smith understands full well that national identity is capable of holding strong sway over the individual. He uses the terms, 'potent and durable', to describe the emotion of attachment that is reinforced by national ceremonies.[5]

Pride or Hostility toward the *Kurdistani* National Flag and the Iraqi National Flag

In mid-2008 the president of the Kurdistan Region, Mas'ud Barzani, banned the raising of the Iraqi national flag beside the Kurdish flag on government and public buildings in Kurdistan. Since the *Rapereen* of 1991, it was the policy of the Kurdistan region to fly the Iraqi national flag along with its own.

The flag for the Kurds represents their nationality and it functions as an important symbol for *Kurdistanyati*. However, the Iraqi flag carries negative associations for many Kurds who recall all too well Saddam's forces hoisting it during the *Anfal* campaigns of bombings, slaughter and chemical warfare against them. Even though these young students would not have been around to witness such atrocities, they most assuredly have heard the stories time and time again as to what acts Iraq's president perpetrated against their people. Mas'ud Barzani banned the Iraqi flag soon after Kurdistan's two administrations were united under his leadership in 2006. This move caused dismay in Baghdad. The issue came to the fore again when President Barzani announced that he would not allow the Iraqi national flag to be raised in March 2008 during a meeting of Iraqi parliamentarians in Erbil, the capital of the Kurdistan region. The reasoning behind President Barzani's decision was the fact that all of the crimes and atrocities against not only the Kurds, but the rest of the Iraqi people as well, had been committed under the leadership of that same flag. Add to this the war against Iran, the invasion of Kuwait and the bombardment of neighboring countries with his deadly rockets and there was no way President Barzani was going to have that flag raised publicly for the Kurds to respect and honor.

The Kurds rightly claimed that it was under this flag that Saddam's regime destroyed more than 5,000 Kurdish villages, used chemical weapons and warfare on Halabja which killed more than 5,000 innocent civilians and waged the *Anfal* campaign in Kurdistan in which more than 180,000 people were slaughtered. It was under this flag that Saddam waged a genocidal war—lasting decades—against the Kurdish citizens of Iraq and the mass graves, which they are still finding, are the proof of these atrocities.[6]

Figure 8.7 indicates that 86.4 per cent of the respondents feel 'very proud' when they see Kurdistan's flag and 7.1 per cent claim to feel a 'bit of pride'

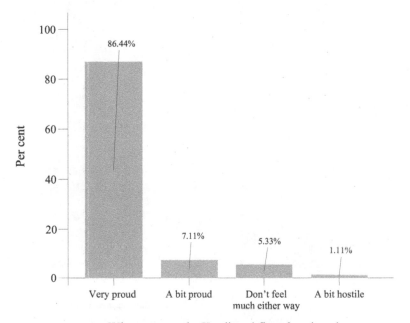

When you see the Kurdistani flag, does it make
you feel proud or hostile or not feel much either way?

Figure 8.7 Respondents' Feelings Toward Seeing Kurdistan's Flag

towards seeing the Kurdish flag; 5.3 per cent of the sample do not feel much
either way and only 1.1 per cent feel a bit hostile. When the same question
was asked regarding perceptions toward the Iraqi flag, opposite results were
obtained (see Figure 8.8). Only a very small percentage (3.7 per cent) indicated that they were 'very proud'. Only 2.6 per cent of them were a 'bit of
proud' and 37.3 per cent indicated that they did not 'feel much either way;'
16.2 per cent felt a bit of hostility towards the Iraqi flag; 40 per cent felt
'very hostile' towards the flag.

Figure 8.9 explains that the majority of students (56.4 per cent) that
consider themselves to be 'middle class' are more attached and/or loyal to
Kurdistan. Almost 24.6 per cent of those who came from the 'upper classes'
saw themselves as attached and/or loyal to Kurdistan. Only six per cent of
the students who came from 'working class' backgrounds saw themselves

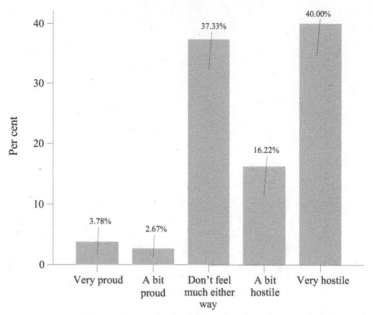

When you see the Iraqi flag, does it make you feel
proud or hostile or not feel much either way?

Figure 8.8 Respondents' Feelings Toward Seeing Iraqi Flag

as attached and/or loyal to Kurdistan. Those students who were 'not very
loyal' or 'not loyal at all' were a very small percentage (four per cent). Class
clearly has a significant role in shaping attitudes toward the nation. As
can be expected, the 'great middle class' consists of those most attached
and loyal to the nation. Comparing the above data to the data that reflect
students' attitudes toward Iraq by class (Figure 8.10), those who consider
themselves to be from the 'middle class' are for the most part the ones who
are not very closely attached to Iraq (50.2 per cent). These are likely the
same respondents who were attached and loyal to Kurdistan. The second
highest percentage of those who are not very closely attached and loyal to
Iraq were those students from upper-class backgrounds (15.33 per cent).
A very small number who were from the 'middle' and 'upper classes' felt
that they were very close to Iraq: (5.1 per cent) and (7.1 per cent) respectively. The lowest number in attachment was among those who came from
working-class backgrounds: 1.1 per cent reported to be 'very close to Iraq',
whereas 4.2 per cent were 'not very close'. A more sophisticated way to

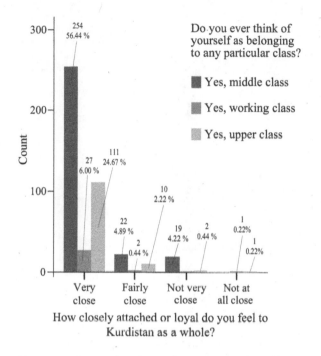

Figure 8.9 Respondents' Attachment to Kurdistan by Class

understand students' attitudes toward Kurdistan is through a measure that is derived from students' responses to four attitudinal statements, which is presented in Table 8.6.

Table 8.6 presents the results of students' opinions on the issues of independence and the separation of Kurdistan from Iraq. The first statement expresses the view of the majority of females and males. Of the female respondents 152 (33.8 per cent) expressed an opinion in favour of independence and separation from Iraq. Also as expected, males felt more strongly on this issue (253: 56.2 per cent) than females (152: 33.8 per cent). The idea of the unification of Iraqi Kurdistan with other parts of Greater Kurdistan is weak among both sexes: only nine per cent of the females and seven per cent of the males expressed this opinion. This response category clearly does not fit into the *Kurdistani* pattern of thinking of the future of their nation. The idea of Kurdistan's remaining part of Iraq while maintaining its own parliament and obtaining more federalist power was also not very strong. It appears that remaining a part

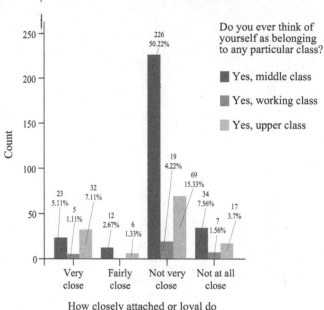

Figure 8.10 Respondents' Attachment to Iraq by Class

of Iraq with a little additional power also does not fit the *Kurdistani* model of thinking. Only 2.7 per cent of the females and 5.6 per cent of the males chose this response. This last view, which expressed the idea of taking Kurdistan back to the pre-1990s era and remaining part of Iraq without having a parliament and a federal system was selected by no one other than one female. This respondent is likely not Kurdish at all. It should be noted that the KRG does not usually talk about separating from Iraq, even if individual members have this sentiment in their hearts. The official policy is to remain part of Iraq. However, this is not the case among the young educated *Kurdistani* generation, particularly when one notes that the referendum movement, in which people sign petitions in favour of some particular issue is very popular in Kurdistan. The data indicate that the young educated generation in Kurdistan is neither sympathetic to, nor attached to, Iraq proper. They have little difficulty imagining Kurdistan as a fully independent state and the *Kurdistani* mode of thinking and being is likely to result in discussing the unutterable: the withdrawal from Iraq and establishing Kurdistan's independence as a nation.

Table 8.6 Opinion on Partition of Iraq and Separation of
Kurdistan by Gender

Question: *Which of these statements come closest to your view?*

	Female	Male	Total
Kurdistan should become independent, separate from Iraq	152 33.8%	253 56.2%	405 90.0%
Kurdistan should become independent, separate from Iraq and the other three parts of Kurdistan join us	4 0.9%	3 0.7%	7 1.6%
Kurdistan should remain part of Iraq, with its own elected parliament, which has more federalist power	12 2.7%	25 5.6%	37 8.2%
Kurdistan should remain part of Iraq, without an elected parliament and federal system	1 0.2%	0 0.0%	1 0.2%
Total responses and percentages	169 37.6%	281 62.4%	450 100%

Source: 2007 Field Survey

Attitudes, Pride, Attachment and Loyalty toward Tribe, Area of Origin, Language and Religion
Respondents' Tribal Identification

Tribal identity, or affiliation and attachment to tribes, does not exist among members of the young educated generation and particularly in urbanized and modernized areas of Iraqi Kurdistan. Table 8.7 illustrates respondents' tribal affiliation by age and class. The data indicate that a clear majority do not have tribal affiliation (379: 84.2 per cent). Only 71 respondents or 15.8 per cent of the sample indicated that they have tribal affiliation. The chi-square test was applied to see if the relationship of tribal belonging with age and class categories was significant. A significant relationship was found to exist between them. See Table 8.8.

The total number of students who were from the 'middle class' was 295. Out of this number 250 or 84.7 per cent did not belong to any tribe. The vast majority of students between the ages of 18–21 that came from 'middle class' families (195: 82.9 per cent) shared that they did not belong to tribes. But 40 respondents (17 per cent) from the same age group and class indicated that they did belong to a tribe. For the 'working class' the number was very small. Out of 31 respondents 30 or 96.8 per cent indicated that they belonged to no tribe. Only 1 respondent (3.2 per cent) confirmed that he belonged to a tribe and he was in the 22–25 age group. This is not surprising since there are no factories in Kurdistan. Those who are self-employed do not consider themselves to be 'working class'. For the 124 students who came from the upper class, 99 (79.8 per cent) said they belonged to no tribe and only 25 (20.2 per cent) indicated that they did belong to a tribe.

Table 8.7 Respondents' Belonging to a Tribe by Age and Class

Questions: *Do you ever think of yourself as belonging to any particular class? Do you belong to any tribe?*

Class Identification	Age Group	Tribal Affiliation		
		Yes	No	Total
Middle Class	18–21	40	195	235
		17.0%	82.9%	100%
	22–25	2	46	48
		4.2%	95.8%	100%
	26–29	3	9	12
		25.0%	75.0%	100%
	Total	45	250	295
		15.3%	84.7%	100%
Working Class	18–21	0	17	17
		0.0%	100%	100%
	22–25	1	12	13
		7.7%	92.3%	100%
	26–29	0	1	1
		0.0%	3.2%	3.2%
	Total	1	30	31
		3.2%	96.8%	100%
Upper Class	18–21	23	86	109
		21.1%	78.9%	100%
	22–25		10	12
		216.7%	83.3%	100%
	26–29	0	3	3
		0.0%	100%	100%
	Total	25	99	124
		20.2%	79.8%	100%
GRAND TOTAL	Number	71	379	450
	Per cent	15.8%	84.2%	100%

Source: 2007 Field Survey

Table 8.8 Chi-Square Test

Question: *Do you ever think of yourself as belonging to any particular class?*

Class		Value	df	Asymp. Sig. (2-sided)
Middle Class	Pearson Chi-Square Continuity Correction	6.014[a]	2	0.049
	Likelihood Ratio	7.437	2	0.024
	Linear-by-Linear Association	0.875	1	0.350
	N of Valid Cases	295		
Working Class	Pearson Chi-Square Continuity Correction	1.431[b]	2	0.489
	Likelihood Ratio	1.784	2	0.410
	Linear-by-Linear Association	0.848	1	0.357
	N of Valid Cases	31		
Upper Class	Pearson Chi-Square Continuity Correction	0.908[c]	2	0.635
	Likelihood Ratio	1.505	2	0.471
	Linear-by-Linear Association	0.765	1	0.382
	N of Valid Cases	124		

Notes

a) 1 cell (16.7%) has expected count less than 5. The minimum expected count is 1.83.

b) 4 cells (66.7%) have expected count less than 5. The minimum expected count is .03.

c) 3 cells (50.0%) have expected count less than 5. The minimum expected count is .60.

What is interesting to note when you look at these numbers is that as you go from 'working class' to 'middle class' to 'upper class', the proportions of those class groups who belong to tribes increases. For example, 3.2 per cent of the 'working class' age groups belong to tribes; 15.3 per cent of the 'middle class' age groups belong to tribes and 20.2 per cent of the 'upper class' age groups have tribal affiliations. One might have expected the opposite trend: that the higher one ascends on the socio-economic ladder, the higher the tendency to leave tribal affiliation behind. But here it is evident that the poorer classes are the ones leaving tribal affiliation behind and the higher classes tend to hang on to the tribal connection. Perhaps with increased human capital in terms of money, education and occupational status, fathers in particular have more invested in the tribal structure and depend on these connections to secure his place in the tribal community. This finding is somewhat surprising and deserves further research.

Belonging to a tribe by gender is presented in Table 8.9. These data indicate that 243 (86.5 per cent) of male respondents do not belong to a tribe. Of the 169 female respondents 136 (80.4 per cent) indicated that they also do not belong to a tribe. A small number of females (33: 19.5 per cent) indicated that they did belong to a tribe and 38 (13.5 per cent) of the males indicated that they belonged to a tribe.

Table 8.9 indicates that 38 males (13.5 per cent of total male respondents) and 33 females (19.6 per cent of total female respondents) for a total of 71 students or 15.8 per cent of the entire sample are tribal members. Alternatively, 243 males (86.5 per cent of total male respondents) and 136 females (80.4 per cent of total female respondents) were not members of a tribe, for a total of 379 student respondents or 84.2 per cent of the entire sample. More females belong to tribes than males do, a difference of 6.1 per cent. It appears that overall the tribe and tribal affiliation is not as salient in the minds of the young educated strata as it might have been for past generations, considering the literary accounts. Kurdish society is not one which can be characterized as a traditional tribal society any longer. If there were an opportunity to compare the data with similar data taken from respondents attending an Iraqi university, for example, different results would likely be obtained because Arabs are generally thought of as being more tribally oriented.

However, in the mid-1990s Amal Obeidi conducted a survey of students from Garyounis University in Libya that dealt with the political culture in that country. Obeidi concluded that more than half of her student respondents affiliated with a tribe and they were not ready to drop that tribal identification.[7] Obeidi's results differ from mine for several reasons. First of all, her study took place sixteen years before this one; secondly the history, culture and political situation of Libya are quite different from that of Kurdistan. It may be that Kurdistan is entering the modern era in terms of time and space well before Libya.

Table 8.9 Respondents' Belonging to Tribe by Gender
Question: *Do you belong to any tribe?*

Gender	Tribe?		
	Yes	No	Totals
Female	33	136	169
	19.6%	80.4%	100%
Male	38	243	281
	13.5%	86.5%	100%
Totals	71	379	450
	15.8%	84.2%	100%

Source: 2007 Field Survey

Attachment and Loyalty to Respondents' Local Areas

Table 8.10 indicates that the vast majority of the respondents (283: 62.9 per cent) see themselves as 'very close' and and loyal to their local areas. Nearly 21 per cent (N = 93) reported not being 'very close' to their local areas. The third-largest category was those who reported to be 'fairly close' to their local areas (49: 10.9 per cent). Only 25 (5.6 per cent) of the respondents affirmed that they were 'not at all close' to their local areas. While students whose fathers worked in the governmental sector and who were 'very close' to their local regions represented the vast majority of the respondents in terms of absolute numbers (151: 33.6 per cent of total sample), their *proportion* of responses in the 'very close' category is actually the lowest at 55.7 per cent. The highest *proportion* of responses that were most closely attached to their local areas was the respondents whose fathers were in the private sector (76 per cent of the 121 students whose fathers worked in the private sector reported being 'very close' to their local areas. The second-highest category of those who reported to be 'very close' to their local regions were respondents whose fathers were retired. A total of 49 respondents' fathers were retired and 34 or 69.4 per cent of those respondents reportedly were 'very close' to their local areas. The 6 respondents whose fathers were unemployed were the third-highest category 'very close' to their local regions at 66.7 per cent. Respondents (N = 151) whose fathers worked for the government sector scored last at being 'very close' to their local areas at 55.7 per cent. Of those nine respondents whose fathers were unemployed, three or 33.3 per cent reported being 'fairly close' to their local areas. But this figure is rather insignificant because the number is so low. What is interesting is

Table 8.10 Attachment to Local Areas by Fathers' Type of Occupation

Question: *How closely attached or loyal do you feel to your local area, city, village or suburb? Does your father work? If so, what is his occupation?*

Father's Occupational Category	Very Closely	Fairly Closely	Not Very Close	Not at all Close	Total
Unemployed	6	3	0	0	9
% of total	1.3%	0.7%	0.0%	0.0%	2.0%
Proportion	66.7%	33.3%	0.0%	0.0%	100.0%
Retired	34	5	7	3	49
% of total	7.6%	1.1%	1.6%	0.7%	10.9%
Proportion	69.4%	10.2%	14.3%	6.1%	100.0%
Government	151	32	68	20	271
% of total	33.6%	7.1%	15.1%	4.4%	60.2%
Proportion	55.7%	11.8%	25.1%	7.4%	100.0%
Private	92	9	18	2	121
% of total	20.4%	2.0%	4.0%	0.4%	26.9%
Proportion	76.0%	7.4%	14.9%	1.7%	100.0%
Total	283	49	93	25	450
	62.9%	10.9%	20.7%	5.5%	100%

Source: 2007 Field Survey

that 68 of the 271 respondents (25.1 per cent) whose fathers worked in the government sector reported not being very close to their local areas. This is not quite half as many as those in the government sector who reported being 'very close' to their local areas. Of the 121 respondents whose fathers worked in the private sector, 18 or 14.9 per cent were not very close to their local regions, compared to seven (14.3 per cent) of those whose fathers were retired. Of the respondents whose fathers worked for the government 20 (7.4 per cent) of were 'not at all close' to their local areas.

Overall, 332 respondents or 73.8 per cent of the total sample reported being close to their local areas; 117 respondents or 26.2 per cent reportedly were 'not very close' or 'not at all close' to their local areas. Since three-quarters of the young generation in Kurdistan are closely attached and loyal to the local areas, it is evident that overall respondents tend to be reasonably content with where they are from. What is somewhat surprising is how many respondents whose fathers worked for the government sector, were not content to be where they live: 68 (25.1 per cent) and 20 (7.4 per cent) reportedly were 'not very close' or 'not at all close' to their local areas respectively. One can't help but wonder if the problem is the location where the government has their fathers working and hence the locale is unsuitable, or if the working conditions are such that it wouldn't matter where they lived, they are just unhappy working in their government jobs. This topic obviously warrants further research.

Attachment and Loyalty to Kurdish, Arabic and English Languages
Table 8.11 shows that the vast majority of students (401: 89.1 per cent overall) feel that speaking in Kurdish is 'very important' for the Kurds. In the Colleges of Arts, 86.7 per cent of the students (N = 195) thought it 'very important' to speak Kurdish. A higher proportion (91.6 per cent) from the Colleges of Science (N = 206) felt it important to speak Kurdish, an increase of 4.9 per cent. Of the 46 students (10.2 per cent) who felt that it was not important to speak Kurdish, 30 or 65.2 per cent of those responses came from the Colleges of Arts and 16 or 34.8 per cent came from the Colleges of Science. It appears that students from the Colleges of Sciences were a bit more sceptical of the idea of speaking Kurdish than students from the Colleges of Arts. Either these 46 students are more 'cosmopolitan' and

Table 8.11 Views on the Importance of Speaking Kurdish
by Type of College

Question: *How important do you think it is to speak*
in the Kurdish language?

Speaking Kurdish	Colleges of Arts	Colleges of Science	Total
Very Important	195	206	401
Proportion	48.6%	51.4%	100%
% of total	86.7%	91.6%	89.1%
Not Important	30	16	46
Proportion	65.2%	34.8%	100%
% of total	13.3%	7.1%	10.2%
Don't Know	0	3	3
Proportion	0.0%	100%	100%
% of total	0.0%	1.3%	0.6%
Total	225	225	450
	100%	100%	100%

Source: 2007 Field Survey

feel that Arabic, English, or some other language will suffice in academe or the marketplace, rather than Kurdish, or these data contain a healthy sub-sample of non-Kurdish student respondents who have little loyalty to the Kurdish language. There is a third possibility and that is that while most of the respondents are indeed Kurdish and tend to identify with national identity, they have heard complaints that the Kurdish language is not useful outside of the Kurdistan area and consequently they are expressing a value that the Kurdish language 'is not important' to speak because they have not yet made the conscious link of the importance of the Kurdish language to national identity. There were three students or 0.6 per cent of the sample that didn't have an opinion, or didn't know if Kurdish was important to speak. In conclusion 90 per cent of the students agreed that it was important to speak Kurdish and this was a robust finding.

Figure 8.11 reflects the fact that the vast majority of the students (166: 36.8 per cent) whose fathers have a preparatory level of education prefer that the university educational system of teaching and studying should be in

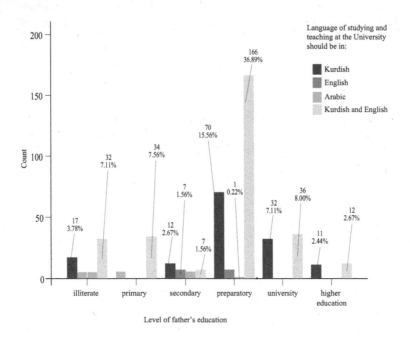

Figure 8.11 Attitudes toward the Language of Learning and Studying at the University by Levels of Fathers' Education

Kurdish and English. The second category among this group of students was those who chose Kurdish alone to be the language of teaching and studying at the university (70: 15.56 per cent). Surprisingly, a very small number of students whose fathers have a higher educational level, such as university and higher, have chosen Kurdish and English to be the languages of teaching and learning at the university (36: 8 per cent) and only 32 (7.1 per cent) of them chose Kurdish. There was little interest in Arabic or in English alone as the main language for teaching and studying at the university. It is significant to emphasize that after 2006 the Kurdish authorities in the educational sector intend to stress the English language from the early primary years and to include it at all levels of the educational system. The above data corroborate what was summarized earlier in this work, namely that Arabic is no longer dominant or considered to be important in Kurdistan, either in education or in daily life.

Table 8.12 shows that in students' opinions Islam does not play a vital role for Kurdish unity. The overwhelming majority (376: 83.6 per cent) strongly disagree that 'the importance of Islam is the vital factor for Kurdish unity.' However, when place of family residence is considered, the data obtained reflect the fact that 81.1 per cent of students who come from the city or urban areas 'strongly disagreed' with the statement. Only 12 respondents or 35 of those who were from the city 'strongly agreed' with the statement while 40 (12.2 per cent) agreed. Even those who come from the villages and suburbs overwhelmingly disagreed with the statement: 91.5 per cent of the

Table 8.12 The Importance of Islam as the Vital Factor for
Kurdish Unity by Place of Family Residence

Question: *Do you agree that Islam is the vital factor for Kurdish unity?*

Family Residence	Strongly Agree	Agree	Strongly Disagree	Don't Know	Total
City	12	40	266	10	328
	3.7%	12.2%	81.1%	3.0%	100%
Village	1	4	65	1	71
	1.4%	5.6%	91.5%	1.4%	100%
Suburb	0	6	45	0	51
	0.0%	11.8%	88.2%	0.0%	100%
Total	13	50	376	11	450
	2.9%	11.1%	83.6%	2.4%	100%

Source: 2007 Field Survey

village respondents (N = 65) and 88.2 per cent of the suburb respondents (N = 45) 'strongly disagreed' with the statement. Only one villager and no suburbanites 'strongly agreed' with the statement; and 4 villagers (5.6 per cent) and 6 (11.8 per cent) suburbanites 'agreed' with the statement. One villager 'didn't know'. If the 'strongly agree' and 'agree' categories are collapsed, then 52 or 15.9 per cent of the respondents from the city agree with the statement that Islam is the vital factor for Kurdish unity; five or seven per cent of the city dwellers agree with the statement; and six or 11.8 per cent of the suburban dwellers agree with the statement. Even if the two 'strongly agree' and 'agree' categories are collapsed for the village and suburban respondents, the total only comes to 12 respondents, or ten per cent of suburban and village respondents who think that Islam is the key to holding Kurdish society together. Comparing this with the 15.8 per cent of the city-dwelling respondents who think that Islam is the key to Kurdish unity, it is clear that the further away from the city you go, the less you are likely to feel that Islam is the key to unity—another surprising finding. Those who live in the village or suburban areas are far less likely to feel that Islam is the key to Kurdish unity.

From these data it is clear that Islam by itself counts for very little in the thinking of the young educated strata of Kurdish citizens. It appears to be *Kurdishness* or *Kurdistanyati* by itself which is considered important. Interestingly, Amal Obeidi's data showed that 84 per cent of the sample she investigated indicated that Arabism and Islam were *equally important* for Libyan students. And for them Islam was the highest ranked reason for being an Arab.[8] Similarly and contrary to the results of this study, Obeidi's survey shows that Islam as a religion for university students in Libyan society was regarded as a vital factor for Arab unity (62 per cent).[9]

Attitudes, Pride, Attachment and Loyalty toward Kurdish Politics

Many aspects of Kurdish politics have been analysed according to students' perceptions and involvement in politics. Indeed, involvement and political activities have a great deal to say about the attitudes that one has in the field of politics. Figure 8.12 records the membership of student respondents in the political parties of Iraqi Kurdistan. It was surprising to find strong negative responses to the question: 'Are you a member of any political party?' This was the case in all the age groups of the sample surveyed. In the first age group (18–21) there were 240 respondents or 53.3 per cent of the entire sample who indicated that they were not a member of any political party, whereas 121 respondents (26.8 per cent) of the sample indicated that they were. Similarly, in the second age group (22–25) the vast majority said they

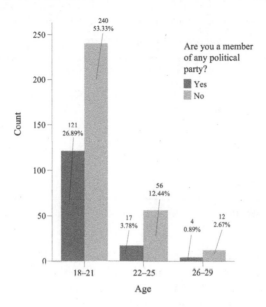

Figure 8.12 Respondents' Membership in a Political Party by Age Groups

were not members of any political party (56: 12.4 per cent), while only 17 or 3.7 per cent said they were. In the third age group (26–29), 12 or 2.6 per cent of the respondents indicated that they were not members of a political party and only four or 0.8 per cent said they were. When calculating the total numbers, it appears that the majority of the students (308: 68.4 per cent) were not involved in any political parties and only 142 or 21.6 per cent were members of political parties.

Table 8.13 reflects the membership of those 142 students who said that they were involved in political parties as members. The majority of the respondents who were involved in politics are involved with the Patriotic Union of Kurdistan (69: 48.6 per cent) and the second party category most frequented was the Kurdistan Democratic Party (57: 40.1 per cent). Only 11 students were members of the Islamic Movement in Kurdistan (7.7 per cent) and a very small number were members of the Kurdistan Communist Party (5: 3.5 per cent). Obviously the PUK and the KDP are the major political parties in the lives of the young educated set in Kurdistan as well as the populace at large.

In order to understand the political climate in Iraqi Kurdistan, it is important to know the degree of loyalty or non-loyalty of the respondents towards

Table 8.13 Students' Membership in Political Parties

Question: *If yes, which party is it?*

Political Party	Number	% of entire sample	% of those involved
Kurdistan Democratic Party	57	12.7%	40.1%
Patriotic Union of Kurdistan	69	15.3%	48.6%
Islamic Movement in Kurdistan	11	2.4%	7.7%
Kurdistan Communist Party	5	1.1%	3.5%
Total	142	31.6%	100.0%

Source: 2007 Field Survey

the two major political parties in Kurdistan, namely the KDP and the PUK. Therefore, two separate questions were asked: 'Please indicate how loyal you feel to the KDP' and 'Please indicate how loyal you feel to the PUK.' Figures 8.13 and 8.14 present the students' responses.

Figure 8.13 shows that the vast majority of the students (375: 83.3 per cent) are not loyal to the KDP at all. However, 48 (10.6 per cent) indicated that they were 'very loyal,' or 'fairly loyal' (13: 2.8 per cent) to the KDP. These data may reflect the fact that although the young generation in Kurdistan are proud of their identity and consider themselves to be *Kurdistani* and they are attached to Kurdistan, they are frustrated with the KDP and do not consider themselves loyalists to the party. The next figure will give us a clear picture on the same issue of attitudes towards the PUK.

Figure 8.14 explains the degree of loyalty of the students towards the PUK. The results indicate that these student respondents were not loyal to the PUK either. In fact, responses were even more negative in nature: (403: 89.5 per cent). Three respondents (0.6 per cent) said they are 'not very loyal'. Those students who consider themselves to be 'very loyal' were 39 or 8.6 per cent and only five respondents or 1.1 per cent claimed to be 'fairly loyal'. The data indicate that the negative attitude towards the PUK was more severe than that towards the KDP. This issue is worthy of investigation as to the reasons behind this sort of attitude toward the two largest and dominating political parties. Why 20 per cent of the student respondents chose to be active in politics at all considering the negativity associated with it is also worth looking into.

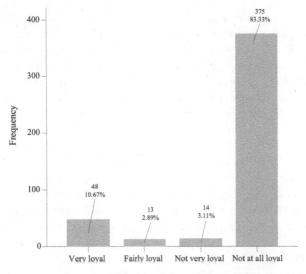

Figure 8.13 Respondents' Loyalty to the KDP

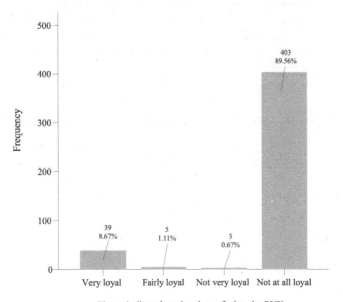

Figure 8.14 Distribution of Respondents' Loyalty to the PUK

Table 8.14 indicates that the vast majority of students (269: 59.8 per cent) do not feel that *Kurdishness* need be 'bound' or tied to political parties, whereas 181 (40.2 per cent) felt that it did. It seems that most of the students, especially those who pride themselves on not having been members of any political parties, may be exhibiting a sort of anger or contention with what is associated with the two ruling parties in Kurdistan. For them, being Kurdish definitely does not equate with involvement with the political *status quo*.

The elections for the National Assembly were held in Iraq on 30 January 2005 when a transitional parliament was elected to draft the country's new constitution. The constitution was adopted through a referendum on 15 October 2005. It is noteworthy to examine which parties the students elected in these elections. The outcomes are shown in Figure 8.15. Contrary to expectation, the overwhelming majority of the students voted for the KDP (252: 56 per cent). The PUK received the second-highest number of votes (145: 32.2 per cent). Expectedly, the other two small parties which the students chose were the Kurdistan Communist Party (KCP) (N = 27, six per cent) and the Islamic Movement (26: 5.7 per cent). These results reflect the ambiguity of the students' negative attitudes toward and dissatisfaction with the two major political parties. It also reveals the cognitive dissonance inherent in having negative attitudes toward the political parties and their decisions to 'elect' them at the same time. More research should be done to tap into what cognitive dissonance reducing mechanisms young people are drawing on to legitimate actions that they have inherent difficulties with.[10]

Table 8.14 Attitudes towards *Kurdishness* and Political Parties

Question: *Does Kurdishness need to be bound to political parties?*

Answer	Number	Percentage
Yes	181	40.2%
No	269	59.8%
Total	450	100.0%

Source: 2007 Field Survey

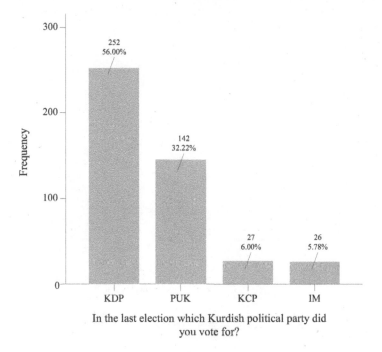

Figure 8.15 Respondents' Voting at the Election of 2005

Figure 8.16 gives a clear picture of respondents' opinions on the 2003 war in Iraq ('Liberation' or 'Invasion,' or 'Invasion but it was good for the Kurds in the end'). The data indicate that 291 or 64.6 per cent view the war in Iraq in 2003 as 'Liberation'. A small proportion of students (46: 10.2 per cent) view it as an 'Invasion'; and 25.1 per cent of the sample (N = 113) saw it as an 'Invasion, but it was good for the Kurds in the end'.

Figure 8.17 represents students' attitudes towards the general standard of living in Kurdistan after 2003. More than half of the respondents (271: 60.2 per cent) thought that the standard of living in Kurdistan had increased a little; 122 respondents (27.1 per cent) thought that the standard of living had 'increased a lot'; 33 respondents, or 7.3 per cent, thought that the standard of living had remained the same and 24 respondents (5.3 per cent) indicated that they thought it had 'fallen a little'. The fact is that the standard of living has indeed increased since 2003, compared to pre-2003 levels. As the majority of the sample were from the middle class that depends on monthly wages to make ends meet, they have undoubtedly seen and experienced

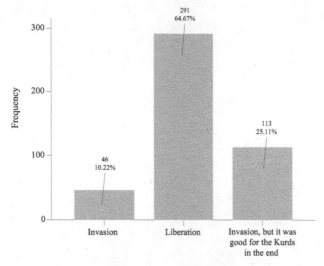

What do you think of the American and British
war of 2003 in Iraq? Was it:

Figure 8.16 Attitudes toward the American/British War of 2003 in Iraq

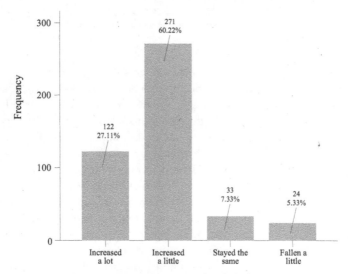

What do you think of the general standard of living in Kurdistan
after 2003? Has it increased or fallen?

Figure 8.17 Attitudes toward the General Standard of Living after 2003

an increase in the standard of living as well as witnessed their families' and parents' comments regarding such. Due to this fact most of respondents' answers were positive.

Regarding the Kurdistan National Assembly and its power, Table 8.15 indicates that students' responses focused on the importance of giving more power to Parliament. The vast majority (382: 84.9 per cent) 'strongly agreed' that Parliament should be given more power; 52 (11.6 per cent) 'agreed' with the statement that Parliament should be given more power. When you add these two categories together, that is a total of over 96 per cent (N = 434) that think that Parliament needs more power. Only ten respondents (11.6 per cent) felt that Parliament did not need more power and only six respondents (1.3 per cent) 'strongly disagreed' with the statement. This totals almost 13 per cent of those who disapproved of Parliament's getting more power (N = 16).

The most heated debates and dilemmas in the Kurdish media were about the Kurdish Parliament in Iraqi Kurdistan not having any real power. It is important to note that during the informal interviews and meetings many students indicated their disappointment with the corruption in many ministerial and political institutions of the Kurdistan Regional Government.

An interesting issue to consider in contemporary Kurdish politics is the unification of the two administrations of the two largest parties (KDP and PUK) and how this will impact the political situation in Iraqi Kurdistan. It took nearly five years for the leadership of the two parties to agree to join forces. Figure 8.18 presents students' attitudes toward the unification process, which culminated with an agreement of the 50–50 division of power between the two parties. The overwhelming majority of the students

Table 8.15 Attitudes toward Kurdistan's Parliament and its Power

Question: *Kurdistan's Parliament should be given more power*

Agreement	Number	Percentage
Strongly Agree	382	84.9%
Agree	52	11.6%
Disagree	10	2.2%
Strongly Disagree	6	1.3%
Total	450	100%

Source: 2007 Field Survey

viewed the agreement as a good action for the Kurds, (375: 83.3 per cent);
62 respondents (13.7 per cent) felt that 'it makes no difference'. Only 13
or 2.8 per cent of the respondents indicated that they 'don't know' whether
this unification is good for the Kurds in the long run or if it makes any
difference.

Table 8.16 shows that more than half of the respondents use the Internet
as a mass media tool for getting news (279: 62 per cent); 87 respondents
or 19.3 per cent indicated that the television was the mass medium they
used; and 54 respondents or 12 per cent indicated that newspapers were
their tool for getting the news. Only six respondents (1.3 per cent) used the
radio for following up on the news, whereas 24 respondents or 5.3 per cent
indicated that they use all of the mentioned mass media for following the
news. Clearly, these young people in the universities are keeping up with

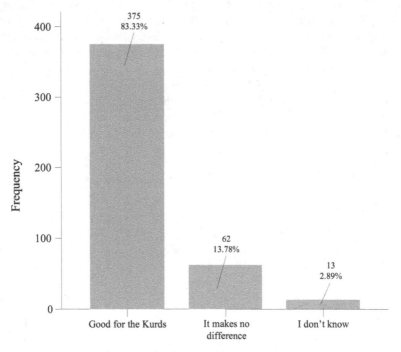

What do you think of the unification of the two
adminstrations of the KDP and the PUK in 2006?

Figure 8.18 Attitudes toward the Unification of the Administrations of the
KDP and the PUK in 2006

the world in making use of the World Wide Web. From my observations in the universities, it is clear that they are using the Web not only for catching up on the news, but for communications with friends and acquaintances, as well as for doing research.

In sum, the general findings of this research indicate that a strong majority of the students (329: 73.1 per cent) in the sample see themselves as *Kurdistani*. This particular type of self-identification in terms of nationality is the outcome of the political socialization process that this educated, young generation has grown up with in Iraqi Kurdistan. Parents' educational levels and occupational status, family income, friends, location in the city/suburb or village, involvement in politics, media usage, tribal affiliation and all the other variables that make a person what he or she is, impact the socialization of the person as he or she grows into adulthood.

As expected, a very small percentage (two per cent) saw themselves as more Iraqi than Kurd. Iraqiness by itself counts for very little in the construction of modern and contemporary Kurdish identity among young people, as does religion. The concept of *Kurdistaniyeti* played a key role in the identification of the majority of the respondents. In Smith's terminology, Kurdish national identity appears to rest upon the unique national, territorial and linguistic bases of the Kurds. In the vast majority of students' views (161: 36.8 per cent), the 'national factor' was the most crucial in determining national identity, especially when comparing it to the other factors such as political, economical, territorial or the linguistic. The second major factor for them was the territorial factor (109: 24.2 per cent), followed by the linguistic factor (89: 19.8 per cent) and then the political factor (86: 19.1 per cent).

Table 8.16 Respondents' Use of Mass Media

Question: *What kind of mass media do you make use of?*

Type of Mass Media	Number	Percentage
Internet	279	62.0%
Radio	6	1.3%
Television	87	19.3%
Newspapers	54	12.0%
All of the above	24	5.3%
Total	450	100.0%

Source: 2007 Field Survey

National, territorial and linguistic factors are very crucial in Kurdistan for consolidating Kurdish national identity, whereas educational and economic factors were not. Ideas of the Kurdish people as a 'nation', with an ancient and historic territory as well as a unique language, weigh heavily as identifying factors for young, educated Kurds.

The students do not as a rule distinguish between Kurdism, *Kurdishness*, *Kurdistanism* or *Kurdistanyeti*. The concepts in students' perceptions have the same meanings. The very Kurdification of Kurdistan's political culture means that Kurdish young people identify strongly with their land, their people, their language and their heritage. They might not like what is going on within the major political parties, but when it comes to national identification, there is little doubt who they think they are. They are *Kurds*, *Kurdistani*, or *Kurdistanyeti*, first and foremost.

9

POST-1990s *KURDISTANIYETI*

A body of work has emerged, especially since the 1990s, which is critical of the view that nationalism can be understood as a fixed and static set of beliefs, emotions and attachments to one's nation. No general theory or paradigm, however, has been developed to address the multiple challenges of present-day national and ethnic realities related to national identification. Research and theoretical contributions to national phenomena tend to be centred on three major paradigms: perennialism, modernism and postmodernism, or put in another way: modernism, ethno-symbolism and social constructivism.

Anthony Smith's theory of ethno-symbolism was applied to the Kurdish case because his theoretical explanation for the origins and development of nations and national identity best fit with the historical understanding of the Kurdish socio-cultural milieu and present-day political dilemmas. Smith rightly judges nation-formation to be a long-term process subject to a great variety of influences: political, economic, social and emotional, all of which require the nation's elites to continuously adjust their means and goals to maintain support and positions of leadership while keeping national identity vital and national goals the focus of the nation.

The Kurdistan territory was explored and its ancient history delved into to expose the significance of language for national identity in Kurdistan. Kurdistan's political culture from the twelfth through the nineteenth century was one in which religious and tribal affiliations were dominant. It was argued that what underlies Kurdish national identity is a 'sense of place' rather than a 'sense of blood.'

Yet, a very significant fact in understanding the question surrounding Kurdish pre-modern history in terms of territoriality suggests that for centuries the Kurds were distinguishable from Arabs or Persians—or even Turks—in that they identify their ethnic identity with a territory, or motherland, i.e., *Kurdistan*, rather than ethnicity. This conception of place rather than blood is crucial in identifying the 'self' (i.e., nation) and differentiating it from the 'other' (nations).

Kurdish-ness is based on living in a common territory. Thus, territory is one of the main elements of Kurdish nationalism—which is why it is difficult for Kurds to see their 'nation' torn apart and distributed to Turkey, Iran, Iraq and Syria. Kirmanj Gundi, said this in his presidential speech at the 21st Annual Conference of the Kurdish National Congress of North America:

> Whether we acknowledge it or not, the reality is that the plight of one part of Kurdistan is tied to other parts of Kurdistan. Sadly, this reality is more recognized by the occupying countries than it is by us. It is mirrored in the brutal measures taken by these central governments against us. They demonstrate that regardless of their differences, they are united in suppressing our Kurdish identity. Therefore, as long as we in each part of Kurdistan adhere to the capital of our respective countries, we will never be able to have a true Kurdish voice.
>
> We need to revive the Kurdish aspiration as a nation, instead of each part thinking separately. For as long as we think separately, we will be treated separately. As long as we are treated separately, we remain ineffective.
>
> We realize that the division of Kurdistan is what makes our situation unique and unlike any other national group that has sought recognition of its national rights. Nevertheless, this must not discourage us from dreaming our sacred dream of independence. This means that the Kurdish political parties in all parts of Kurdistan must stop bickering and come to terms with each other and together strengthen Kurdish unity. We must do this to promote our common interests on the diplomatic front...
>
> So while we can continue to press our claims for our rights as autonomous people within the nations to which we have been consigned, we must see this as only an interim step toward a final goal of a free and united Kurdistan.[1]

Without a doubt, it is the fear that the Kurds do intend to have their 'free and united Kurdistan' that helps to explain the treatment that the Kurds have been given by their host nations for the past hundred years.

To summarize, up to the sixteenth century the Kurds had no ethnic self-consciousness. The main divisions used to differentiate the Kurds from 'others' were generally based on social hierarchy, religious separation of the *Shi'i* and *Sunni* groups and economic-cultural categories between the settled mountainous, nomadic, family or tribal groups. It was the events of the 1990s that coalesced to ripen a sense of *Kurdistani* identity that currently defines the character of Kurdish society—and this, it seems evident, is now irreversible.

The reason is this: Kurdistan, as well as many regions in the Middle East, lacks an established civil society. Because it lacks an established civil society, it lacks a solid base upon which to build or develop a sense of responsible citizenship and the democratic mindset that would enable it to stand on its own without relying on the props of titular ethnicity. It is difficult to address the lack of civil societal apparatuses without acknowledging an element that very few scholars are willing to address but which blocks the path toward building civil society structures. Let us begin by defining what 'civil society' is.

The London School of Economics' Centre for Civil Society refers to 'civil society' as an atmosphere where 'uncoerced collective action around shared interests, purposes and values' is made possible. Its institutional forms are distinct from those of the state, family and market, though the boundaries between them are often blurred and negotiated. 'Civil society embraces a diversity of spaces, actors and institutional forms which all vary in their degree of formality, autonomy and power. Civil societies consist of organizations such as registered charities, development non-governmental organizations, community groups, women's organizations, faith-based organizations, professional associations, trade unions, self-help groups, social movements, business associations, coalitions and advocacy groups.'[2]

In a nutshell then, civil society refers to voluntary participation by average citizens and thus it does not include behaviour that is imposed or coerced by the state. There is a high degree of nongovernmental organizational (NGO) involvement, a strong measure of voluntary participation in the public and private sector and it includes individual action as well as the institutions and organizations they participate in. Sometimes these institutions are called 'civil society organizations' or CSOs. Thus, 'civil society is strong to the degree that those CSOs are large and powerful.'[3] A civic culture is one in which most people believe that their government is legitimate and their institutions can be trusted. Civil societies operate to assist in democratic institution building, in strengthening communities, in promoting equitable access to resources and ensuring respect of human rights and diversity.

Having laid out the groundwork for understanding what a civil society is, let us address one of the roadblocks in Kurdistan (and throughout other parts of the Middle East) that may stand in the way of Kurdistan's building the necessary framework that must be established for a long-lasting democratically oriented civic culture. The issue is the enigma of the ancient practice of cousin marriage.

In nearly half of all marriages in Arab Muslim cultures the spouses are first or second cousins to each other.[4] Steve Sailer refers to a 1986 study of 4,500 married hospital patients and staff in Baghdad where they found that '46 per cent were wed to a first or second cousin, while a smaller 1989 survey found that 53 per cent were "consanguineously married."'[5] For example, Saddam Hussein and his first wife, Sajida, were first cousins. Sailer says, 'By fostering intense family loyalties and strong nepostistic urges, inbreeding causes the development of civil society to be nearly impossible.'[6]

Stanley Kurtz addresses the centrality of men to the Muslim kinship system and how that sets up the problem. 'The women who marry into a lineage pose a serious threat to the unity of the band of brothers. If a husband's tie to his wife should become more important than his solidarity with his brothers, the couple might take their share of the property and leave the larger group, thus weakening the strength of the lineage.'[7]

'There is a solution to this problem, however—a solution that marks out the kinship system of the Muslim Middle East as unique in the world. In the Middle East, the preferred form of marriage is between a man and his cousin (his father's brother's daughter). Cousin marriage solves the problem of lineage solidarity. If, instead of marrying a woman from a strange lineage, a man marries his cousin, then his wife will not be an alien, but a trusted member of his own kin group. Not only will this reduce a man's likelihood of being pulled away from his brothers by his wife, a woman of the lineage is less likely to be divorced by her husband and more likely to be protected by her own extended kin in case of a rupture in the marriage. Somewhere around a third of all marriages in the Muslim Middle East are between members of the same lineage and in some places the figure can reach as high as 80 per cent.'[8]

Consanguineous marriages are the solution if you live in an insecure land and are subject to unexpected invasions. Clan and tribal support systems based on trust served to protect the extended family, served as a form of social insurance and offered help to avenge the wrong done to one of your members by an outsider. They also allowed a tribe to keep wealth within the family as there were fewer heirs to divide the wealth between.[9] Security is enhanced because it is incumbent upon the tribe to take care of 'their own', but not necessarily outsiders.

King Faisal reportedly described his subjects as being 'devoid of any patriotic idea ... they had ears given to [hear] evil; [they were] prone to anarchy and perpetually ready to rise against any government whatever'.[10]

Sailer relates the corruption inherent in 'clannishness' and coups to the high rates of inbreeding.[11] The well-known lack of trust among tribes and clans for those outside their own kinship structure adversely affects the development of civil society. Randall Parker asks, 'How can we transform Iraq into a modern liberal democracy if every government worker sees a government job as a route to helping out his clan at the expense of other clans?'[12]

> Extended families that are incredibly tightly bound are really the enemy of civil society because the alliances of family override any consideration of fairness to people in the larger society. Yet, this obvious fact is missing from 99 per cent of the discussions about what is wrong with the Middle East.[13]

US Army Colonel (Ret.) Norvell De Atkine spent many years in the Middle East during his military career. He wrote about his observations in the *Middle East Quarterly:*

> In the modern Middle East, networks of kin are still the foundation of wealth, security, and personal happiness. That, in a sense, is the problem. As we've seen in Afghanistan, loyalty to kin and tribe cuts against the authority of the state. And the corrupt dictatorships that rule much of the Muslim Middle East often function themselves more like self-interested kin groups than as rulers who take the interests of the nation as a whole as their own. That, in turn, gives the populace little reason to turn from the proven support of kin and tribe, and trust instead in the state.[14]

Jon Utley states that building democracy in lands with high rates of cousin marriage is a slow process, but can come about with education, economic prosperity and a lot of intermingling. He suggests that whereas the goal of obtaining a truly 'civil society' in lands with high consanguineous marriage rates might be out of reach, perhaps the goal of a society based on the rule of law may not be. 'Successful transitions to modern societies can come about in countries where there is a 'good' semi-dictator or ruler who has stayed in power long enough to effect the change. 'Justice' is a very basic part of Muslim teachings and so lends itself to the rule of law. The modern societies in Asia have all experienced stable governments and laws first, then economic development and more freedom.'[15]

The Roman Catholic Church has waged a long war against cousin marriage, even out to fourth cousins or higher. By halting the custom of consanguineous marriages, especially among royalty, the extended families of Europe weakened and the advantages of arranged marriages lessened. It also strengthened broader institutions like the Church and the nation state as well as other 'grass-roots' organizations.[16]

The point is not that Islam is necessarily responsible for the high rates of inbreeding in Muslim countries. The custom pre-dated Islam and was found among the ancient Jews, such as Abraham, who married his half-sister, Sarah; Isaac married Rebekah, a cousin once removed; and Jacob married his two first cousins, Leah and Rachel. The Hindus of India have high consanguinity rates and some Christians in the Middle East practise the custom also, though less so than Muslims.[17]

So why do so many people around the world prefer endogamous marriages in the family? Sailer explains the answer to this question by sharing a discussion he had with a Pakistani lecturer named Rafat Hussain. Hussain told him: 'In patriarchal societies where parents exert considerable influence and gender segregation is followed more strictly, marriage choice is limited to whom you know. While there is some pride in staying within the inner bounds of family for social or economic reasons, the more important issue is: Where will parents find a good match? Often it boils down to whom you know and can trust.'[18]

Is it true that the closer the genetic relationship between two people, the more likely they are to feel a sense of loyalty and altruism toward one another? This was William D. Hamilton's thesis in 1964 when he claimed that nepotism was biologically inspired.[19] The level of nepotistic feeling depends upon the degree of genetic similarity. The more similar you are genetically speaking the normal family feelings will be multiplied accordingly.[20] But nepotism is a zero sum game. 'The flip side of being materially nicer toward your relatives is that you have fewer resources with which to be civil or even fair toward non-kin. So nepotism corruption is rampant in countries such as Iraq where Saddam appointed members of his extended family from his hometown of Tikrit to key positions in the national government, those whom he could "trust."'[21]

'The tendency toward inbreeding can also turn an extended family into a miniature racial group with its partially isolated gene pool. This process has been going on for thousands of years in the Middle East. Not just the Jews, but other ancient inbreeding groups such as the Samaritans, the John the Baptist-worshipping Sabeans and the Yezidis still survive.'[22]

The point to be made here with regard to civil society structure building is that diversity needs to be encouraged, as well as marriages based on exogamous qualities; and the young people and citizenry need to have more personal and social choices—whether they be in the university setting or in the family setting, if modern, democratic-oriented and civic-minded institutions are to be developed that will last for a very long time in Kurdistan.

The political and cultural cohesions growing within and among the young *Kurdistanis* appear to be strong and the sense of community they feel with the nation is solid. Attempts to create a nation based on the predominant ethnicity are bound to continue. However, with the aid of free choice of marriage partners and the encouragement of intermarriage and associations with voluntary organizations, the evolution toward civil society will grow stronger.

The political events of the 1920s, 40s, 60s, 70s and the 90s particularly had the effect of consolidating Kurdish national identity and strengthening Kurdish pride in Kurdistan. In the twentieth century, especially after the 40s and up to 1990, political history and politics in Iraqi Kurdistan brought to bear some tremendous challenges and changes. The notion of *Kurdistanism* (Kurdistani-ness) or *Kurdistaniyeti* began to take root. This helps to explain why the Iraqi state under the various ruling regimes (i.e., the monarchies, Qasim, the Arif brothers and Saddam Hussein) could not incorporate the Kurds into Iraq's fold, socially, politically, or economically speaking.

None of the various regimes and governments that ruled Iraq since its formation in the 1920s until the removal of Saddam Hussein from power in 2003, succeeded in assimilating the Kurds into the state of Iraq and its Arab dominant population. This was due to the failure of these regimes to instil a normative sense of Iraqiness in the Kurdish people. The identity that was fostered and imposed continually on the Kurdish people served to differentiate the Kurds from the centre, keep them on the fringes of society and prevent the formation of Iraqi identification. From the start the monarchy failed to formulate an Iraqi identity among the Kurds. Evidently they didn't see the importance of this for the future, or they simply did not care. Keeping the Kurds on the sidelines, they missed an opportunity to enlarge the Iraqi nation to include the Kurds and their territory called Kurdistan.

Qasim's regime failed to consolidate the territory that was given Iraq into the Iraqi identity. His era was short, chaotic and politically unstable. More than any previous regime in Iraq's modern history, the ongoing Arabization policies, *Anfal* and massive deportations which the *Ba'th* strategically adopted and systematically applied in Kurdistan, could not melt the Kurds' growing sense of ethnic identity or integrate the inclusive national identity of the Kurds into the Iraqi Arab culture and the *Ba'thist* pan-Arab ideology.

The post-1990s era in Iraqi Kurdistan was the era of *Kurdistaniyeti*. *Kurdistaniyeti* means the promotion of *Kurdistani* in its ethnic, territorial and traditional conceptions. It is also a condition in which the territorial and political imagination of Kurdistan have been consolidated. The real history of the consolidation of a Kurdish national identity and nation-building in Iraqi Kurdistan began after March 1990 and the elections of 1992, which effectively put an end to the tyranny of the *Ba'thist* regime in Kurdistan. In the early 1990s following the uprising in Iraq, Saddam and his regime were shown to be isolated regionally and internationally.

This can now be seen clearly, but was visible from 1998 when the best period of political institutions in Kurdistan began. Since the 1990s the Kurds have entered into a new era of nation-building. After the withdrawal of the Iraqi army, the biggest change in the governmental institutions of Kurdistan was the election of the Kurdistan National Assembly and the power-sharing arrangement between the two major parties in ruling Kurdistan. After 2003 this transformation expanded as the Kurdish political system consolidated itself nationally and internationally.

In conclusion, modern nationalism for the Kurds since the 1990s may be regarded as a state-seeking and nation-building movement. The political and administrative experience of the last twenty years have made it clear that Iraqi Kurdistan is institutionalized politically—not in a fully self-sufficient, independent manner as a UN-recognized State, but as a *de facto* Kurdish state. There is an organized political leadership which has risen to power through democratic elections and which has received popular support. This political leadership has achieved sufficient capacity to provide governmental services, maintain effective control internally and regionally and it is capable of entering into relations with other states. Findings from the present investigation indicate that the Kurdistan Region of Iraq does not at present possess a broad-based democratic culture or fully developed civil society. This leaves unanswered the questions about the prospects for the emergence of a *de jure* Kurdish political state in the future.

That is not to say that there are not level-headed voices of democracy in Kurdistan. There certainly are. In 2006 the state of Turkey put pressure on the Kurdistan Regional Government as well as the US to attack the PKK bases in southern Kurdistan (north of Iraq). Iran, who needed Turkey's support in the event that the US interfered with its nuclear ambitions, for the first time openly expressed support for Turkey in its war against the PKK and PJAK. The US opposed Turkey's intention to send troops into Iraq to destabilize Kurdistan as it had in the past. Dr. Saman Shali, then president of the Kurdish National Congress of North America, called upon the Kurdish leaders to be prudent in their decision-making, especially with regard to the volatile events surrounding Turkey and the PKK. Shali urged

Kurdish leaders to cease all military activity and to pursue diplomatic measures that would protect the rights of the Kurds and ensure a lasting peace.
War was the 'harbinger of destruction and despair', but by resisting the call
to war, which appeared to be Turkey's aim, Kurdistan could 'light the way
to peace'.[23]

Kurdish Prime Minister Mr. Nechirvan Barzani proposed mediation
between the Turkish Government and the PKK, but the Turkish government refused, just as it had refused earlier offers of mediation proposed by
Deputy Prime Minister of Iraq, Dr. Barham Salih and the Iraqi Foreign
Minister, Mr. Hoshyar Zebari. President Mas'ud Barzani of the Kurdish
region and Prime Minister Nechirvan Barzani informed the Turkish government of their opposition to and resistance toward any military operation
inside of Iraqi Kurdistan. With pressure from the US, who were also opposed
to Turkey's interference in the physical territory of Iraqi Kurdistan, Turkey
and Iran backed off and the invasion never happened.

There are many other examples of moderate and temperate responses to
agitating circumstances and signs are evident that Kurdistan is making its
way toward becoming a civic-oriented society. The research demonstrates
that tribal affiliation, identification with and connections to tribes appear
to be lessening. As Kurdistan enters into and interacts with the international community and bright Kurdish students and scholars go abroad to
study, there will be more intermingling, intermarriage and the embracing of
democratic ideals. It is believed that Kurdistan is on the path to democratic
and civic-minded methods and procedures that will enable it, as Shali said,
to be a 'beacon of light on the way to peace'.

APPENDIX

Appendix 1
The Treaty of Sèvres of 1920, Articles 62–4

Article 62

A commission sitting at Constantinople and composed of three members appointed by the British, French and Italian Governments respectively shall draft within six months from the coming into force of the present Treaty a scheme of local authority for the predominantly Kurdish areas lying east of the Euphrates, south of the southern boundary of Armenia as it may hereafter be determined and north of the frontier of Turkey with Syria and Mesopotamia...

Article 63

The Turkish Government hereby agrees to accept and execute the decisions of both the Commissions mentioned in Article 62 within three months from their communication to the said Government.

Article 64

If within one year from the coming into force of the present Treaty the Kurdish peoples within the areas defined in Article 62 shall address themselves to the Council of the League of Nations in such a manner as to show a majority of the population of these areas desires independence from Turkey and if the Council then considers that it should be granted to them, Turkey hereby agrees to execute such a recommendation and to renounce all rights and title over these areas... If and when such renunciation takes place, no objection will be raised by the principal Allied Powers to the voluntary adhesion to such an independent Kurdish state of the Kurds inhabiting that part of Kurdistan which has hitherto been included in the Mosul Vilayet.

Appendix 2
The Agreement of 11 March 1970

1 Participation of Kurds in government, including the appointment of Kurds to key posts in the state.
2 Recognition of Kurdish in those areas where Kurds constitute the majority. Kurdish and Arabic would be taught together in all schools.
3 Furtherance of Kurdish education and culture.
4 Requirement that officials in the Kurdish areas speak Kurdish.
5 Right to establish Kurdish student, youth, women's and teachers' organisation.
6 Economic development of the Kurdish area.
7 Return of Kurds to their villages or financial compensation.
8 Agrarian reform.
9 Amendment of the constitution to read 'the Iraqi people consist of two main nationalities: the Arab and Kurdish nationalities.'
10 Return of the clandestine radio and heavy weapons to the government.
11 Appointment of a Kurdish vice-president.
12 Amendment of provincial laws in accordance with this declaration.
13 Formation of a Kurdish area with self government.

Appendix 3
General Provisions of the Autonomy Declaration of 1974

1   The area of Kurdistan shall enjoy autonomy, limited by the legal, political and economic integrity of the Republic of Iraq. The area shall be defined in accordance with the 11 March 1970 manifesto and the 1957 census records.

2   Kurdish will be the official language beside Arabic in the region and the language of education, although the teaching of Arabic will also be compulsory.

3   The rights of non-Kurdish minorities within the region will be guaranteed, with proportional representation in local autonomy.

4   The judiciary will conform to the legal system of Iraq.

5–9   Covered fiscal aspects of autonomy, within the financial integrity of the state.

10–15 Provided for the establishment of a Legislative and an Executive Council as government organs of the autonomous area.

16–21 Established the relationship between the Central authority and the Autonomous Administration, defined by the government as one of supervision and co-ordination.

Appendix 4
Resolution 688 of 5 April 1991

Adopted by the Security Council at its 298 meeting on 5 April 1991. The Security Council, mindful of its duties and its responsibilities under the Charter of the United Nations for the maintenance of international peace and security, Recalling of Article 2, paragraph 7, of the Charter of the United Nations, Gravely concerned by the repression of the Iraqi civilian population in many parts of Iraq, including most recently in Kurdish populated areas, which led to a massive flow of refugees towards and across international frontiers and to cross-border incursions, which threaten international peace and security in the region, deeply disturbed by the magnitude of the human suffering involved, taking note of the letters sent by the representatives of Turkey and France to the United Nations dated 2 April 1991 and 4 April 1991, respectively (S/22435 and S/22442), taking note also of the letters sent by the permanent Representative of the Islamic Republic of Iran to the United Nations dated 3 and 4 April 1991, respectively (S/22436 and S/22447), reaffirming the commitment of all Member States to the sovereignty, territorial integrity and political independence of Iraq and of all States in the area, bearing in mind the Secretary-General's report of 20 March 1991 (S/22366). 1. Condemns the repression of the Iraqi civilian population in many parts of Iraq, including most recently in Kurdish populated areas, the consequences of which threaten international peace and security in the region; 2. Demands that Iraq, as a contribution to remove the threat to international peace and security in the region, immediately end this repression and express the hope in the same context that an open dialogue will take place to ensure that the human and political rights of all Iraqi citizens are respected; 3. Insists that Iraq allow immediate access by international humanitarian organisations to all those in need of assistance in all parts of Iraq and to make available all necessary facilities for their operations; 4. Requests the Secretary-General to pursue his humanitarian efforts in Iraq and to report forthwith, if appropriate on the basis of a further mission to the region, on the plight of the Iraqi civilian population and in particular the Kurdish population, suffering from the repression in all its forms inflicted by the Iraqi authorities; 5. Requests further the Secretary-General to use all the resources at his disposal, including those of the relevant United Nations agencies, to address urgently the critical needs of the refugees and displaced Iraqi population; 6. Appeals to all Member States and to all humanitarian organisations to contribute to these humanitarian relief efforts; 7. Demands that Iraq cooperate with the Secretary-General to these ends; 8. Decides to remain seized of the matter.

Appendix 5
The Unification Agreement between the KDP and the PUK

On 21 January 2006, (KDP) and (PUK), on the basis of partnership, consensus and equity, agreed on what follows:

1 A new post of Vice President of the Region will be established by amendment to the Law of the Presidency of the Region. The Vice President will be from the PUK and will also serve as the Deputy Commander-in-Chief of the Peshmerga forces of the Kurdistan Region.

2 The Prime Minister and his Deputy will be identified by the Kurdistan National Assembly (KNA) and will be charged by the President of the Kurdistan Region with forming a joint cabinet. The Prime Minister will submit the names of his cabinet to the KNA.

3 The Speaker of the KNA will be from the PUK and the Prime Minister will be from the KDP until the next election of the KNA at the end of 2007. For the next election, the KDP and PUK will participate in a joint slate as equals and at that time the post of the Speaker of the KNA will go to the KDP and the Prime Minister will be from the PUK. This will be for two years. After that, the KDP and PUK will rotate the posts of Speaker and Prime Minister. If by the end of 2007 elections are not conducted due to delay, the posts of Speaker and Prime Minster will rotate.

4 If either of the ministerial blocs withdraws from the joint cabinet, the entire cabinet will be considered as resigned.

5 The ministerial posts will be divided as follows:

a The Ministers of Interior, Justice, Education, Health, Social Affairs, Religious Affairs, Water Resources, Transportation, Reconstruction, Planning and Human Rights will be from the PUK.

b The Ministers of Finance, Peshmerga Affairs, Higher Education, Agriculture, Martyrs, Culture, Electricity, Natural Resources, Municipalities, Sports and Youth and Minister of Region for the affairs of areas outside the Region will be from the KDP.

c The remaining ministries will be assigned to other parties of the Kurdistan Region.

d The Ministries of Finance, Peshmerga Affairs, Justice and Interior should unite within one year. These four ministries, until they unite, will have both a cabinet minister and a minister of the region for the affairs of the concerned ministry. Each minister will have responsibility for the part of the ministry which is currently under their control.

6 The budget of 2006 will be managed as it has been decided, but the share of the budget of the Presidency of the Kurdistan Region, the KNA, the Council of Ministers and the Judicial Council and any other joint items from each side will be allocated equally. Afterwards, in the coming years, the Kurdistan regional budget will be prepared by the unified KRG and submitted to the KNA. After approval, the budget will be allocated to various areas according to population percentage and agreement within the unified KRG.

7 Under the auspices of the Presidency of the Kurdistan Region there will be established a Supreme Commission to institutionalize the police and security agencies of the Kurdistan Region. These united agencies will be removed from political considerations. After the unified KRG takes office in the capital of the Kurdistan Region, Erbil, a special programme will be instituted for university graduates with the aim of recruiting new candidates to the security services of the governorates for the sake of unification and re-establishment of these important agencies for our people.

8 The KRG representations abroad, according to agreement of both the KDP and PUK, will be assigned by the Prime Minster and his Deputy.

9 In all the Governorates of the Kurdistan Region a joint committee will be established between the KDP and PUK to resolve issues as they may arise.

10 Both sides, KDP and PUK, will present Mr. Jalal Talabani as their candidate for the sovereign post in the Iraqi Federal Government.

Appendix 6
The Questionnaire in English

All the questions can be answered with a simple tick/number.
All your answers will be treated as confidential and anonymous.

1. Place of family residence
☐ City ☐ Village ☐ Suburb

2 Place of birth
☐ Urban ☐ Rural

3 Age
☐ 18–21 ☐ 22–25 ☐ 26–29
☐ 30–33 ☐ 34+

4 Gender
☐ Female ☐ Male

5 Marital status
☐ Married ☐ Single ☐ Divorced ☐ Widow

6 Year of university study
☐ First ☐ Second ☐ Third ☐ Fourth

7 In which College do you study?
☐ College of Arts ☐ College of Science

8 a) Does your father work?
☐ Yes ☐ No
b) If so, what is his occupation?
☐ Unemployed ☐ Retired
☐ Government Sector ☐ Private Sector

9 Level of father's education
☐ Illiterate ☐ Primary ☐ Secondary
☐ Preparatory ☐ University ☐ Higher education

10 a) Does your mother work?

☐ Yes   ☐ No

   b) If yes, what is her occupation?

☐ Unemployed   ☐ Retired

☐ Government Sector   ☐ Private Sector

11 Level of mother's education

☐ Illiterate   ☐ Primary   ☐ Secondary

☐ University and over

12 Who is usually responsible for making decisions in your family?

☐ Father   ☐ Mother   ☐ Both   ☐ All the family

13 How many people live in your household?

☐ Less than 2   ☐ 2–4   ☐ 5–7   ☐ 8–10

☐ 11–13   ☐ 14–16   ☐ 17–19

14 a) What is your family income (per month in thousand Dinars)?

☐ Less than 120 ☐ 121–199   ☐ 200–300

☐ 301–500   ☐ 501 and over

   b) How would you classify/categorise the social status of your family?

☐ Working Class   ☐ Lower Middle   ☐ Middle

☐ Upper Middle   ☐ Upper

15 What kind of house do you live in?

☐ Villa   ☐ Apartment/flat   ☐ An old house

16 Do you feel free to talk to your parents about your or your family's issues/concerns?

☐ Yes   ☐ No

   b) If yes whom do you talk to?

☐ Father   ☐ Mother   ☐ Both

17 Do you ever think of yourself as belonging to any particular class?

☐ Yes, Middle class   ☐ Yes, Working class   ☐ Yes, Upper class

18   a) Do you belong to any tribe?

☐   Yes   ☐   No

    b)   If yes, please indicate how loyal you are to your tribe?

☐   Very loyal   ☐   Fairly loyal

☐   Not very loyal   ☐   Not at all loyal

19   If it were possible, would you like the Kurds to drop their tribal identifications and think of themselves only as Kurds?

☐   Yes   ☐   No

20   How closely attached or loyal do you feel to your local area city or village?

☐   Very closely   ☐   Fairly closely

☐   Not very close   ☐   Not at all close

21   What do you consider your national identity to be?

☐   Kurd   ☐   Iraqi Kurd

☐   Kurdistani   ☐   Kurdistani but not Iraqi

☐   Iraqi   ☐   More Iraqi than Kurd

☐   Iraqi not Kurd   ☐   I don't know

22   How closely attached or loyal do you feel to Kurdistan as a whole?

☐   Very close   ☐   Fairly close

☐   Not very close   ☐   Not at all close

23   How closely attached or loyal do you feel to Iraq as a whole?

☐   Very close   ☐   Fairly close

☐   Not very close   ☐   Not at all close

24   How proud are you of being a Kurdistani?

☐   Very proud   ☐   Not very proud

☐   Not at all proud   ☐   Not a Kurd

25   How proud are you of being an Iraqi?

☐   Very proud   ☐   Not very proud

☐   Not at all proud   ☐   Not Iraqi

26 When you see the Iraqi flag, does it make you feel proud or hostile
    or do you not feel much either way?

☐ Very proud   ☐ A bit proud   ☐ Don't feel much either way
☐ A bit hostile   ☐ Very hostile

27 When you see the Kurdistani flag, does it make you feel proud or
    hostile or do you not feel much either way?

☐ Very proud   ☐ A bit proud   ☐ Don't feel much either way
☐ A bit hostile   ☐ Very hostile

28 Which of these statements comes closest to your view?
☐ Kurdistan should become independent, separate from Iraq.
☐ Kurdistan should become independent, separate from Iraq and
   the other three parts of Kurdistan should join us.
☐ Kurdistan should remain part of Iraq, with its own elected
   parliament, but with more federalist power.
☐ Kurdistan should remain part of Iraq, without an elected
   parliament or federal system.

29 The Kurdish Parliament has no power compared with the two
    major Political Parties.
☐ Strongly agree   ☐ Agree   ☐ Disagree
☐ Strongly disagree   ☐ Don't know

30 Is it necessary for a Kurd to learn and speak Arabic?
☐ Yes   ☐ No   ☐ I don't know

31 How important do you think it is to share the same religion with
    a mate?
☐ Very important   ☐ Not very important

32 Do you think that Islam is the vital factor for Kurdish unity?
☐ Strongly agree   ☐ Agree
☐ Strongly disagree   ☐ Don't know

33 How important do you think it is to be Kurdish or Kurdistani?

☐ Very important   ☐ Not important   ☐ Don't know

34 How important do you think it is to speak the Kurdish language?

☐ Very important   ☐ Not important   ☐ Don't know

35 What are the major factors, which consolidate Kurdish National Identity?

☐ National Factor   ☐ Political Factor

☐ Economic Factor   ☐ Linguistic Factor

☐ Territorial Factor   ☐ Educational Factor

☐ Other Factors. Please identify

36 Language of teaching and studying at the university should be in

☐ Kurdish   ☐ English   ☐ Kurdish & English

☐ Arabic   ☐ Kurdish & Arabic

37 University education ought to be less under the control of the government

☐ Strongly agree   ☐ Agree   ☐ Disagree

☐ Strongly disagree   ☐ Don't know

38 a) Are you a member of any political party?

☐ Yes   ☐ No

   b) If yes which party is it?

   c) If not, why not?

39 Please indicate how loyal you feel to the KDP?

☐ Very loyal   ☐ Fairly loyal

☐ Not very loyal   ☐ Not at all loyal

40 Please indicate how loyal you feel to the PUK?

☐ Very loyal   ☐ Fairly loyal

☐ Not very loyal   ☐ Not at all loyal

41 Does 'Kurdishness' need to be bound to political parties?

☐ Yes   ☐ No

42 In the last election which Kurdish political party did you vote for?
☐ KDP   ☐ PUK   ☐ KCP   ☐ IM
☐ I didn't vote

43 Do you discuss political affairs, local or international?
☐ Yes   ☐ No

44 What do you think of the American and British war of 2003 in Iraq? Was it:
☐ Invasion   ☐ Liberation
☐ Invasion but it was good for the Kurds in the end

45 What kind of mass media do you make use of?
☐ Internet   ☐ Radio   ☐ Newspapers
☐ Television   ☐ Magazines ☐ All of the above

46 Do you think that the current situation in Iraq is directly relevant to Kurdistan?
☐ Yes   ☐ No

47 Has the general standard of living in Kurdistan after 2003 increased or fallen?
☐ Increased a lot   ☐ Increased a little
☐ Stayed the same   ☐ Fallen a little   ☐ Fallen a lot

48 Kurdistan's Parliament should be given more power
☐ Strongly agree   ☐ Agree
☐ Disagree   ☐ Strongly disagree

49 What do you think of the unification of the two administrations of the KDP and the PUK in 2006?
☐ Good for the Kurds   ☐ It makes no difference
☐ I don't know

Appendix 7
Map of Greater Kurdistan

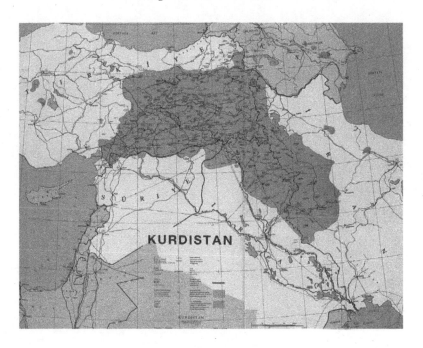

Map A.1 The Boundaries of the Greater Kurdistan Region

Source: www.institutkurde.org.

NOTES

The Construction of Kurdish National Identity in Iraqi Kurdistan

1   'Ethnonationalism' is useful because it distinguishes state-seeking nationalism from the nationalism of existing states; and it captures the ethnic-cultural dimension of the former. Ethnonationalism is the action of a group that claims some degree of self-government on the grounds that it is united by a special sense of solidarity emanating from one or more shared features that makes it a 'nation.' The manifestation of ethnonationalism is a nationalist movement which consists of nationalist parties and organizations. See Walker Connor, *Ethnonationalism: The Quest for Understanding* (Princeton, New Jersey: Princeton University Press, 1994).

2   Walker Connor, 'The Politics of Ethnonationalism,' *Journal of International Affairs*, Vol. 27, No. 1, 1973: 1–21; Walker Connor, 'Ethnonationalism.' In *Understanding Political Development*, edited by Myron Weiner and Samuel Huntington (Massachusetts: Little Brown and Company, 1987), 196–220.

3   Walker Connor, 'Beyond Reason: The Nature of the Ethnonational Bond,' *Ethnic and Racial Studies*, Vol. 16, No. 3, July 1993: 373–89.

4   Stephen Cornell, 'The Variable Ties that Bind,' *Ethnic and Racial Studies*, Vol. 19, No. 2, April 1996: 265–89.

5   Rogers Brubaker, *Nationalism Reframed: Nationhood and the National Question in the New Europe* (Cambridge: Cambridge University Press, 1996), 1–10. Brubaker's study of the recent history of nationalisms in Eastern Europe and the former Soviet Union explores how particular representations of the nation are institutionalized as part of a process of nation-state building. See p. 1.

6   Connor, *Ethnonationalism*, p. 223.

7   Anthony D. Smith, *Theories of Nationalism*, p. 27; and John Hutchinson and Anthony D. Smith, (eds.), *Nationalism* (Oxford: Oxford University Press, 1994), p. 3.

8   David McCrone, *et al.*, (eds.), 'Who Are We? Problematising National Identity,' *Sociological Review*, Vol. 4, No. 46, 1998: 629–52, at 629.

9   Mark Muller and Sharon Linzey, *The Internally Displaced Kurds of Turkey: Ongoing Issues of Responsibility, Redress and Resettlement* (London: Kurdish Human Rights Project, Bar Human Rights Committee of England and Wales, 2007), pp. 17–8, at 18. The number of Kurds worldwide is believed to be around 30 million, though some think it as high as 40 million.

10   Nezan Kendal, 'The Kurds: Current Position and Historical Background.' In
     Kurdish Culture and Identity, edited by Philip G. Kreyenbroek and Christine
     Allison (London and New Jersey: Zed Books Ltd, 1996), p. 14.

11   On 5 April 1991 the UN Security Council passed Resolution 688 condemning
     the repression of the Iraqi civilian population throughout Iraq. On 19 May
     1992 the Kurds had their first free election in Kurdistan. See Gareth R. V.
     Stansfield, *Iraqi Kurdistan: Political Development and Emergent Democracy*
     (London: RoutledgeCurzon, 2003), pp. 95–6.

12   Our treatment of the *Kurdistani* concept is distinguished from that of Gareth
     Stansfield and Hashem Ahmadzadeh. They refer to civic regionalism as part of
     Kurdistani identity; the dichotomy of civic and ethnic conceptions of *Kurdistani*
     identity is the focus. *Cf.* Gareth Stansfield and Hashem Ahmadzadeh, 'Kurdish
     or Kurdistanis? Conceptualizing Regionalism in North Iraq.' In *An Iraq of Its
     Region, Cornerstones of a Federal Democracy?* edited by Reidar Visser and Gareth
     Stansfield (London: Hurst Publishers Ltd, 2007), 123–49.

13   Erbil, or Arbil ('Hawler' in Kurdish), is the capital of Iraqi Kurdistan. This
     city has been regarded as one of the world's oldest continuously settled towns,
     having been continuously inhabited for about 8,000 years. The earliest records
     referring to 'Arab'ilu' belong to the late 3rd millennium BC. It lies on a flat,
     rich and fertile plain between the Great Zab and the Lesser Zab rivers. 'Erbil'
     was mentioned in the Sumerian holy writings (about 2,000 BC) as 'Orbelum'
     or 'Urbilum' and in the Arab and Assyrian texts as 'Arba-Elu'. The name can
     also refer to Helios, the sun god, making the city a place of worship of the sun.
     Hawler is famous for its ancient citadel (*Qala*) and minaret. For more informa-
     tion on Erbil and how it developed, see Mahir Abdulwahid Aziz, *al-Tatawur
     al-Hathari fi madinat Erbil, (Urban Development in Erbil City)*, Unpublished
     Master's Thesis, University of Baghdad, 1990, pp. 5–6. Suleimaniya is the
     second-largest city in the region. According to some nationalist Kurds, it is
     the capital of Kurdish nationalism. Dohuk is the third city in terms of size and
     population.

14   *Rapareen* is the Kurdish word for uprising and *intifada* is the Arabic word for
     it.

15   Sami Zubaida, 'Introduction.' In *The Kurds: A Contemporary Overview*, edited
     by Philip G. Kreyenbroek and Stefan Sperl (London: Routledge, 1992), p. 4.

16   Mehrdad R. Izady, *The Kurds: A Concise Handbook* (London: Taylor and Francis,
     1992), p. 133; and Sa'ad Jawad, *Iraq and the Kurdish Question: 1958–1970*
     (London: Ithaca Press, 1981), p. 3.

17   UNDP Iraq Living Condition Survey, Vol. 1. Tabulation Report, Table 1.6,
     2004 (cited on KRG website: http://www.krg.org).

18   Oil-for-Food Distribution Plan, approved by the UN, December 2002 (cited
     on KRG website: http://www.krg.org).

19   Figures taken from the Commission of the European Communities, Regular
     Report on Turkey's Progress Towards Accession (2007) European Commission
     p. 39; accessed at http://ec.europa.eu/-enlargement/archives/pdf/key_docu-
     ments/2004/rr)tr_2004_en.pdf. Retrieved on 3 September 2007.

20   Muller and Linzey, *The Internally Displaced Kurds*, p. 18.

21   David L. Phillips, 'Power-Sharing with Iraqi Kurds,' Center for Preventive
     Action, Council on Foreign Relations. 10 June 2004, p. 11.

22 UNDP Iraq Living Conditions Survey, Vol. 1, Tabulation Report, Table 1.12: Displacement due to war, 2004 (cited on KRG website: http://www.krg.org).

23 The International Covenant on Civil and Political Rights. Concluded at New York, Dec. 16, 1966. Entered into force, Mar. 23, 1976. 999 U.N.T.S. 171. In *Human Rights*, edited by Louis Henkin, Gerald L. Neuman, Diane F. Orentlicher, David W. Leebron (New York: Foundation Press, 2001), pp. 57–74.

24 Taken from KRG's old website: http://old.krg.org/about/ministries/reconstruction/index.asp.

25 Izady, *The Kurds*, p. 131; Michiel Leezenberg, 'Political Islam among the Kurds,' paper presented for the International Conference 'Kurdistan: The Unwanted State,' Jagiellonian University, Polish-Kurdish Society, Cracow, Poland, 29–31 March 2001: 1–26, at 1. For an account of Zoroastrianism, see Philip G. Kreyenbroek, 'Religion and Religions in Kurdistan.' In *Kurdish Culture*, edited by Kreyenbroek, *et al.*, pp. 96–9. For an analysis of Kurdistan before Islam, see Maria T. O'Shea, *Trapped Between the Map and Reality: Geography and Perception of Kurdistan* (London: Routledge, 2004), pp. 71–3.

26 John Bulloch and Harvey Morris, *No Friends but the Mountains: The Tragic History of the Kurds* (London: Penguin Books, 1993), p. 59.

27 Mahir Abdulwahid Aziz, '*al A'ila wadawruhu fi ul Tanshi'a al Igtima'ia*,' (The Family Role in Socialization), *Gulan Al-Arabi*: Monthly General Political-Cultural Magazine, No. 74. 31 July 2002: 98–105, at 101–2; and Leezenberg, 'Political Islam,' *op.cit.*, pp. 1–6.

28 On the role of the Mullas, see Bruinessen *Agha, Shaikh*, pp. 209–10; and Leezenberg, 'Political Islam,' pp. 1–2.

29 Kreyenbroek, 'Religion and Religions in Kurdistan,' *op.cit.*, pp. 92–105; Entessar, *Kurdish Ethnonationalism*, p. 9; and Bruinessen, *Agha, Shaikh*, pp. 270–98.

30 See Rayyan Al-Shawaf, 'The Destruction of Iraq's Christians,' *Daily News: Egypt*, 20 July 2007; Buckenmeyer, Jacob, 'US Commission Hears Testimony on Christians in Iraq,' *Catholic News Service*, 26 July 2007; Julia Duin, 'Iraq's Perils Dire for Minority Faiths,' *The Washington Times*, 26 July 2007; and 'USCRIF to Secretary Rice: US Must Address Threats to Religious Minorities in Iraq,' USCRIF Press Release, 6 September 2007.

31 Kreyenbroek, 'Religion and Religions in Kurdistan,' *op.cit.*, pp. 92–3. This figure is Bruinessen's estimate. McDowall assesses it at 75%. See David McDowall, *A Modern History of the Kurds*, (London: I.B.Tauris, 1996), p. 10; and Bruinessen, *Agha, Shaikh*, pp. 35–6.

32 Bruinessen, *Agha, Shaikh*, pp. 205 64; and Leezenberg, 'Political Islam,' *op.cit.*, p. 1.

33 Accessed at http://news.bbc.co.uk/2/hi/middle-east/1501327.stm, retrieved on 5 April 2006.

34 Carl-Mikael A. Teglund, *Economic Sanctions as Warfare: A Study about the Economic Sanctions on Iraq: 1990–2003*, Bachelor's thesis, Uppsala University, 2006, p. 38.

35 Accessed at http://www.un.org/depts/oip/background/index.html, retrieved on 29 April 2006.

36 Acting under Chapter VII of the UN Charter, the Security Council adopted Resolution 986 on 14 April 1995; establishing the Oil-for-Food programme.

This resolution provided Iraq with another opportunity to sell oil to finance the purchase of humanitarian goods and carry out UN mandated activities. The programme was intended to be a 'temporary measure to provide for the humanitarian needs of the Iraqi people until Iraq fulfilled relevant Security Council resolutions, notably Resolution 687 of 3 April 1991.' Accessed at http://news.bbc.co.uk/2/hi/middle_east/1501327.stm on 4.5.2006.

37 See Michiel Leezenberg, 'Economy and Society in Iraqi Kurdistan: Fragile Institutions and Enduring Trends.' In *Iraq at the Crossroads: State and Society in the Shadow of Regime Change*, edited by Toby Dodge and Steven Simon, International Institute of Strategic Studies, Adelphi Paper 354 (Oxford: Oxford University Press, 2003), 149–60.

38 David Pollock, *The Kurdish Regional Government in Iraq: An Inside Story.* In *The Future of the Iraqi Kurds*, edited by Soner Cagaptay, The Washington Institute for Near East Policy, Policy Focus 85, July 2008: 1–38, at 8.

39 *Ibid.*

40 *Ibid.*, pp. 8–9.

41 Data were obtained from the Directorate of Planning Office of Salahaddin University in 2007.

Nationalism, Nation, State, Nation State and Stateless Nation

1 Liah Greenfeld, *Nationalism: Five Roads to Modernity* (Cambridge, Mass: Harvard University Press, 1992), pp. 7–9. According to Miroslav Hroch, the term 'nationalism' entered academe rather late, perhaps no earlier than the work of the American historian Carlton Hayes with his *Historical Evolution of Modern Nationalism* (New York, 1931). See Miroslav Horch, 'From National Movement to the Fully-formed Nation: The Nation-building Process in Europe.' In *Mapping the Nation*, edited by Gopal Balakrishnan (London: Verso, 1996), 78–97, at 96, fn 2. It was mostly the historians, rather than sociologists or political scientists, who first paid attention to national phenomena at the beginning of the last century. The pioneering works of Carlton Hayes, Hans Kohn and Louis Snyder made national phenomena a subject of a sustained academic inquiry. For more information, see Umut Ozkirimli, *Theories of Nationalism: A Critical Introduction* (New York: Palgrave, 2000).

2 Paul Latawski, 'The Problem of Definition: Nationalism, Nation and Nation-State in East Europe.' In *Contemporary Nationalism in East Central Europe*, edited by Paul Latawski (New York: St. Martin's Press, 1995), p. 2.

3 Smith, *National Identity.* See also Peter Alter, *Nationalism* (London: Edward Arnold, 1989), 56–93.

4 Smith, *National Identity*, p.74. The italics are in the original text. See Anthony D. Smith, *Myths and Memories of the Nation* (Oxford and New York: Oxford University Press, 1999), p. 103.

5 Ernest Gellner, *Nations and Nationalism* (Ithaca, New York: Cornell University Press, 1983), p. 6.

6 *Ibid.*

7 Katherine Verdery, 'Whither "Nation" and "Nationalism"?' In *Mapping the Nation*, p. 229.

8 Connor, *Ethnonationalism*, chapter 4.

9 Smith, *National Identity*, pp. 8–15.

10   E. J. Hobsbawm, *Nations and Nationalism since 1780: Programme, Myth, Reality* (Cambridge: Cambridge University Press, 2d ed., 1997), p. 3.

11   Godfrey Baldacchino, 'A Nationless State? Malta, National Identity and the EU', *West European Politics*, Vol. 25, No. 4, October 2002: 191–206, at 192.

12   Alter, *Nationalism*, p. 18.

13   Connor, *Ethnonationalism*, p. 40. Nation-building is wrongly used to refer to what is usually and correctly known as 'state-building,' because the term 'state' is confused with the 50 states that comprise the United States.

14   Philip Abrams, 'Notes on the Difficulty of Studying the State,' *Journal of Historical Sociology*, Vol. 1, No. 1, March 1988: 58–89.

15   David Held, 'Introduction: Central perspectives on the Modern State.' In *States and Societies*, edited by David Held, *et al.*, (Oxford: Martin Robertson, 1983), p. 1.

16   *Ibid.*, p. 42.

17   Max Weber, 'Politics as Vocation.' In *From Max Weber: Essays in Sociology*, edited by H. H. Gerth and C. Wright Mills (London: Routledge, 1991), p. 78.

18   Stansfield, *Iraqi Kurdistan* , pp. 14–5.

19   Philip Schlesinger, 'On National Identity: Some Conceptions and Misconceptions Criticised,' *Social Science Information*, Vol. 26, No. 2, 1987: 219–64.

20   Michael Billig, *Banal Nationalism* (London: Sage Publications, 1995), pp. 24, 60 and 69. Billig treats national identity and nationalism from the understanding of the behaviourist school of psychology, which is avoided in this study.

21   Smith, *Nationalism: Theory*, p. 17.

22   Thomas K. Fitzgerald, *Metaphors of Identity* (Albany: State University of New York Press, 1993), p. 186.

23   Bhikhu Parekh, 'Defending National Identity in a Multicultural Society.' In *People, Nation and State: The Meaning of Ethnicity and Nationalism*, edited by Edward Mortimer and Robert Fine, (London: I.B.Tauris, 1999), 66–74, at 69.

24   Stuart Hall, 'Introduction: Who Needs 'Identity?' In *Questions of Cultural Identity*, edited by Stuart Hall and Paul Du Gay (London: Sage Publications, 1996), p. 4.

25   Michael Rush and Phillip Althoff, *An Introduction to Political Sociology* (London: Nelson, 1971), pp. 68–9.

26   Iain McLean, *Oxford Concise Dictionary of Politics* (Oxford: Oxford University Press, 1996), p. 379.

27   Rod Hague and Martin Harrop, *Comparative Government and Politics: An Introduction* (London: Palgrave, 2001), p. 78.

Approaches to the Study of Nationalism and National Identity

1   Smith, *National Identity*, p. 15.

2   *Ibid.*, p. 13.

3   Smith, *The Ethnic Origins*, pp. 134–5.

4   *Ibid.*, pp. 137–8.

5   *Ibid.*, p. 138.

6   Smith, *National Identity*, pp. 79–84.
7   John Hutchinson, *The Dynamics of Cultural Nationalism* (London: Allen and Unwin, 1987), p. 12.
8   *Ibid*, pp. 12–3.
9   Anthony D. Smith, *The Ethnic Revival* (Cambridge: Cambridge University Press, 1981), p. xii.
10 Smith, *Nationalism: Theory*, p.13; Smith, *National Identity*, p.14; Anthony D. Smith, 'The Origins of Nations,' *Ethnic and Racial Studies*, Vol. 12, No. 3, July 1989: 340–67; and Hutchinson, *The Dynamics*, pp. 12–3.
11 Smith prefers the French term *ethnie* to 'ethnic community'. He doesn't consider himself a 'primordialist', but calls his account of nationalism 'ethno-symbolic', which links modern nations to premodern *ethnies* through myth, symbol, memory, value and tradition. For more on Smith's ethno-symbolism paradigm, see Smith, *Nationalism: Theory*, pp. 4 and 57–8.
12 Smith, *The Ethnic Origins,* pp. 21–2.
13 Smith, *National Identity*, p. 39.
14 *Ibid.*, p. 40.
15 Anthony D. Smith, 'The Myth of the "Modern Nation" and the Myths of Nations', *Ethnic and Racial Studies*, Vol. 11, No. 1, January 1988: 1–26.
16 Smith, *National Identity*, pp. 39–40, and Smith, *Nationalism*, p. 13.
17 For more on these six dimensions see Smith, *The Ethnic Origins*, pp. 22–31.
18 Smith, *National Identity*, p. 73.
19 *Ibid.*, p. 74. See also, Smith, *Myths and Memories*, pp. 188–9.
20 *Ibid.*
21 *Ibid.*, pp. 13–6.
22 *Ibid.*, pp. 153–200.
23 Anthony D. Smith, *Nations and Nationalism in a Global Era* (Cambridge: Polity Press, 1995), p. xiii.
24 *Ibid.*
25 *Ibid.*, p. 40.
26 *Ibid.*, p. 13.
27 *Ibid.*, p. 14.
28 *Ibid.*, p. viii.
29 *Ibid.*, pp. 5–6.
30 Smith, *The Ethnic Revival*, pp. 66 and 85.
31 Anthony D. Smith, 'Culture, Community and Territory: The Politics of Ethnicity and Nationalism', *International Affairs*, Vol. 72, No. 3, July 1996: 445–58, at 450–1.
32 *Ibid.*, p. 451.
33 Smith, *Nations and Nationalism*, p. 13
34 *Ibid.*, p. 158.
35 *Ibid.*, pp. 80–1.
36 Smith, *The Ethnic Origins*, p. 129.
37 *Cf.*, David McDowall, *The Kurds: A Nation Denied* (London: Minority Rights Publication, 1992), p. 11.
38 Smith, *The Ethnic Origins*, pp. 22–3.
39 *Ibid.*, p. 23.
40 *Ibid.*, p. 24.

41 *Ibid.*, pp. 24–25.
42 *Ibid.*, pp. 211–2.
43 Abdul Rahman Ghassemlou, *Kurdistan and the Kurds* (London: Collet's Publishers, 1965), p. 35.
44 Stephen C. Pelletiere, *The Kurds: An Unstable Element in the Gulf* (London: Westview Press, 1984), p. 22.
45 Mir Sharafkhani Bdlisi, *Sharafnama: Mezhuy Mala Mirani Kurdistan,* (Sharafnama: The History of Mula Mir's of Kurdistan), Kurdish trans. by Mamosta Hazhar, (Hawler, Aras Publishing House, No. 410, 2006). Most Persians in Iran regard Karim Khan-e-Zand as a Persian, not a Kurd.
46 Jwaideh, *The Kurdish National Movement*, p. 37, cited in Hassanpour, *Language*, p. 50.
47 *Mami Alan* or *Mam u Zin* is an epic drama that Ahmadi Khani (1650–1706) refers to in 1696. *Mam* of the Alan clan and *Zin* of the rival *Botan* clan are two lovers whose union is prevented by a certain Bakir of the *Bakran* clan. *Mam* eventually dies. While mourning the death of her lover on his grave, *Zin* falls dead of grief and is buried next to him. See Izady, *The Kurds*, p. 176.
48 Hakan Ozoglu, *Kurdish Notables and the Ottoman State: Evolving Identities, Competing Loyalties and Shifting Boundaries* (Albany: State University of New York Press, 2004), p. 22; Ghassemlou, *Kurdistan*, pp. 41–4; and Bulloch, *et al., No Friends but the Mountains*, p. 50.
49 In 614 BC Assur, the first capital of Assyria was sacked by the Medes under King Cyaxares. The Medes and the Persians defeated the Assyrians in 612 BC after a mere three-month siege. The Babylonian army defeated the Assyrian–Egyptian alliance at the Battle of Carchemish in 605 BC and Assyria never again existed as an independent nation.
50 Izady, *The Kurds*, p. 34.
51 Smith, *The Ethnic Origins*, p. 26.
52 *Ibid*, pp. 26–7. For our account of the Kurdish language as an important marker of ethnicity and national identity, see Chapter 4.
53 The Yezidi religion is a syncretistic combination of Zoroastrian, Manichaean, Jewish and Nestorian Christian with Islamic *Shi'a* and *Sufi* elements and has many variants. They believe that they were created separately from the rest of mankind and are descended from Adam only—not from Adam and Eve like the rest of humanity. They have therefore kept themselves isolated from others where they live and do not intermarry. They call themselves 'children of Adam' and see themselves as a chosen people. See Sharon F. Linzey, *Turkey's Compliance with Its Obligations: The Context of Turkey's Law on Compensation for Damage arising from Terrorist Acts,* Unpublished L.L.M. Thesis, Cornell Law School, 2006.
54 However, Yezidism is probably the only truly ethnic religion in the world. It is practiced *only* by the Kurds. So while all Kurds are not Yezidi, all Yezidis are Kurds. See Linzey Ibid.
55 Camille Overson Hensler and Mark Muller, *Freedom of Expression and of Association in Turkey* (London: Kurdish Human Rights Project & Bar Human Rights Committee of England and Wales, November 2005), p. 17.
56 *Ibid.*, p. 28
57 *Ibid.*, p. 29.

58   *Ibid.*
59   *Ibid.,* p. 31.
60   Smith, *National Identity,* p. 75.
61   Guibernau, *Nationalisms,* p. 80.
62   Pal Kolsto, 'National Symbols as Signs of Unity and Division,' *Ethnic and Racial Studies,* Vol. 29, No. 4, July 2006: 676–701 at 676.
63   See Benedict Anderson, *Imagined Communities: Reflections on the Origin and Spread of Nationalism* (Revised Edition. London: Verso, 1991).
64   Emile Durkheim, *Elementary Forms of Religious Life.* Trans. by J. W. Swain (London: Allen & Unwin, 1957), p. 220.
65   On 5 February 2008 Iraq removed the three stars from the Iraqi national flag, which referred to the three aims of the *Ba'th* Party (unity, freedom and socialism). Since then, the new Iraqi flag has been raised on the governmental buildings in Kurdistan.
66   Kolsto, 'National Symbols as Signs', p. 679. The Kurdish poem, *Ay Raqib,* (*Oh Enemy*), by Dildar, (also known as Younis Ra'uf, 1917–48), is a most effective nationalist symbol for the Iraqi Kurds, as is the marching song or national anthem of the Kurds asserting their origin as Medes ('We are the sons of Medes' and *Kay Khusraw,* 'Our religion and faith is Kurdistan').
67   Smith, *The Ethnic Origins,* p.154. I disagree with Smith here. The demand for autonomy appeared alongside the struggle for participation in legislative and executive power in Iraq. In the mid-seventies Kurdish leadership accepted autonomy as the best solution and as a political means for obtaining political ends. But the Kurdish aspiration for independence has always been the ultimate dream. The result of the referendum of 2002 is a good example of this fact.
68   Ozoglu, *Kurdish Notables,* pp. 47–51.
69   Hobsbawm, *Nations and Nationalism,* p. 78.
70   *Ibid.,* pp. 46–79.
71   *Ibid.,* p. 64.
72   *Ibid.,* pp. 64, 73 and 77.
73   Smith, *Nationalism: Theory,* p.48.
74   McCrone, *The Sociology,* p. 5.
75   Anderson, *Imagined Communities,* p. 6.
76   *Ibid.,* p. 6. Italics in the original.
77   *Ibid.,* p. 4.
78   Seton-Watson, *Nations and States,* p. 5.
79   Anderson, *Imagined Communities,* pp. 3–6.
80   *Ibid.,* p. 7.
81   *Ibid.,* pp. 7 and 9–36.
82   *Ibid.,* p. 12.
83   *Ibid.,* pp. 12–8.
84   *Ibid.,* pp. 12 and 19.
85   Smith, *Nationalism: Theory,* p. 48.
86   Anderson, *Imagined Communities,* pp. 42–4.
87   *Ibid.,* p. 36.
88   *Ibid.*
89   Guibernau, *Nationalisms,* p. 66.
90   Anderson, *Imagined Communities,* pp. 44–6.

91 *Ibid.,* pp. 17–49.
92 Smith, *Myths and Memories,* p. 6.
93 Anthony D. Smith, *Nationalism and Modernism: A Critical Survey of Recent Theories of Nations and Nationalism* (London: Routledge, 1998), p. 145.

Making Sense of Kurdish History:
Territory, Language and Proto-Nationalism

1   Anthony D. Smith, 'The Crises of Dual Legitimation.' In *Nationalism,* pp. 113–21, at 113 and 117.
2   Smith, *Nations and Nationalism,* pp. 5–6
3   Referring to the Scottish case, David McCrone confirms that in Scotland a 'sense of tribe' (defining Scottishness in terms of blood and genealogy) is perhaps weaker than the 'sense of place' (residence, territory). See McCrone, *The Sociology,* p. 42.
4   McDowall, *A Modern History,* pp. 2–3.
5   Smith, *The Ethnic Origins,* p. 135.
6   *Ibid.,* pp. 76–77.
7   *Ibid.,* pp. 81–3.
8   Izady, *The Kurds,* pp. 32–4.
9   Smith, *The Ethnic Origins,* pp. 83–5.
10 Izady, *The Kurds,* p. 34; and O'Shea, *Trapped Between,* p. 66. Izady claims too much for the Kurds and his periodization is exaggerated.
11 O'Shea, *Trapped Between,* pp. 63–92. From a geopolitical point of view O'Shea sees Greater Kurdistan as a buffer zone between the Persians and Ottomans. Martin van Bruinessen shares the same idea. According to Eskander, it was at the Cairo conference (12 March 1921) that the British government favoured a separate Kurdish entity in the shape of a 'buffer zone'. See Saad Eskander, 'Southern Kurdistan under Britain's Mesopotamian Mandate: From Separation to Incorporation 1920–3,' *Journal of Middle Eastern Studies,* Vol. 37, No. 2, April 2001: 153–80, at 154–6.
12 Godfrey Rolles Driver, 'The Name "Kurd" and its Connexions,' *Journal of Royal Asiatic Society of Great Britain and Ireland (JRAS),* July, Part III, 1923: 393–404, at 393ff, cited also in Ozoglu, *Kurdish Notables,* p. 23.
13 See Genesis 10:2 in *The New Oxford Annotated Bible: New Revised Standard Version with the Apocrypha.* Michael D. Coogan, Marc Zvi Brettler, Carol A. Newsom and Pheme Perkins, (eds.), 3rd edition (New York: Oxford University Press, 2007). Scholars estimate the timeline of Japheth's birth to be approximately 2500 BC.
14 Robert L. Brenneman, *As Strong as the Mountains,* (Long Grove, IL: Waveland Press, 2007), p. 18. Dutch theologian Ellen Van Wolde traces the sons of Japheth to their ancestral places of residence and states that *Madai* was the father of the Medes who migrated south of the Caspian Sea and north of the Tigris River. See Ellen Van Wolde, *Stories of the Beginning* (Ridgefield, CT: Morehouse, 1997).
15 Brenneman, *As Strong as the Mountains,* p. 18.
16 Godfrey Rolles Driver, 'The Name "Kurd" and its Connexions,' *op.cit.*
17 Ghassemlou, *Kurdistan,* p. 34; Bulloch, *et al., No Friends but the Mountains,* p. 55; Izady, *The Kurds,* p. 35; and Pelletiere, *The Kurds,* p. 20.

18   Jemal Rashid Ahmad, *Dirasat Kurdiyah fi bilad Subartu*, (Kurdish Studies in
      the Country of Subartu), Baghdad, 1984; and Jemal Rashid Ahmad, *Tarikh
      al-Kurd al-Qadim*, (The Ancient History of the Kurds), (Hawler: Salahaddin
      University Publisher, 1990).
19   Ghassemlou, *Kurdistan*, p. 34.
20   Martin van Bruinessen, 'Kurdish Society, Ethnicity, Nationalism and Refugee
      Problems.' In *The Kurds*, edited by Kreyenbroek, *et al.*, p. 48.
21   Derk Kinnane, *The Kurds and Kurdistan* (London: Oxford University Press,
      1964), p. 12; Kerim Yildiz, *The Kurds in Iraq: The Past, Present and Future*
      (London: Pluto Press, 2004), p. 7; McDowall, *A Modern History*, p. 6; Kendal,
      'The Kurds,' p. 10; and Ozoglu, *Kurdish Notables*, p. 26.
22   Izady, *The Kurds*, p. 41.
23   *Ibid.*, p. 46.
24   Boris James, *Uses and Values of the Term 'Kurd' in Arabic Medieval Literary
      Sources*, paper presented in the World Congress of Kurdish Studies, University
      of Salahaddin, Erbil, 6–9 September 2006.
25   *Ibid.*
26   Bruinessen, *Agha, Shaikh*, p. 111.
27   Bruinessen, *Kurdish Ethno-Nationalism versus Nation-Building States: Collected
      articles* (Istanbul: The ISIS Press, 2000), pp. 16–8.
28   Cecil John Edmonds, 'Kurdish Nationalism,' *Journal of Contemporary History*,
      Vol. 6, No. 1, Nationalism and Separatism, 1971: 87–107, at 87.
29   *Ibid.*, p. 26; and Khasbak, *al Kurd wal-Mas'ala al-Kurdiyai fil Iraq*, p. 13.
30   Ozoglu, *Kurdish Notables*, pp. 22–6.
31   Muhammad Rashid Al-Feel, *al Akrad fi Nathar al Elm*, (The Kurds from the
      Viewpoint of Science), Baghdad, 1965.
32   Guibernau, *Nationalisms*, pp. 66–71.
33   Anderson, *Imagined Communities*, pp. 37–46.
34   *Ibid.*, p. 45.
35   Gellner, *Thought and Change*, p. 195.
36   Smith, *The Ethnic Origins*, pp. 6–16.
37   Manuel Castells, *The Power of Identity: The Information Age: Economy, Society
      and Culture.* (Oxford, United Kingdom: Blackwell Publication Ltd., Vol. 2,
      2nd edition, 2004), p. 52.
38   Philip G. Kreyenbroek, 'On the Kurdish Language.' In *The Kurds*, p. 70;
      Ghassemlou, *Kurdistan*, p. 26; McDowall, *A Modern History*, p. 9; Joyce
      Blau, 'Kurdish Written Literature.' In *Kurdish Culture and Identity*, Philip G.
      Kreyenbroek and Christine Allison, (eds.) (London, New Jersey: Zed Book
      Ltd, 1996), p. 20; Izady, *The Kurds*, p. 167. Izady's classification and analysis
      of the Kurdish language are very confusing and misleading as he divides the
      Kurdish language into two major groups: Kurmanji and Pahlawani. Kurmanji
      is further divided into two branches, Bahdinani and Sorani, whereas Pahlawani
      is divided into the two branches of Dimili (or Zaza) and Gurani. *Ibid.*, p.167.
39   Mahir Abdulwahid Aziz, 'al Shakhsia al Kurdia: Dirasa Igtima'ia fi thaw' al
      Anthropologia al Hatharia,' (Kurdish Personality: A Social Study in Cultural
      Anthropology), *Gulan Al-Arabi*, Monthly General Political-Cultural Magazine,
      Erbil Kurdistan, No. 73, 30 June 2002: 61–6.; and Aziz, 'al A'ila wadawruha fi
      al Tanshi'a al Igtima'ia,' (Family Role in Socialization), at 103.

40   Bruinessen, *Agha, Shaikh*, pp. 21–2; and Bruinessen, 'Kurdish Society,' *op.cit.*, p. 35.

41   Arfa, *The Kurds*, p. 4.

42   McDowall, *A Modern History*, pp. 9–10. 'Despite not having a single systematized written or spoken language, the Kurdish language is composed of two major dialects: Kirmanji and Sorani and four sub-dialects: Kirmanshahi, Leki, Gurani and Zaza.' For more on this, see McDowall, *The Kurds*, pp. 12–13.

43   Kreyenbroek, 'On the Kurdish Language,' *op.cit.*, pp. 70–1.

44   Entessar, *Kurdish Ethnonationalism*, p. 4.

45   *Ibid.*, pp. 4–5.

46   *Ibid.*, p. 4.

47   *Ibid.*, p. 5. See also, Amir Hassanpour, 'Kurdish Studies: Orientalist, Positivist and Critical Approaches: Review of Nader Entessar's *Kurdish Ethnonationalism*, *Middle East Journal*, Vol. 47, No. 1 Winter, 1993: 119–22.

48   Stansfield, *Iraqi Kurdistan*, p. 37. Stansfield's and other Western scholars' assessment of these dialects as languages is disputed. The diversity of dialects is natural in such mountainous regions where pre-twentieth century communications are difficult. In June 2008 the KRG Parliament passed a law which mandates the use of the Latin alphabet, rather than Arabic, for writing in Kurdish. There is discussion in cultural and academic centres in Kurdistan regarding uniting the major two dialects.

49   Ghassemlou, *Kurdistan*, p. 27.

50   Izady, *The Kurds*, p. 178.

51   Kreyenbroek, 'On the Kurdish Language,' *op.cit.*, p. 69.

52   Sajadi, *Mejouy Adabi Kurdi*, pp. 146–287.

53   *Ibid.*, p. 72.

54   Anderson, *Imagined Communities*, p. 45.

55   Hobsbawm, *Nations and Nationalism*, p. 60.

56   *Ibid.*, p. 61.

57   Jwaideh, *The Kurdish National Movement*, pp. 37–42. *Mirnisheen* is the Kurdish word for 'principality' and *Imara* (Emirate) is the Arabic word for it. *Mir* is the Kurdish version for *Amir* which means 'the Prince'.

58   *Ibid.*, p. 39.

59   McDowall, *The Kurds*, pp. 26–7.

60   Ioannis N. Grigoriadis, 'Turkey's Political Culture and Minorities,' paper presented at the International Conference 'Nationalism, Society and Culture in post-Ottoman South East Europe' May 29–30, 2004, St Peter's College, Oxford University, Oxford, 1–24 at 7–11.

61   Bruinessen, *Agha, Shaikh*, pp. 138–40; and Ghassemlou, *Kurdistan*, pp. 36–9.

62   See Bdlisi, *Sharafnama*.

63   Bruinessen, 'Kurdish Society,' p. 48. Also see Hassanpour, *The Making of Kurdish Identity*, pp. 111–4.

64   Martin van Bruinessen, '*Ehmedi Xani's Mem u Zin* and Its Role in the Emergence of Kurdish National Awareness.' In *Essays on the Origins of Kurdish Nationalism*, edited by Abbas Vali (Costa Mesa, California: Mazda Publishers, 2003), pp. 40–57.

65   *Ibid.*, p. 41.

66   Sajadi, *Mejouy Adabi Kurdi*, pp. 204–06; Vali, 'Genealogies of the Kurds,' *op.cit.*, p. 22. For an account of *Mam u Zin*, see Martin Strohmeier, *Crucial*

Images in the Presentation of a Kurdish National Identity: Heroes and Patriots, Traitors and Foes (Leiden: Brill, 2003), 27–35.

67 Hassanpour, 'The Making of Kurdish Identity,' *op.cit.*, p. 120.

68 Sajadi, *Mejouy Adabi Kurdi*, pp. 324–7

69 Saad Basheer Eskander, '*Qiyam al-Nitham al-Imarati fi Kurdistan wa Suqutuhu: Mabain Muntasaf al-Qarn al-Ashir wa Muntasaf al-Qarn al- Tasi' Ashar,*' (The Rise and Fall of the Principality System in Kurdistan: Between the Tenth and Mid-Nineteenth Centuries), *Dar al-Shu'un al-Thaqafia al-Ama*, Baghdad, 2005: 378–98.

70 Robert Olson, *The Emergence of Kurdish Nationalism and the Sheikh Said Rebellion*, 1880–1925 (Austin: University of Texas Press, 1989).

71 Janet Klein, 'Kurdish Nationalists and Non-nationalist Kurdists: Rethinking Minority Nationalism and the Dissolution of the Ottoman Empire, 1908–1909,' *Nations and Nationalism*, Vol. 13, No. 1, 2007: 135–53 at 137.

72 *Ibid.*, p. 145.

73 *Ibid.*, p. 146.

74 The essence of the Kurdish 'question' for the Kurds is being a nation without a state. Many scholars refer to 1880 as the first time the Kurdish leaders appeared to have explicit ideas as to a separate Kurdish state. For more on this, see Jwaideh, *The Kurdish National Movement*, and Olson, *The Emergence of Kurdish Nationalism*.

75 Hobsbawm, *Nations and Nationalism*, p. 46. (Italics in the original.)

76 Ozoglu, *Kurdish Notables*, p. 70.

The Historical and Socio-Political Conditions for the Development of Kurdish Nationalism: 1921–91

1 Gareth Stansfield, 'The Kurdish Question in Iraq: 1914–1947,' Middle East, On Line, Series 2, Introductory Essays, The National Archives, UK, 2007, p. 2. For more on the Mosul question, see Charles Tripp, *A History of Iraq* (Cambridge: Cambridge University Press, 2000), pp. 58–60; and O'Shea, *Trapped Between*, pp. 141–5.

2 Ghareeb, 'The Kurdish Issue,' In *Iraq: Its History, People and Politics*, p. 168; and Tripp, *A History of Iraq*, pp. 58–9.

3 O'Shea *Trapped Between*, p. 116. For more on the British policy in Iraqi Kurdistan, see Saad Eskander, 'Britain's Policy in Southern Kurdistan: The Formation and the Termination of the First Kurdish Government, 1918–9,' *British Journal of Middle Eastern Studies*, Vol. 27, No. 2, 2000: 129–63; see also, Eskander, 'Southern Kurdistan,' *op.cit.*

4 O'Shea *Trapped Between*, pp. 128–39.

5 Jwaideh, *The Kurdish National Movement*, pp. 471–516; Arfa, *The Kurds*, pp. 112–13; and McDowall, *A Modern History*, p. 156.

6 Jwaideh, *The Kurdish National Movement*, pp. 511–12; Arfa, *The Kurds*, p. 113; and McDowall, *A Modern History*, p. 156.

7 McDowall, *The Kurds*, pp. 81–3.

8 Edgar O'Ballance, *The Kurdish Struggle: 1920–94* (London: Macmillan Press Ltd, 1996), p. 20; and Chaliand, *The Kurdish Tragedy*, pp. 54–5.

9 The British Ambassador to Iran made this statement, chastising his council in Tabriz who was sympathetic toward some Kurdish nationalist projects. See McDowall, *A Modern History*, p. 199; and Romano, *The Kurdish Nationalist*, p. 36.

10   Muller and Linzey, *The Internally Displaced Kurds*, p. 19.
11   President Woodrow Wilson's *Fourteen Point Programme for World Peace* (1918) made clear the Great Powers' concern that minorities of the Ottoman Empire be 'assured of an absolute unmolested opportunity of autonomous development.' Accessed at, http://usinfo.state.gov/usa/infousa/facts/demo-crac/51.htm. The United States Department of State, in September 2007.
12   Jwaideh, *The Kurdish National Movement*, p. 539; and McDowall, *The Kurds*, p. 33.
13   Muller and Linzey, *The Internally Displaced Kurds*, p. 19.
14   *Ibid.*
15   O'Shea, *Trapped Between*, pp. 139–40.
16   Muller and Linzey, *The Internally Displaced Kurds*, p. 19.
17   McDowall, *A Modern History*, p. 130; O'Shea, *Trapped Between*, p. 141; Muller and Linzey, *The Internally Displaced Kurds*, p. 19; and Bruinessen, *Kurdish Society*, pp. 272–3.
18   O'Shea, *Trapped Between*, pp. 80–3 and 141. Gertrude Margaret Lowthian Bell was a British writer, traveller, political analyst, administrator in Arabia and an archaeologist who mapped and identified Anatolian and Mesopotamian ruins. She was appointed Commander of the Order of the British Empire in 1917.
19   Jwaideh, *The Kurdish National Movement*, p. 567; and Bruinessen, *Kurdish Society*, p. 273.
20   Ghareeb, 'The Kurdish Issue,' In *Iraq: Its History, People and Politics*, p. 168.
21   O'Shea, *Trapped Between*, p. 143; and Stansfield, 'The Kurdish Question,' *op.cit.*, p. 2.
22   McDowall, *A Modern History*, p. 140.
23   *Ibid.*, p. 142.
24   O'Shea, *Trapped Between*, p. 143.
25   John Ciment, *The Kurds: State and Minority in Turkey, Iraq and Iran* (New York: Facts On File, Inc., 1996), p. 80.
26   Stansfield, *Iraqi Kurdistan*, p. 61.
27   McDowall, *A Modern History*, p. 174.
28   Edmonds, 'Kurdish Nationalism,' *op.cit.*, p. 88.
29   Michael M. Gunter, *The Kurds of Iraq: Tragedy and Hope* (New York: St. Martin's Press, 1992), p. 3. Sheikh Mahmud was an *Agha* and *Sheikh*, as well as a member of the *Naqshbandi* order.
30   McDowall, *A Modern History*, p. 158.
31   Gunter, *The Kurds*, p. 3.
32   McDowall, *The Kurds*, p. 82. The italics are in the original text.
33   McDowall, *A Modern History*, pp. 178–80.
34   Marion Farouk-Sluglett and Peter Sluglett, *Iraq since 1958: From Revolution to Dictatorship* (London: I.B.Tauris, 1990), p. 291.
35   Quoted in *Ibid.*, p. 290.
36   *Ibid.*
37   On the role of these religious schools, see Bruinessen, *Agha, Shaikh*, Chapter Four.
38   Amir Hassanpour, 'The Creation of Kurdish Media Culture.' In *Kurdish Culture and Identity*, pp. 53, 72.

39 Denise Natali, *The Kurds and the State: Evolving National Identity in Iraq, Turkey and Iran* (Syracuse, New York: Syracuse University Press, 2005), p. 27.

40 Gunter, *The Kurds*, p. 2; and McDowall, *A Modern History*, p. 172.

41 Blau, 'Kurdish Written,' *op.cit.*, p. 22. For a detailed and vivid account of the prints and publications of newspapers, magazines, journals and books on Kurdistan during this period, see Hassanpour, 'The Creation,' *op.cit.*, pp. 48–84.

42 Natali, *The Kurds*, p. 34.

43 *Ibid.*, p. 35.

44 Stansfield, *Iraqi Kurdistan*, p. 64; McDowall, *A Modern History*, p. 289; and Edmund Ghareeb, *The Kurdish Question in Iraq* (New York: Syracuse University Press, 1981), p. 27.

45 McDowall, *A Modern History*, pp. 293–4.

46 *Cf.*, Abdel Satar Tahir Shareef, '*al-Jamiyat wal Munathamat wal Ahzab al Kurdiya fi Nisf Qarn: 1908–58,*' (Associations, Organizations and Kurdish Political Parties in Half a Century: 1908–58), (Baghdad: *Sharikat al Ma'rifa*, 1989), pp. 87–208. Shareef was a member of the KDP in the 1960s and later became the head of *al Hizb al Democraty al Kurdistani al thawri* (The Revolutionary Kurdistan Democratic Party) in Baghdad. This party was supported by the *Ba'thists* as an alternative to the KDP after 1975. Shareef was assassinated in Kirkuk in 2008. See Stansfield, *Iraqi Kurdistan*, pp. 63–4; Romano, *The Kurdish Nationalist*, p. 189; and McDowall, *A Modern History*, pp. 293–4. According to Salih al-Haidari, (cited in Shareef), the *Hiwa* Party was first announced in Erbil by leftist Kurds of Erbil. This party first organized under the name of *Darker*, which was adopted from an Italian nationalist organization. *Shorish* as a party was also established in Erbil before becoming the *Rizgari Kurd*. The KDP was established from the amalgamation of *Shorish* and *Rizgari Kurd*. See Shareef, '*al-Jamiyat wal Munathamat*', p. 155.

47 David McDowall, 'The Kurdish Question.' In *The Kurds*, p. 25; and Gunter, *The Kurds*, p. 9.

48 Ismet Sheriff Vanly, 'Kurdistan in Iraq.' In *People without a Country: The Kurds and Kurdistan*, edited by Gerard Chaliand. Trans. by Michael Pallis (London: Zed Books Ltd, 1993), p. 149; McDowall, 'The Kurdish Question', *op.cit.*, p. 26; and Gunter *The Kurds*, pp. 3 and 9–10.

49 Stansfield, *Iraqi Kurdistan*, p. 63; Romano, *The Kurdish Nationalist*, pp. 224–9; and Jwaideh, *The Kurdish National Movement*, p. 709.

50 For an account of the establishment of the KDP, see Stansfield, *Iraqi Kurdistan*, p. 66.

51 Romano, *The Kurdish Nationalist Movement*, p. 189.

52 Stansfield, *Iraqi Kurdistan*, p. 63.

53 Natali, *The Kurds*, pp. 28–9.

54 *Ibid.*, pp. 43–4.

55 Stansfield, *Iraqi Kurdistan*, pp. 61–7; and Natali, *The Kurds*, p. 47.

56 Phebe Marr, *The Modern History of Iraq* (Boulder, Colorado: Westview Press, 2nd ed., 2004), p. 81.

57 Bruinessen, *Agha, Shaikh*, p. 26. Apart from Brigadier General Abdul Karim Qasim who became the President of Iraq, (Prime Minister, Minister of Defence

and Commander in Chief of the Army), the rest of the Free Officers were Arab nationalists. Colonel Abdul Salam Arif, who became the Vice-President, (Deputy Prime Minster and Minister of the Interior), was a Nasserite nationalist. See Michael Eppel, *Iraq from Monarchy to Tyranny: From Hashemites to the Rise of Saddam* (Gainesville: University Press of Florida, 2004), p. 153.

58 Eppel, *Iraq from Monarchy*, p. 153; Bruinessen, *Agha, Shaikh*, p. 26.
59 Eppel, *Ibid.*
60 Natali, *The Kurds*, p. 49.
61 Ghareeb, *The Kurdish Question*, p. 38, (cited in Stansfield, *Iraqi Kurdistan*, p. 67); Vanly, 'Kurdistan in Iraq.' In *People without a Country*, p. 150; and Bruinessen, *Agha, Shaikh*, pp. 26–7;
62 Marr, *The Modern History*, pp. 104–5.
63 Eppel, *Iraq from Monarchy*, p. 186; and Entessar, *Kurdish Ethnonationalism*, p. 117.
64 Marr, *The Modern History*, *op.cit*, p. 105; and Eppel, *Iraq from Monarchy*, p. 188.
65 For an in-depth account of the Mosul and Kirkuk insurgents see Hanna Batatu, *The Old Social Classes and the Revolutionary Movements of Iraq: A Study of Iraq's Old Landed and Commercial Classes and its Communists, Ba'thists and Free Officers* (New Jersey: Princeton University Press, 1978), pp. 890–925.
66 Stansfield, *Iraqi Kurdistan*, pp. 68–9; Bruinessen, *Agha, Shaikh*, p. 27; and Natali, *The Kurds*, p. 52.
67 Smith, *National Identity*, p. 137.
68 *Ibid.*
69 For a detailed account of the September 1961 revolution, see Stansfield, *Iraqi Kurdistan*, pp. 68–9, and Vanly, 'Kurdistan in Iraq.' In *People without a Country*, pp. 151–2.
70 Vanly, 'Kurdistan in Iraq.' In *People without a Country*, pp. 151–2; and Stansfield, *Iraqi Kurdistan*, pp. 69–70.
71 Stansfield, *Iraqi Kurdistan*, pp. 69–70; Eppel, *Iraq from Monarchy*, pp. 288–9; and Marr, *The Modern History*, p. 131.
72 Marr, *The Modern History*, p. 130; Stansfield, *Iraqi Kurdistan*, pp. 73–4; Eppel, *Iraq from Monarchy*, pp. 229–30; and Tripp, *A History*, pp. 185–9.
73 In Iraq's modern era, there is not one single example of a natural or smooth transition of power from a ruler or regime to another. Transfers have either been unexpected, bloody, or both. During the monarchical era of the Kings (1921–58), Faysal I, Gazi and Faysal II died or were killed at a young age: 48, 27 and 23 respectively. Abdel Karim Qasim was killed in 1963, Abdel Salam Arif died in a helicopter crash. Saddam Hussein was hanged on 31 Dec. 2006. Abdel Rahman Arif was the only leader or president who was not killed in a *coup d'état*. Arif was allowed to go into exile in Turkey. He lived there until 1988 when Saddam allowed him to return to Iraq. However, Arif died in 2007 in Jordan. See Ofra Bengio, 'A Republican Turning Royalist? Saddam Husayn and the Dilemmas of Succession,' *Journal of Contemporary History*, Vol. 35, No. 4, 2000: 641–53, at 641–2.
74 Brendan O'Leary and Khaled Saleh, 'The Denial, Resurrection and Affirmation of Kurdistan.' In *The Future of Kurdistan in Iraq*, Brendan O'Leary, *et al.*, (eds.), (Philadelphia, Pennsylvania: University of Pennsylvania Press, 2005), p. 22.

75 *Cf.*, Hanna Batatu, *The Old Social Classes*, p. 1073; Eppel, *Iraq from Monarchy*, p. 241; Anderson, *et al.*, *The Future of Iraq: Dictatorship, Democracy, or Division?* (New York: Palgrave Macmillan, 2004), pp. 51–2; and Pelletiere, *The Kurds*, pp. 160–1.

76 Ghareeb, *The Kurdish Question*, pp. 138–42; and Tripp *A History of Iraq*, pp. 94–9.

77 Smith, *The Ethnic Origins*, p. 156.

78 Batatu, *The Old Social Classes*, p. 1102.

79 *Ibid.*, pp. 1109–10; and Vanly, 'Kurdistan in Iraq.' In *People without a Country*, p. 157.

80 Pelletiere, *The Kurds*, pp. 162–3.

81 Marr, *The Modern History*, p. 154; Ghareeb, 'The Kurdish Issue,' In *Iraq: Its History, People and Politics*, p. 171; and Stansfield, *Iraqi Kurdistan*, p. 75. For more on Saddam's meeting with Barzani, see Bulloch, *et al.*, *No Friends*, pp. 129–30.

82 McDowall, *The Kurds*, pp. 89–91; Stansfield, *Iraqi Kurdistan*, p. 75; McDowall, *A Modern History*, pp. 325–8; Marr, *The Modern History*, p. 154; and Vanly, 'Kurdistan in Iraq.' In *People without a Country*, pp. 153–4.

83 Vanly, 'Kurdistan in Iraq.' In *People without a Country*, pp. 153–7; and Marr, *The Modern History*, p. 155.

84 Ofra Bengio, *Saddam's Word: Political Discourse in Iraq* (Oxford: Oxford University Press, 1998).

85 Stansfield, *Iraqi Kurdistan*, p. 75; Marr, *The Modern History*, p. 155; and Chaliand, *The Kurdish Tragedy*, p. 62.

86 Ghareeb, 'The Kurdish Issue,' In *Iraq: Its History, People and Politics*, p. 172; and Stansfield, *Iraqi Kurdistan*, p. 76.

87 Bulloch, *et al.*, *No Friends but the Mountains*, p. 137; and Eppel, *Iraq*, p. 248. For more on the 1975 Algiers Agreement and what followed, see Vanly, 'Kurdistan in Iraq.' In *People without a Country*, pp. 167–76.

88 Farouk-Sluglett, *et al.*, *Iraq*; Stansfield, *Iraqi Kurdistan*, pp. 77–9; and Eppel, *Iraq*, p. 248.

89 Ghareeb, 'The Kurdish Issue,' In *Iraq: Its History, People and Politics*, p. 73; and Bulloch, *et al.*, *No Friends but the Mountains*, p. 141.

90 Gunter, *The Kurds*, pp. 46–7; Anderson, *et al.*, *The Future of Iraq*, pp. 167–8; and Stansfield, *Iraqi Kurdistan*, p. 79;

91 Guiding Principles on Internal Displacement, U.N. Doc. E/CN.4/1998/53/ Add.2 (1998), noted in Comm. Hum. Rts. Res. 1998/50. [hereinafter 'Guiding Principles.']

92 Muller and Linzey, *The Internally Displaced Kurds*, p. 15.

93 *Ibid.*, p. 29.

94 Some scholars hold that the Arabization policy started in 1963 during Abdel Salam Arif's rule. Others date this policy to an earlier period. Anderson and Stansfield hold that the policy goes back to the British mandate era of the 1920s and 1930s when they backed the Iraqi government in bringing in huge numbers of Arab workers to satisfy the expanding oil industry needs in Kirkuk, in addition to settling the area with several large nomadic Arab tribes such as *Al Jbur*. See Anderson, *et al.*, *The Future of Iraq*, p. 156. The *Ba'th* policy encouraged the Arabs (mostly *Shi'a*) to live in Kirkuk by giving every family a piece

of land free of charge and 10,000 dinars to build a house on it. The Kirkukis called them *Ashertalaf* immigrants, or 'the Arabs who got 10,000 dinars'. The government also gave large sums of money to any Arab who married a Kurdish woman.

95 Vanly, 'Kurdistan in Iraq.' In *People without a Country*, pp. 185–7; and Chaliand, 'Introduction.' In *People without a Country*, p. 7. Forced assimilation and internal displacement result in massive oppression and widespread poverty. See, Muller and Linzey, *The Internally Displaced Kurds*, pp. 24–9.

96 Tripp, *A History of Iraq*, p. 214; and Gunter, *The Kurds*, p. 35.

97 Vanly, 'Kurdistan in Iraq.' In *People without a Country*, pp. 185–6.

98 *Ibid.*

99 Stansfield, *Iraqi Kurdistan*, p. 79.

100 Chaliand, (ed.) 'Introduction.' In *People without a Country*, p. 8.

101 McDowall, *A Modern History*, pp. 342–3; Stansfield, *Iraqi Kurdistan*, pp. 79–81. Talabani was the KDP representative in Lebanon from 1974–5. The word *Mam* in Kurdish means 'uncle'.

102 Stansfield, *Iraqi Kurdistan*, p. 80.

103 Vanly, 'Kurdistan in Iraq.' In *People without a Country*, p. 188.

104 Foreign and Commonwealth Office, *Background Brief on the Iraqi Opposition*, London, Private Paper, 1993: 1–6, at 2.

105 A. Sherzad, 'The Kurdish Movement in Iraq: 1975–88'. In *The Kurds: A Contemporary Overview*, edited by Philip G. Kreyenbroek and Stefan Sperl (London: Routledge, 1992), pp. 134–69, at 137–8.

106 In July 1979 Saddam pushed Al-Bakir from power and took his place as President of the Republic, Prime Minister and Commander in Chief of the Armed Forces, the Chairman of the RCC and Secretary of Regional Command. For a good discussion of the Iraqi totalitarian state under Saddam, see Stansfield, *Iraq: People*, pp. 96–8.

107 Ahmed S. Hashim, 'Military Power and State Formation in Modern Iraq,' *Middle East Policy*, Vol. 10, No. 4, 2003: 20–47, at 35.

108 For a detailed assessment of Saddam's family rule, see the in-depth essay by Bengio, 'A Republican Turning Royalist,' *op.cit.*, pp. 641–53, at 644–5.

109 Stansfield, *Iraq, People*, pp. 107–8; and O'Ballance, *The Kurdish Struggle*, p. 123.

110 O'Ballance, *The Kurdish Struggle*, pp. 123–46; and Stansfield, *Iraqi Kurdistan*, p. 90.

111 McDowall, 'The Kurdish Question,' *op.cit.*, p. 55; and Marr, *The Modern History*, p. 199.

112 Chaliand, *The Kurdish Tragedy*, p. 70

113 While pursuing undergraduate studies at Salahaddin University from 1982 to 1987, I witnessed years of fear, threats and harassment by the *Ba'th* Student Union and its security agents. Students were daily urged to join the *Ba'th* and the popular Army. As a result of refusing to join the *Ba'th*, many of us were suspended from the University for a year. (The author was in his second year of studies in 1983.) In April 1984 a mass student demonstration was held, in which the author participated, that was supported by small underground cells of communists, PUK's *Komala* and *Alay Shoresh*. Many students were captured by the secret police in the city centre of Erbil. Other than two Arab communist students, the rest were leftist Kurdish nationalists. During these years many

Iraqi Kurd graduates fled the country (mostly to Iran) to escape compulsory military service.

114 See, 'Guiding Principles,' *op.cit.*

115 Chaliand, *The Kurdish Tragedy*, p. 70. This was also a violation of the International Convention on the Elimination of All Forms of Racial Discrimination. Entered into force, Jan. 4, 1969. 660 U.N.T.S. 195. In *Human Rights*, Louis Henkin, Gerald L. Neuman, Diane F. Orentlicher, David W. Leebron, (eds.), (New York: Foundation Press, 2001), pp. 180–91.

116 Sophia Wanche, 'Awaiting Liberation: Kurdish Perspectives on a Post-Saddam Iraq.' In *The Future of Kurdistan*, p. 187. For more on this policy see Resolution no. 850 of the RCC 27 November 1988 and Resolution no. 199 of the RCC 6 September 2001 which allows any Kurd or Turkmen to change to Arab nationality. This information is based on Report no. 58 of the PUK's Organisational Branch 2, Kirkuk, Private Paper, 2005.

117 Denise Natali, 'Manufacturing Identity and Managing Kurds in Iraq.' In *Right-Sizing the State: The Politics of Moving Borders*, Brendan O'Leary, Ian S. Lustick and Thomas Callaghy, (eds.), (Oxford: Oxford University Press, 2001), 253–88, at 277.

118 For more on the *Anfal* Operation, see McDowall, *A Modern History*, pp. 353–64; Stansfield, *Iraqi Kurdistan*, p. 90; Tripp, *A History of Iraq*, pp. 243–5; and Bruinessen *Agha, Shaikh*, pp. 42–3. During the 1980s *Anfal* campaign, the *Jash* (*Fursan*, or *Jehush* in Arabic), who came mostly from tribal rural uneducated backgrounds, assisted the Iraqi Army. A number of them were used as Special Forces (*Mafariz Khasa* in Arabic), attached to the General Security in the Kurdish cities of Erbil, Suleimaniya, Dohuk and Kirkuk. For a comprehensive account of their involvement in *Anfal* and as an apparatus of the security forces of the *Ba'th* in Kurdistan, see McDowall, *A Modern History*, pp. 354–63.

119 The term *Anfal* means 'the spoils.' Taken from the eighth *Sura* of the *Qur'an* (*Surat al-Anfal*), it refers to the first Muslim battle (Battle of *Badr*) with unbelievers in AD 624. The *Sura* claims that the spoils of the battle belong to God and the messenger (Muhammad). It gives the right to plunder an enemy's life, wealth and property. For the Iraqi Army *Anfal* was a military code-name for the operation of genocide launched against the Kurds. See McDowall, *A Modern History*, p. 366; and Sheri Laizer, *Martyrs, Traitors and Patriots: Kurdistan after the Gulf War* (London: Zed Books, 1996), p. 27.

120 The IKF was formed during November–December 1987. Its formation was announced in May 1988.

121 Stansfield, *Iraqi Kurdistan*, p. 92; and Gunter, *The Kurds*, pp. 39–40.

Reconstructing and Consolidating National Identity: 1991–2008

1 At the time of the Gulf war the entire Gulf Cooperation Council (Saudi Arabia, Kuwait, Bahrain, the United Arab Emirates [UAE], Qatar and Oman) took strong positions against Iraq, as did Egypt, Syria, Morocco and Lebanon in spite of the often expressed pro-Iraqi public opinion. By the mid-1990s only Saudi Arabia and Kuwait publicly remained strongly supportive of American policy toward Iraq (even if many of the Arab leaders privately continued to support the containment of Iraq). By the end of the 1990s most Arab leaders opposed the sanctions in private as well as in public. On March 2002 an Arab summit in

Beirut brought about a public Arab consensus on restoring Iraq to the Arab order, while a succession of Arab leaders pointedly rejected US Vice President Dick Cheney's suggestion that they privately supported the American agenda of war against Iraq. For more on this see Marc Lynch, 'Beyond the Arab Street: Iraq and the Arab Public Sphere,' *Politics and Society*, Vol. 31, No.1, 2003: 55–91, at 57.

2   Ghareeb, 'The Kurdish Issue,' In *Iraq: Its History, People and Politics*, p. 176.

3   For a detailed account of the uprising in the south see Faleh Abd al-Jabbar, 'Why the Intifada Failed.' In *Iraq Since the Gulf War: Prospect for Democracy*, edited by Fran Hazelton, The Committee Against Repression and for Democratic Rights in Iraq (CARDRI), (London: Zed Books, 1994), pp. 97–117.

4   It is not surprising then that apart from Baghdad and the three *Sunni* cities of Anbar, Tikrit and Mosul, all the other cities in Iraq rose up against the Regime.

5   The idiomatic translation of *Peshmarga* is 'those who face death.' *Pesh* means 'to stand in front of' and *marga* means 'death'.

6   McDowall, *A Modern History*, pp. 371–2. Early in the morning on 7 March the Governor of Erbil and Director of Security of Erbil (accompanied by many other *Ba'thist* and Army officers) fled to Mosul by helicopter. Only the *Ba'thist* security headquarters, which resisted until 10 a.m. in Erbil, was the Directory of Northern Region's security. All the security police officers who resisted were killed by the rebels in the same building.

7   On April 1991 James Baker, the US Secretary of State reached the Turkish border where many Kurds complained and requested the help of the United States.

8   Stansfield, *Iraqi Kurdistan*, p. 95; and McDowall, *A Modern History*, pp. 373–5.

9   O'Ballance, *The Kurdish Struggle*, pp.188–90; Stansfield, *Iraqi Kurdistan*, pp. 95–6; and Marr, *The Modern History*, p. 255.

10 Marr, *The Modern History*, p. 256.

11 McDowall, *A Modern History*, pp. 376–9.

12 For an in-depth account of the negotiation, see Ghareeb, 'The Kurdish Issue.' In *Iraq: Its History, People and Politics*, p. 178.

13 McDowall, *A Modern History*, pp. 382–3.

14 See Amnesty International, 'Iraq: Human Rights Abuse in Iraqi Kurdistan since 1991', 28 February 1995, p. 9.

15 Romano, *The Kurdish Nationalist Movement*, p. 209. For a vivid analysis of the result of the election, organs and administration of the government, see Stansfield, *Iraqi Kurdistan*, pp. 121–44.

16 Cited in Romano, *The Kurdish Nationalist*, p. 208.

17 Stansfield, *Iraqi Kurdistan*, pp. 146–52; and Ghareeb, 'The Kurdish Issue.' In *Iraq: Its History, People and Politics*, p. 179.

18 Romano, *The Kurdish Nationalist Movement*, p. 209.

19 Stansfield, *Iraqi Kurdistan*, p. 210; and Ghareeb, 'The Kurdish Issue.' In *Iraq: Its History, People and Politics*, p. 180.

20 Stansfield, *Iraqi Kurdistan*, p. 121.

21 *Ibid.*, p. 175.

22 *Ibid.*, p. 177.

23 Ofra Bengio, 'Autonomy in Kurdistan in Historical Perspective.' In *The Future of Kurdistan*, pp. 179–80; and Stansfield 'Governing Kurdistan.' In *The Future of Kurdistan in Iraq*, pp. 201–3.

24 Stansfield, Gareth, R. L. and Hashem Ahmadzadeh, *The Kurdish Policy Imperative*, Middle East Programme Briefing Paper 07/04, December 2007, accessed at http://www.chathamhouse.org.uk/publications/papers/view/-/id/584/.

25 *Ibid.*

26 Kenneth Katzman, 'The Kurds in Post-Saddam Iraq,' CRS Report for Congress, 27 September 2008: 1–6, at 3.

27 Ian S. Spears, 'Understanding Inclusive Peace Agreements in Africa: The Problems of Sharing Power,' *Third World Quarterly*, Vol. 21, No. 1, 2000: 105–18, at 105.

28 Henri J. Barkey and Ellen Laipson, 'Iraqi Kurds and Iraq's Future,' *Middle East Policy*, Vol. XII, No. 4, Winter 2005, p. 68.

29 Pollock, *The Kurdish Regional Government in Iraq*, pp. 8–9.

30 *Ibid.*, p. 4.

31 *Ibid.*

32 *Ibid.* In the 2009 elections, women achieved 29 per cent of the seats, constituting nearly a third of the seats in Parliament.

33 Stansfield, *Iraqi Kurdistan*, p. 119.

34 Stansfield, *et al., The Kurdish Policy Imperative*, pp. 4–5.

35 The Oil for Food Programme was created as a humanitarian counterweight to the sanctions imposed against Iraq by the 1991 UN Security Council Resolution 687.

36 Stansfield, *Iraq, People*, p. 149.

37 Stansfield, 'Governing Kurdistan.' In *The Future of Kurdistan in Iraq*, p. 204.

38 Information was obtained from various governmental sections in the region during our last field trip of 2007. See also, Anderson, *et al., The Future of Iraq*, pp. 114 and 177; Stansfield, 'Governing Kurdistan.' In *The Future of Kurdistan in Iraq*, p. 205; and Peter W. Galbraith, 'What Went Wrong?' In *The Future of Kurdistan in Iraq*, pp. 241–2.

39 Anderson *et al., The Future of Iraq*, pp. 177–8. Politically speaking, for those born in the early 1960s, Iraq under the rule of Saddam Hussein represents the 'bad memories' of the past.

40 Galbraith, 'What Went Wrong?' In *The Future of Kurdistan in Iraq*, p. 243.

41 *Ibid.*, pp. 241–2.

42 US Senator Sam Brownback outlined a plan for a federal Iraq where '*Sunnis, Shi'a* and Kurds would manage their own affairs within a unified state.' It appears to be the concern with Kirkuk and its oil that has kept other politicians and world leaders from supporting this solution. See 'Brownback Outlines "Diplomatic Surge" for Iraq' on the Kurdish National Congress of North America website accessed 9/4/2007 at http://www.kncna.org/docs/k_view-article.asp?date=8/15/2007.

43 *Ibid.*, p. 28.

Nationalism and National Identity amongst University Students

1 During May and June 2007 the Iraqi dinar's value increased slightly. Accordingly, 500,000 Iraqi dinars was equivalent to $700. During the time of the survey, however, 500,000 Iraqi dinars was equivalent to $600.

Toward an UnderstAnding of Modern Kurdish Nationalism
and National Identity

1 Smith, *The Ethnic Origins*, p. 21.
2 Smith, *Nations and Nationalism,* p. 139.
3 Smith, *Nationalism: Theory*, p. 31
4 Smith, *National Identity*, p. 77.
5 *Ibid.*, p. 78.
6 Whereas the Iraqi Constitution of 2005 is silent when it comes to which flag is considered to be the national flag, it is clear and straightforward in Article 12 that the flag and national anthem, along with all the national emblems, would be regulated by law. This article should have been implemented long ago. See Eamad J. Mazouri, *The Flag Controversy in Iraq*, Kurdishaspect.com, Kurdish News and Points of View, 2007: http://chinese-school.netfirms.com/other-article-flags.html. It is significant that on 5 February 2008 the Iraqi Parliament decided to change the flag by removing the three stars, which were emblems of *Ba'th* Party goals. This was a compromise that the Kurds had agreed on. It was after this that Barzani allowed the Iraqi flag to fly next to the Kurdish flag on public and governmental buildings.
7 Amal Obeidi, *Political Culture in Libya* (Surrey: Curzon Press, 2001), p. 219.
8 *Ibid.*, pp. 90, 218.
9 *Ibid.*, p. 203.
10 See Leon Festinger, *A Theory of Cognitive Dissonance* (Palo Alto, California: Stanford University Press, 1962).

Post-1990s *Kurdistaniyeti*

1 Gundi, Kirmanj, Presidential Address, Twenty-first Annual Conference of the Kurdish National Congress of North America, Washington: D.C., 28 March 2009.
2 See 'What Is Civil Society?' Centre for Civil Society, London School of Economics, http://www.lse.ac.uk/collections/CCS/what_is_civil_society.htm. Retrieved 29 Nov. 2009.
3 '"Civil Society" An Agreed Definition' (2003) available at http://pages.british-library.net/blww3/3way/civilsoc.htm. (cited by Charles (Chip) Hauss, 'What is Civil Society?' *Beyond Intractibility*, accessed on http://www.beyondintractability.org/essay/civil_society. Retrieved 29 Nov. 2009.
4 Sailer, Steve, 'Cousin Marriage Conundrum: The Ancient Practice Discourages Democratic Nation-Building,' *The American Conservative*, 13 January 2003, pp. 20–?
5 *Ibid.*
6 *Ibid.*
7 Kurtz, Stanley, 'Veil of Tears,' *National Review*, 28 January 2002.
8 *Ibid.*
9 Jon Basil Utley, 'Tribes, Veils and Democracy: Understanding Muslim Society,' 26 April 2006. Available at http://www.antiwar.com/utley/?articleid=8900. Retrieved 3 Dec. 2009.
10 Sailer, 'Cousin Marriage Conundrum,' p. 20.
11 *Ibid.*
12 Cited in Sailer, *op.cit.*, p. 21.

13   Utley, 'Tribes, Veils and Democracy'.
14   Novell B. De Atkine, 'Why Arabs Lose Wars,' *Middle East Quarterly*, Dec. 1999, Vol. 6, No. 2.
15   *Ibid.*
16   Sailer, 'Cousin Marriage Conundrum,' p. 22.
17   *Ibid.*
18   *Ibid.*
19   William D. Hamilton, 'Kin Selection,' (1964), cited in Sailer, *Ibid.*
20   *Ibid.*
21   Sailer, 'Cousin Marriage Conundrum,' p. 22.
22   *Ibid.*
23   Shali, Saman, 'The Kurds and the Middle East Crisis,' KurdishMedia.com, 13 August 2006.

BIBLIOGRAPHY

Literature in Kurdish and Arabic

Ahmad, Jemal Rashid, *Dirasat Kurdiyah fi bilad Subartu*. (*Kurdish Studies in the Country of Subartu*). (Baghdad, 1984).

Ahmad, Jemal Rashid, *Tarikh al-Kurd al-Qadim*, (*The Ancient History of the Kurds*). (Hawler: Salahaddin University Publisher, 1990).

Al-Feel, Muhammad Rashid, *al-Akrad fi Nathar al-Elm*, (*The Kurds from the Viewpoint of Science*). (Baghdad, 1965).

Aziz, Mahir A., *al-Tatawur al-Hathari fi Madinat Erbil*, (*Urban Development in Erbil City*), Unpublished Master's thesis. (University of Baghdad, College of Arts, Sociology Department), 1990.

Aziz, Mahir Abdulwahid, '*al-Shakhsia al-Kurdia: Dirasa Igtima'ia fi thaw' al-Anthropologia al-Hatharia*', (*Kurdish Personality: A Social Study in Cultural Anthropology*). *Gulan Al-Arabi*, (Monthly General Political-Cultural Magazine). (Erbil, Iraq, No. 73, 30 June 2002), pp. 61–6.

Aziz, Mahir Abdulwahid, '*al-A'ila wadawruha fi al-Tanshi'a al-Igtima'ia*', (*Family Role in Socialization*). *Gulan Al-Arabi* (Monthly General Political-Cultural Magazine). (Erbil, Iraq, No. 74, 31 July 2002), pp. 98–105.

Aziz, Mahir Abdulwahid, '*Islami Siyasi u Moderniti la Roghhalati nawarast'*. (*Political Islam and Modernity in the Middle East*). Translated by Saman Halabjayi, *Tiwejinewe*, Issue No. 3. (Irbil, 2005), pp. 221–32.

Bdlisi, Mir Sharafkhani, *Sharafnama: Mezhuy Mala Mirani Kurdistan*, (*Sharafnama*: *The History of Mula Mirs of Kurdistan*). Translated by Mamosta Hazhar. (Hawler: Aras Publishing House, No. 410, 2006).

Eskander, Saad Basheer, '*Qiyam al-Nitham al-Imarati fi Kurdistan wa Suqutuhu: Mabain Muntasaf al-Qarn al-Ashir wa Muntasaf al-Qarn al-Tasi' Ashar*', (*The Rise and Fall of the Principality System in Kurdistan: between the Tenth and Mid-Nineteenth Centuries*), *Dar al-Shu'un al-Thaqafia al-Ama*. (Baghdad, 2005).

Huzni, Husein, *Sarjami Barhami Hussein Huzni,* (*The Collected Works of Hussein Huzni*), Vol. 1, edited by Kurdistan Mukeryani. (Hawler: Aras Publishing House, 2007).

Khasbak, Shakir, *alKurd wal-Mas'ala al-Kurdiyai fil Iraq,* (*Kurds and the Kurdish Question in Iraq*). *Al-Mu'asasa al-Arabia le al-Dirasat wal-Nashr.* (Beirut, 1959, 2nd edition, 1989).

Sajadi, Ala'ddin, *Mejouy Adabi Kurdi,* (*The History of Kurdish Literature*). (Baghdad, 1952).

Sajadi, Ala'ddin, *Shoreshakani Kurd wa Kurdu Komari Iraq,* (*Kurdish Revolutions, Kurds and the Republic of Iraq*). (Tehran: Atlas Publisher, 2005).

Shareef, Abdel Satar Tahir, '*al-Jamiyat wal Munathamat wal Ahzab al-Kurdiya fi Nisf Qarn: 1908-1958',* (*Associations, Organizations and Kurdish Political parties in half a century: 1908—58*). (Baghdad: Sharikat al-Ma'rifa, 1989).

Zaki, Muhammad Amin, *Khulasayeki Tarikhi Kurdu Kurdistan,* (*A Brief History of the Kurds and Kurdistan*). (Vol. 1, Baghdad, 1931; Vol. 2, Baghdad, 1937).

Literature in English

Abd al-Jabbar, Faleh, 'Why the Intifada Failed'. In *Iraq since the Gulf War: Prospect for Democracy,* edited by Fran Hazelton. The Committee Against Repression and for Democratic Rights in Iraq (CARDRI). (London: Zed Books, 1994).

Abrams, Philip, 'Notes on the Difficulty of Studying the State,' *Journal of Historical Sociology,* Vol. 1, No. 1, March, 1988: 58–89.

Al-Shawaf, Rayyan, 'The Destruction of Iraq's Christians,' *Daily News: Egypt* 20 July 2007.

Alter, Peter, *Nationalism.* (London: Edward Arnold, 1989).

Anderson, Benedict, *Imagined Communities: Reflections on the Origin and Spread of Nationalism.* (Revised Edition. London: Verso, 1991).

Anderson, Benedict, 'Introduction'. In *Mapping the Nation,* edited by Gopal Balakrishnan. (London: Verso, 1996).

Anderson, Liam and Gareth Stansfield, *The Future of Iraq: Dictatorship, Democracy, or Division?* (New York: Palgrave Macmillan, 2004).

Arfa, Hassan, *The Kurds: An Historical and Political Study.* (London: Oxford University Press, 1966).

Baldacchino, Godfrey, 'A Nationless State? Malta: National Identity and the EU', *West European Politics,* Vol. 25, No. 4, October 2002: 191–206.

Barkey, Henri J. and Ellen Laipson, 'Iraqi Kurds and Iraq's Future,' *Middle East Policy,* Vol. 12, No. 4, Winter, 2005: 66–76.

Batatu, Hanna, *The Old Social Classes and the Revolutionary Movements of Iraq: A Study of Iraq's Old Landed and Commercial Classes and of its Communists, Ba'thists and Free Officers.* (Princeton, New Jersey: Princeton University Press, 1978).

Bellah, Robert N., 'Civil Religion in America,' *Daedalus, Journal of the American Academy of Arts and Sciences*, Vol. 96. No. 1, Winter 1967: 1–21.

Bengio, Ofra, 'Autonomy in Kurdistan in Historical Perspective', In *The Future of Kurdistan in Iraq*, edited by Brendan O'Leary, *et al.* (Philadelphia, PA: University of Pennsylvania Press, 2005).

Bengio, Ofra, 'A Republican Turning Royalist? Saddam Husayn and the Dilemmas of Succession', *Journal of Contemporary History*, Vol. 35, No. 4, 2000: 641–53.

Bengio, Ofra, *Saddam's Word: Political Discourse in Iraq.* (Oxford: Oxford University Press, 1998).

Billig, Michael, *Banal Nationalism.* (London: Sage Publications, 1995).

Blau, Joyce, 'Kurdish Written Literature'. In *Kurdish Culture and Identity*, edited by Philip G. Kreyenbroek and Christine Allison. (London: Zed Books Ltd, 1996).

Brenneman, Robert L., *As Strong as the Mountains* (Long Grove, IL: Waveland Press, 2007).

Brubaker, Rogers, *Nationalism Reframed: Nationhood and the National Question in the New Europe.* (Cambridge: Cambridge University Press, 1996).

Bruinessen, Martin van, *Agha, Shaikh and State: The Social and Political Structures in Kurdistan.* (London: Zed Books Ltd, 1992).

Bruinessen, Martin van, *Kurdish Ethno-Nationalism versus Nation-Building States: Collected Articles.* (Istanbul: The ISIS Press, 2000).

Bruinessen, Martin van, '*Ehmedi Xani's Mem u Zin* and Its Role in the Emergence of Kurdish National Awareness'. In *Essays on the Origins of Kurdish Nationalism*, edited by Abbas Vali. (Costa Mesa, California: Mazda Publishers, 2003)

Bruinessen, Martin van, 'Kurdish Society, Ethnicity, Nationalism and Refugee Problems.' In *The Kurds: A Contemporary Overview*, edited by Philip G. Kreyenbroek and Stefan Sperl. (London: Routledge, 1992).

Bulloch, John and Harvey Morris, *No Friends but the Mountains: The Tragic History of the Kurds.* (London: Penguin Books, 1993).

Castells, Manuel, *The Power of Identity: The Information Age: Economy, Society and Culture.* (Oxford, United Kingdom: Blackwell Publications Ltd, Vol. 2, 2nd edition, 2004).

Chaliand, Gerard, 'Introduction'. In *People without a Country: The Kurds and Kurdistan,* edited by Gerard Chaliand. Translated by Michael Pallis. (London: Zed Books Ltd, 1993).

Chaliand, Gerard, *The Kurdish Tragedy.* Translated by Philip Black. (London: Zed Books Ltd, 1994).

Ciment, John, *The Kurds: State and Minority in Turkey, Iraq and Iran.* (New York: Facts On File, Inc, 1996).

Connolly, William. E., *Identity–Difference: Democratic Negotiations of Political Paradox.* (London: University of Minnesota Press, 1991).

Connor, Walker, 'The Politics of Ethnonationalism', *Journal of International Affairs,* Vol. 27, No. l, 1973: 1-21.

Connor, Walker, 'Beyond Reason: The Nature of the Ethnonational Bond', *Ethnic and Racial Studies,* Vol. 16, No. 3, July 1993: 373–89.

Connor, Walker, 'Ethnonationalism'. In *Understanding Political Development,* edited by Myron Weiner and Samuel Huntington. (Massachusetts: Little, Brown and Company, 1987).

Connor, Walker, *Ethnonationalism: The Quest for Understanding.* (Princeton, New Jersey: Princeton University Press, 1994).

Connor, Walker, 'A Nation is a Nation, is a State, is an Ethnic Group, is a....' In *Nationalism,* edited by John Hutchinson and Anthony D. Smith. (Oxford: Oxford University Press, 1994).

Cornell, Stephen, 'The Variable Ties that Bind,' *Ethnic and Racial Studies,* Vol. 19, No. 2, April 1996: 265–89.

De Atkine, Novell B., 'Why Arabs Lose Wars', *Middle East Quarterly,* Vol. 6, No. 2, Dec. 1999.

Driver, Godfrey Rolles, 'The Name "Kurd" and its Connexions', *Journal of Royal Asiatic Society of Great Britain and Ireland (JRAS),* Part III, July 1923: 393–404.

Durkheim, Emile, *Elementary Forms of Religious Life.* Translated by J. W. Swain. (London: Allen & Unwin, 1957).

Edmonds, Cecil John, 'Kurdish Nationalism', *Journal of Contemporary History,* Vol. 6, No. 1, Nationalism and Separatism, 1971: 87–107.

Entessar, Nader, *Kurdish Ethnonationalism.* (Boulder, Colorado: Lynne Rienner Publishers, 1992).

Eppel, Michael, *Iraq from Monarchy to Tyranny: From Hashemites to the Rise of Saddam.* (Gainesville, Florida: University Press of Florida, 2004).

Eskander, Saad, 'Britain's Policy in Southern Kurdistan: The Formation and the Termination of the First Kurdish Government, 1918-1919', *British Journal of Middle Eastern Studies,* Vol. 27, No. 2, 2000: 129–63.

Eskander, Saad, 'Southern Kurdistan under Britain's Mesopotamian Mandate: From Separation to Incorporation 1920-23', *Journal of Middle Eastern Studies*, Vol. 37, No. 2, April 2001: 153–80.

Farouk-Sluglett, Marion and Peter Sluglett, *Iraq since 1958: From Revolution to Dictatorship*. (London: I.B.Tauris, 1990).

Festinger, Leon, *A Theory of Cognitive Dissonance*. (Stanford, California: Stanford University Press, 1962).

Fitzgerald, Thomas K., *Metaphors of Identity* (Albany, New York: State University of New York Press, 1993).

Galbraith, Peter W., 'What Went Wrong'. In *The Future of Kurdistan in Iraq*, edited by Brendan O'Leary, *et al.* (Philadelphia, PA: University of Pennsylvania Press, 2005).

Galetti, Mirella, 'Kurdistan and its Christians', World Congress of Kurdish Studies conference, University of Salahaddin, Irbil, 6–9 September 2006.

Gellner, Ernest, *Thought and Change*. (London: Weidenfeld & Nicolson, 1964).

Gellner, Ernest, *Nations and Nationalism*. (Ithaca, New York: Cornell University Press, 1983).

Ghareeb, Edmund, *The Kurdish Question in Iraq*. (Syracuse, New York: Syracuse University Press, 1981).

Ghareeb, Edmund, 'The Kurdish Issue.' In *Iraq: Its History, People and Politics*, edited by Shams C. Inati., (New York: Humanity Press, 2003).

Ghassemlou, Abdul Rahman, *Kurdistan and the Kurds*. (London: Collet's Publishers, 1965).

Gleason, Philip, 'Identifying Identity: A Semantic History'. *The Journal of American History*, Vol. 69, No. 4, March, 1983: 910–31.

Greenfeld, Liah, *Nationalism: Five Roads to Modernity*. (Cambridge, Massachusetts: Harvard University Press, 1992).

Grigoriadis, Ioannis N., 'Turkey's Political Culture and Minorities'. Paper presented for the International Conference 'Nationalism, Society and Culture in Post-Ottoman South East Europe, 29–30 May 2004, St Peter's College, Oxford University, Oxford, 1–24.

Guibernau, Montserrat, 'Anthony D. Smith on Nations and National Identity: a Critical Assessment', *Nations and Nationalism*, Vol. 10, No. 1/2, 2004: 125–41.

Guibernau, Montserrat, *Nationalisms: The Nation-State and Nationalism in the Twentieth Century*. (Cambridge: Polity Press, 1996).

Gundi, Kirmanj, Presidential Address, Twenty-first Annual Conference of the Kurdish National Congress of North America. Washington: D.C., 28 March 2009.

Gunter, Michael M., *The Kurds of Iraq: Tragedy and Hope*. (New York: St. Martin's Press, 1992).

Hall, John A., 'Nationalism, Classified and Explained'. In *Notions of Nationalism*, edited by Sukumar Periwal. (Budapest: Central European University Press, 1995).

Hall, Stuart, 'The New Ethnicities'. In *Ethnicity*, edited by John Hutchinson and Anthony D. Smith. (Oxford: Oxford University Press, 1996).

Hall, Stuart, 'Introduction: Who Needs "Identity"?' In *Questions of Cultural Identity*, edited by Stuart Hall and Paul Du Gay. (London: Sage Publications, 1996).

Hamilton, William D., 'The Genetic Evolution of Social Behaviour I and II', *Journal of Theoretical Biology*, 7: 1–16, 17–32, (quoted in Steve Sailer, 'Cousin Marriage Conundrum: The Ancient Practice Discourages Democratic Nation-Building', *The American Conservative*, 13 January 2003: 20–2).

Hashim, Ahmed S., 'Military Power and State Formation in Modern Iraq,' *Middle East Policy*, Vol. 10, No. 4, 2003: 20-47.

Hassanpour, Amir, *Language and Nationalism in Kurdistan: 1918–1985*. (San Francisco: Mellen Research University Press, 1992).

Hassanpour, Amir 'The Creation of Kurdish Media Culture'. In *Kurdish Culture and Identity*, edited by Philip G. Kreyenbroek and Christine Allison. (London: Zed Books Ltd, 1996).

Hassanpour, Amir, 'Kurdish Studies: Orientalist, Positivist and Critical Approaches.' Review of Nader Entessar's *Kurdish Ethnonationalism*, *Middle East Journal*, Vol. 47, No. 1, Winter, 1993: 119–22.

Hassanpour, Amir, 'The Making of Kurdish Identity: Pre-20th Century Historical and Literary Discourses'. In *Essays on the Origins of Kurdish Nationalism*, edited by Abbas Vali. (Costa Mesa, California: Mazda Publishers, 2003).

Hassanpour, Amir, Review of Hakan Ozoglu, *Kurdish Notables and the Ottoman State: Evolving Identities, Competing Loyalties and Shifting Boundaries*, SUNY Series in Middle Eastern Studies. (Albany: State University of New York Press, 2004), in H-Turk, H-Net, Reviews, (September 2007). http://www.h net.org- /reviews/showrev. php?id=13540.

Hauss, Charles (Chip), 'What is Civil Society?' *Beyond Intractibility*, accessed on http://www.beyondintractability.org/essay/civil_society. Retrieved 29 Nov. 2009.

Hayes, Carlton, *Historical Evolution of Modern Nationalism*. (New York: Richard R. Smith Pub., 1931).

Held, David, 'Introduction: Central Perspectives on the Modern State'. In *States and Societies*, edited by David Held, *et al.* (Oxford: Martin Robertson, 1983).

Henkin, Louis, Gerald L. Neuman, Diane F. Orentlicher, David W. Leebron, (eds.) *Human Rights*. (New York: Foundation Press, 2001).

Hensler, Camille Overson and Mark Muller, *Freedom of Expression and of Association in Turkey*. (London: Kurdish Human Rights Project & Bar Human Rights Committee of England and Wales, November 2005).

Hoberman, R. D., *The Syntax and Semantics of Verb Morphology in Modern Aramaic: A Jewish Dialect of Iraqi Kurdistan*. (New Haven: American Oriental Society, 1989).

Hobsbawm, Eric J. 'Ethnicity and Nationalism in Europe Today'. In *Mapping the Nation*, edited by Gopal Balakrishnan. (London: Verso. 1996).

Hobsbawm, Eric, 'Introduction: Inventing Traditions'. In *The Invention of Tradition*, edited by Eric Hobsbawm and Terence Ranger. (Cambridge: Cambridge University Press, 1983).

Hobsbawm, Eric J., 'The Nation as Invented Tradition'. In *Nationalism*, edited by John Hutchinson and Anthony D. Smith. (Oxford: Oxford University Press, 1994).

Hobsbawm, Eric J., *Nations and Nationalism Since 1780: Programme, Myth, Reality.* (Cambridge: Cambridge University Press, 2nd edition, 1997).

Horch, Miroslav, 'From National Movement to the Fully-formed Nation: The Nation-building Process in Europe'. In *Mapping the Nation, edited by Gopal Balakrishnan. (London: Verso, 1996).

Hughes, Michael, *Nationalism and Society: Germany 1800-1945.* (London: Edward Arnold, 1988).

Hutchinson, John, *The Dynamics of Cultural Nationalism*. (London: Allen and Unwin, 1987).

Hutchinson, John and Anthony D. Smith, (eds.), *Nationalism*. (Oxford: Oxford University Press, 1994).

Izady, Mehrdad R., *The Kurds: A Concise Handbook*. (London: Taylor and Francis, 1992).

James, Boris, 'Uses and Values of the Term Kurd in Arabic Medieval Literary Sources'. Paper presented in the World Congress of Kurdish Studies, Salahaddin University, Erbil, 6–9 September 2006.

Jawad, Sa'ad, *Iraq and the Kurdish Question: 1958–1970.* (London: Ithaca Press, 1981).

Jwaideh, Wadie, *The Kurdish National Movement: Its Origin and Development*. (Syracuse, NY: Syracuse University Press, 2006).

Jwaideh, Wadie, 'The Kurdish Nationalist Movement: Its Origins and Development'. Unpublished PhD Dissertation, Syracuse University, 1960.

Katzman, Kenneth, 'The Kurds in Post-Saddam Iraq'. CRS Report for Congress, 27 September 2008: 1–6.

Kedourie, Elie, *Nationalism*. (Oxford: Blackwell Publishers, 1993).

Kendal, Nezan, 'The Kurds: Current Position and Historical Background'. In *Kurdish Culture and Identity*, edited by Philip G. Kreyenbroek and Christine Allison. (London: Zed Books Ltd, 1996).

Kinnane, Derk, *The Kurds and Kurdistan*. (London: Oxford University Press, 1964).

Klein, Janet, 'Kurdish Nationalists and Non-Nationalist Kurdists: Rethinking Minority Nationalism and the Dissolution of the Ottoman Empire, 1908-1909'. *Nations and Nationalism*, Vol. 13, No. 1, 2007: 135–53.

Kolsto, Pal, 'National Symbols as Signs of Unity and Division', *Ethnic and Racial Studies*, Vol. 29, No. 4, July 2006: 676–701.

Kreyenbroek, Philip G., 'On the Kurdish Language'. In *The Kurds: A Contemporary Overview*, edited by Philip G. Kreyenbroek and Stefan Sperl. (London: Routledge, 1992).

Kreyenbroek, Philip G., 'Religion and Religions in Kurdistan'. In *Kurdish Culture and Identity*, edited by Philip G. Kreyenbroek and Christine Allison. (London: Zed Books Ltd, 1996).

Kuntz, J. Kenneth, *The People of Ancient Israel*. (New York: Harper and Row, 1974).

Kupchan, Charles A., 'Introduction: Nationalism Resurgent'. In *Nationalism and Nationalities in the New Europe*, edited by Charles A. Kupchan. (London: Cornell University Press, 1995).

Kurtz, Stanley, 'Veil of Tears,' *National Review*, 28 January 2002: 36–40.

Latawski, Paul, 'The Problem of Definition: Nationalism, Nation and Nation-State in East Europe'. In *Contemporary Nationalism in East Central Europe*, edited by Paul Latawski. (New York: St. Martin's Press, 1995).

Leezenberg, Michiel, 'Economy and Society in Iraqi Kurdistan: Fragile Institutions and Enduring Trends'. In *Iraq at the Crossroads: State and Society in the Shadow of Regime Change*, edited by Toby Dodge and Steven Simon. (Adelphi Paper 354. Oxford: IISS, Oxford University Press, 2003).

Leezenberg, Michiel, 'Political Islam among the Kurd'. Paper originally presented for the International Conference 'Kurdistan: The Unwanted State', Jagiellonian University, Polish-Kurdish Society, Cracow, Poland, 29–31 March 2001: 1–26.

Lijphart, Arend, *Democracy in Plural Societies: A Comparative Exploration*. (New Haven: Yale University Press, 1977).

Lijphart, Arend, *The Politics of Accommodation: Pluralism and Democracy in the Netherlands*. (Berkeley: University of California Press, 1968).

Linzey, Sharon F., Turkey's Compliance with its Obligations: The Context of Turkey's Law on Compensation for Damage arising from Terrorist Acts. Unpublished L.L.M. Thesis, Cornell Law School, (2006).

Lynch, Marc, 'Beyond the Arab Street: Iraq and the Arab Public Sphere'. *Politics and Society*, Vol. 31, No.1, 2003: 55–91.

Malesevic, Sinisa, '"Divine Ethnies" and "Sacred Nations:" Anthony D. Smith and the Neo-Durkheimian Theory of Nationalism', *Nationalism and Ethnic Politics*, Vol. 10, No. 4, Winter, 2004: 561–93.

Marr, Phebe, *The Modern History of Iraq*. (Boulder, Colorado: Westview Press, 2nd edition, 2004).

Mazouri, Eamad J., *The Flag Controversy in Iraq*, Kurdishaspect.com, Kurdish News and Points of View, (2007). Accessed at http://chinese-school.netfirms.com/other-article-flags.html.

McCrone, David, *The Sociology of Nationalism: Tomorrow's Ancestors*. (London: Routledge, 2000).

McCrone, David, *et al.*, 'Who Are We? Problematising National Identity'. *Sociological Review*, Vol. 46, No. 4, 1998: 629–52.

McDowall, David, *A Modern History of The Kurds*. (London: I.B.Tauris, 1996).

McDowall, David, *The Kurds: A Nation Denied*. (London: Minority Rights Publication, 1992).

McDowall, David, 'The Kurdish Question: a Historical Review'. In *The Kurds: A Contemporary Overview*, edited by Philip G. Kreyenbroek and Stefan Sperl. (London: Routledge, 1992).

McLean, Iain, *Oxford Concise Dictionary of Politics*. (Oxford: Oxford University Press, 1996).

Muller, Mark and Sharon Linzey, *The Internally Displaced Kurds of Turkey: Ongoing Issues of Responsibility, Redress and Resettlement*. (London: Kurdish Human Rights Project, Bar Human Rights Committee of England and Wales, 2007).

Natali, Denise, 'Manufacturing Identity and Managing Kurds in Iraq'. In *Right-Sizing the State: The Politics of Moving Borders*, edited by Brendan O'Leary, Ian S. Lustick and Thomas Callaghy. (Oxford: Oxford University Press, 2001), 253–88.

Natali, Denise, *The Kurds and the State: Evolving National Identity in Iraq, Turkey and Iran*. (Syracuse, New York: Syracuse University Press, 2005).

O'Ballance, Edgar, *The Kurdish Struggle: 1920-1994*. (London: Macmillan Press Ltd, 1996).

Obeidi, Amal, *Political Culture in Libya.* (Surrey: Curzon Press, 2001).

O'Leary, Brendan, 'Power-Sharing, Pluralist Federation and Federacy'. In *The Future of Kurdistan in Iraq*, edited by Brendan O'Leary, *et al.* (Philadelphia: University of Pennsylvania Press, 2005).

O'Leary, Brendan and Khaled Saleh, 'The Denial, Resurrection and Affirmation of Kurdistan.' In *The Future of Kurdistan in Iraq*, edited by Brendan O'Leary, *et al.* (Philadelphia: University of Pennsylvania Press, 2005).

Olson, Robert, *The Emergence of Kurdish Nationalism and the Sheikh Said Rebellion, 1880-1925.* (Austin: University of Texas Press, 1989).

Olson, Robert, (ed.), *The Kurdish Nationalist Movement in the 1990s: Its Impact on Turkey and the Middle East.* (Lexington: The University Press of Kentucky, 1996).

O'Shea, Maria T., *Trapped Between the Map and Reality: Geography and Perception of Kurdistan.* (London: Routledge, 2004).

Ozkirimli, Umut, *Theories of Nationalism: A Critical Introduction.* (New York: Palgrave, 2000).

Ozoglu, Hakan, *Kurdish Notables and the Ottoman State: Evolving Identities, Competing Loyalties and Shifting Boundaries* (Albany: State University of New York Press, 2004).

Parekh, Bhikhu, 'Defending National Identity in a Multicultural Society.' In *People, Nation and State: The Meaning of Ethnicity and Nationalism*, edited by Edward Moretimer and Robert Fine. (London: I.B.Tauris, 1999).

Pelletiere, Stephen C., *The Kurds: An Unstable Element in the Gulf.* (London: Westview Press, 1984).

Phillips, David L., 'Power-Sharing with Iraqi Kurds,' Center for Preventive Action, Council on Foreign Relations. 10 June 2004, p. 11.

Pollock, David, 'The Kurdish Regional Government in Iraq: An Inside Story'. In *The Future of the Iraqi Kurds*, edited by Soner Cagaptay, The Washington Institute for Near East Policy, Policy Focus 85, July 2008: 1–38.

Romano, David, *The Kurdish Nationalist Movement: Opportunity, Mobilization and Identity.* (Cambridge: Cambridge University Press, 2006).

Rush, Michael and Phillip Althoff, *An Introduction to Political Sociology.* (London: Nelson, 1971).

Sailer, Steve, 'Cousin Marriage Conundrum: The Ancient Practice Discourages Democratic Nation-Building', *The American Conservative*, 13 January 2003: 20–2.

Schneckener, Ulrich, 'Models of Ethnic Conflict Regulation: The Politics of Recognition'. In *Managing and Settling Ethnic Conflicts: Perspectives* on *Successes and Failures in Europe, Africa and Asia*, edited by Ulrich Schneckener and Stefan Wolff. (London: Hurst & Company, 2004).

Seton-Watson, Hugh, *Nations and States: An Inquiry into the Origins of Nations and the Politics of Nationalism*. (London: Methuen, 1982).

Shafer, Boyd C., *Faces of Nationalism: New Realities and Old Myths*. (New York: Harcourt Brace Jovanovich, 1972).

Shali, Saman, 'The Kurds and the Middle East Crisis', KurdishMedia.com, 13 August 2006.

Sherzad, A., 'The Kurdish Movement in Iraq: 1975-88'. In *The Kurds: A Contemporary Overview*, edited by Philip G. Kreyenbroek and Stefan Sperl (London: Routledge, 1992).

Smith, Anthony D., 'The Crises of Dual Legitimation'. In *Nationalism*, edited by John Hutchinson and Anthony D. Smith. (Oxford: Oxford University Press, 1994).

Smith, Anthony D., 'Culture, Community and Territory: The Politics of Ethnicity and Nationalism', *International Affairs*, Vol. 72, No. 3, July 1996: 445–58.

Smith, Anthony D., *The Ethnic Origins of Nations*. (Oxford: Blackwell Publishers, 1986).

Smith, Anthony D., 'Ethnic Myths and Ethnic Revivals', *Journal of European Sociology*, Vol. 25, 1984: 283–305.

Smith, Anthony D., 'National Identity and Myths of Ethnic Descent', *Research in Social Movements, Conflict and Change*, Vol. 7, 1984: 95–130.

Smith, Anthony D., *National Identity*. (London: Penguin Books, 1991).

Smith, Anthony D., *The Ethnic Revival*. (Cambridge: Cambridge University Press, 1981).

Smith, Anthony D., 'The Myth of the "Modern Nation" and the Myths of Nations', *Ethnic and Racial Studies*, Vol. 11, No. 1, January 1988: 1–26.

Smith, Anthony D., *Nationalism and Modernism: A Critical Survey of Recent Theories of Nations and Nationalism*. (London: Routledge, 1998).

Smith, Anthony D., *Nationalism: Theory, Ideology, History*. (Cambridge: Polity Press, 2004).

Smith, Anthony D., *Nations and Nationalism in a Global Era*. (Cambridge: Polity Press, 1995).

Smith, Anthony D., *Theories of Nationalism*. (London: Harper & Row, 2nd edition, 1983).

Smith, Anthony D., 'The Origins of Nations', *Ethnic and Racial Studies*, Vol. 12, No. 3, July 1989: 340–67.

Smith, Anthony D., *Myths and Memories of the Nation*. (Oxford: Oxford University Press, 1999).

Spears, Ian S., 'Understanding Inclusive Peace Agreements in Africa: The Problems of Sharing Power', *Third World Quarterly*, Vol. 21, No. 1, 2000: 105–18.

Stansfield, Gareth R. V., 'Governing Kurdistan: The Strength of Division'. In *The Future of Kurdistan in Iraq*, edited by Brendan O'Leary, *et al.* (Philadelphia: University of Pennsylvania Press, 2005).

Stansfield, Gareth R. V., *Iraqi Kurdistan: Political Development and Emergent Democracy.* (London: RoutledgeCurzon, 2003).

Stansfield, Gareth R. V., *Iraq: People, History, Politics.* (Cambridge: Polity Press, 2007).

Stansfield, Gareth R. V., 'The Kurdish Question in Iraq'. In *Iraq: 1914- 1947*; Middle East, On Line, Series 2, introductory essays. The National Archives, UK, 2007.

Stansfield, Gareth, R. V. and Hashem Ahmadzadeh, 'Kurdish or Kurdistanis? Conceptualizing Regionalism in the North Iraq'. In *An Iraq of Its Region, Cornerstones of a Federal Democracy?* Edited by Reidar Visser and Gareth Stansfield (London: Hurst Publishers Ltd, 2007).

Stansfield, Gareth, R. V., Robert Lowe and Hashem Ahmadzadeh, *The Kurdish Policy Imperative.* Middle East Programme Briefing Paper 07/04, (December 2007). Accessed at http://www.chathamhouse.org.uk/ publications/papers/view/-/id/584.

Strohmeier, Martin, *Crucial Images in the Presentation of a Kurdish National Identity: Heroes and Patriots, Traitors and Foes.* (Leiden: Brill, 2003).

Tripp, Charles, *A History of Iraq.* (Cambridge: Cambridge University Press, 2000).

Utley, Jon Basil, 'Tribes, Veils and Democracy: Understanding Muslim Society', 26 April 2006. Available at http://www.antiwar.com/ utley/?articleid=8900. Retrieved 3 Dec. 2009.

Vali, Abbas, 'Genealogies of the Kurds: Constructions of Nation and National Identity in Kurdish Historical Writing'. In *Essays on the Origins of Kurdish Nationalism*, edited by Abbas Vali. (Costa Mesa, California: Mazda Publishers, 2003).

Vali, Abbas, 'The Kurds and Their "Others:" Fragmented Identity and Fragmented Politics', *Comparative Studies of South Asia, Africa and the Middle East*, Vol. xviii, No. 2, 1998: 82–95.

Van Wolde, Ellen, *Stories of the Beginning.* (Ridgefield, Connecticut: Morehouse, 1997).

Vanly, Ismet Sheriff, 'Kurdistan in Iraq'. In *People without a Country: The Kurds and Kurdistan*, edited by Gerard Chaliand. Translated by Michael Pallis. (London: Zed Books Ltd, 1993).

Verdery, Katherine, 'Whither "Nation" and "Nationalism"?' In *Mapping the Nation*, edited by Gopal Balakrishnan. (London: Verso, 1996).

Wanche, Sophia, 'Awaiting Liberation: Kurdish Perspectives on a Post-Saddam Iraq'. In *The Future of Kurdistan in Iraq*, edited by Brendan O'Leary, *et al.* (Philadelphia: University of Pennsylvania Press, 2005).

Weber, Max, 'Politics as Vocation'. In *From Max Weber: Essays in Sociology*, edited by H. H. Gerth and C. Wright Mills. (London: Routledge, 1991).

Wilson, Woodrow, *Fourteen Point Programme for World Peace* (1918). The United States Department of State. Accessed at http://usinfo.state.gov/usa/infousa/facts/democrac/51.htm. Retrieved 9 September 2007.

Yildiz, Kerim, *The Kurds in Iraq: The Past, Present and Future*. (London: Pluto Press, 2004).

Zubaida, Sami, 'Introduction'. In *The Kurds: A Contemporary Overview*, edited by Philip G. Kreyenbroek and Stefan Sperl. (London: Routledge, 1992).

Reports and Theses

Amnesty International, 'Iraq: Human Rights Abuse in Iraqi Kurdistan since 1991'. 28 February 1995.

'Brownback Outlines "Diplomatic Surge" for Iraq'. Kurdish National Congress of North America website: http://www.kncna.org/docs/k_viewarticle.asp?date=8/15/2007.

'"Civil Society" An Agreed Definition', (2003) available at http://pages.britishlibrary.net/blww3/3way/civilsoc.htm, (cited by Charles (Chip) Hauss, 'What is Civil Society?' *Beyond Intractability*, accessed on http://www.beyondintractability.org/essay/civil_society. Retrieved 29 Nov. 2009.

Commission of the European Communities, Regular Report on Turkey's Progress Towards Accession (2007) European Commission, p. 39; accessed at http://ec.europa.eu/enlargement/archives/pdf/key_documents/2004/rr)tr_-2004_en.pdf. Retrieved 3 September 2007.

Foreign and Commonwealth Office, 'Background Brief on the Iraqi Opposition'. London, Private Paper, 1993: 1–6.

Guiding Principles on Internal Displacement. U.N. Doc. E/CN.4/1998/53/Add.2 (1998), noted in Comm. Hum. Rts. Res. 1998/50.

PUK's Organisational Branch 2, 'Report no. 58'. Kirkuk, Private Paper, 2005.

UNDP Iraq Living Condition Survey, Vol. 1, Tabulation Report, Table 1.6, (2004). Accessed at http:// www.krg.org.

UNDP Iraq Living Conditions Survey Vol. 1, Tabulation Report, Table 1.12: Displacement due to war, (2004). http:// www.krg.org.

USCRIF to Secretary Rice: 'US Must Address Threats to Religious Minorities in Iraq'. USCRIF Press Release, 6 September 2007.

'What is Civil Society?' Centre for Civil Society, London School of Economics, accessed at http://www.lse.ac.uk/collections/CCS/what_is_civil_society.htm. Retrieved 29 Nov. 2009.

INDEX